Elite Recruitment and Coherence of the Inner Core of Power in Finland

Elite Recruitment and Coherence of the Inner Core of Power in Finland

Changing Patterns during the Economic Crises of 1991–2011

Ilkka Ruostetsaari

LEXINGTON BOOKS
Lanham • Boulder • New York • London

Published by Lexington Books
An imprint of The Rowman & Littlefield Publishing Group, Inc.
4501 Forbes Boulevard, Suite 200, Lanham, Maryland 20706
www.rowman.com

Unit A, Whitacre Mews, 26-34 Stannary Street, London SE11 4AB

British Library Cataloguing in Publication Information Available

Library of Congress Control Number: 2015939024
ISBN: 978-1-4985-1029-5 (cloth: alk. paper)
ISBN: 978-1-4985-1030-1 (ebook)

∞™ The paper used in this publication meets the minimum requirements of American National Standard for Information Sciences—Permanence of Paper for Printed Library Materials, ANSI/NISO Z39.48-1992.

Printed in the United States of America

Contents

Preface   vii

1   Introduction   1

2   Theoretical Premises   17

3   Approach of the Study   33

4   Recruitment into Elites   49

5   Coherence of the Elite Structure   109

6   Discussion   193

Bibliography   213

Index   229

About the Author   233

Preface

It's said that in today's increasingly complex and globalized society, the only constant is change. For the past two decades, this has certainly been true of Finland and its immediate international environment. In this time we have seen the breakdown of the Soviet Union; the great recession and the banking crisis that ensued; cutbacks in welfare services, and a deepening of social divisions; Finland's accession to the European Union and the eurozone, the recession triggered by the international financial crisis; the eurozone debt crisis; and the reconfiguration of the political field in the 2011 parliamentary election. Finland's recent history since 1990 is well captured by the concept of peripety, as employed by Göran Therborn (1995) to analyze Europe's social upheavals since World War II. Depending on the viewpoint, peripety may mean either a positive or negative turning point in development.

Finland is not, of course, the only country that has seen major upheavals. What makes the Finnish case so interesting is the way that these upheavals are interwoven with social stability. According to US think tank Fund for Peace (FfP), Finland was the world's most stable state in 2014, closely followed by the other Nordic countries, that is, Sweden, Denmark, and Norway. One year earlier, Sweden was ranked alongside Finland in the "highly stable" category, but in 2014 Finland was the sole country listed in this category. PfP rankings are based on 12 criteria, including security, income inequality, and political situation (*Helsingin Sanomat*, Dec 28, 2014).

This book explores to what extent and how elites at the highest echelon of the Finnish power structure have changed in the turbulent environment of social change and crisis, and how this has impacted democracy. It looks at how routes to the highest levels of power in society have changed, and asks whether social mobility has increased or decreased. Another concern is with the changes that have happened in the coherence of the Finnish power elite and its constituent groups, that is, the political, administrative, business, organizational, mass media, scientific, and cultural elites: have elite networks become more centralized or fragmented, has it become easier or harder to retain elite positions, and to what extent do elite members move across from one group to another? Third, the book asks whether the attitudinal gap between elites has grown, and whether the gulf between elites and citizens has widened, as is often argued.

This work is the result of a quarter of a century of my own research on elites. The data comes from postal surveys I conducted in 1991, 2001, and 2011 among elites and citizens, which makes it a unique piece of research both in Finland and internationally. In putting together this book I have also drawn on earlier texts I have written on the subject over the years. This work would not have been possible without the input of thousands of elite members and ordinary citizens, to whom I owe a huge debt of gratitude. All the surveys employed in this work were funded by the Academy of Finland. The 2011 data set was collected as part of an Academy-funded project under the supervision of professor Heikki Paloheimo, entitled Political Power in Finland. My research assistant in this project has been Jari Holttinen, Master of Social Science. The book was originally published for a Finnish audience by Vastapaino in October 2014.

Just as Gallup polls cannot capture the future electoral success of political parties, so this work cannot (nor does it attempt to) predict future changes in the national power structure. However, I hope that it will inspire reflection and debate about the direction in which our national power structures are changing in an increasingly turbulent climate where economic and political crises are constantly throwing up new challenges for the political system. What we must ask is to what extent are the crises we see in our society having an impact on citizens, on the one hand, and on the highest, elite echelons, on the other.

1

Introduction

MOBILITY AT ELITE LEVEL

Social mobility and its counterpart, social inheritance, are among the most popular themes of research conducted with social sciences. The research interest in social mobility ties in closely with the idea of the openness of society and meritocracy. In a meritocratic society, success depends on the individual's talent and effort: all individuals, regardless of their family background, have equal opportunities. The perfect meritocratic society does not exist, but meritocracy is still considered an ideal worth pursuing (Härkönen 2010, 52).

Given the apparent connection between social mobility and equal opportunity, social mobility is generally considered a measure of the openness of society. However, parental social class is associated with children's social class in all societies. Part of the explanation for the association between parents' and their children's social position lies in the inheritance of skills and abilities and differences in the appreciation of education. Complete independence between parents' and their children's social positions would probably require coercive measures, which are at variance with the basic values of democracy. Nevertheless countries with higher social mobility are generally thought to be more open societies than countries with lower social mobility, and equality of opportunity through social mobility is considered a major objective from both a justice and democracy point of view. Social mobility tends to be high in transitional periods when the economy and the social structure are in flux, when new occupations are emerging to replace old ones, and the focus of the economy is shifting from one sector to another, for instance from agriculture to industry and further to services (Ibid., 52–54, 65–66).

This study aims to find out to what extent there has been mobility at the highest echelons of the Finnish power structure since the early 1990s, a period of much turmoil including the "great recession" of the early 1990s, Finland's accession to the European Union in 1995, and the international financial crisis and eurozone debt crisis in the 2000s. The purpose is to explore how the elite structure in Finland has changed in terms of vertical social mobility or openness, on the one hand, and horizontal mobility or coherence, on the other.

Elite theory ranks alongside pluralism and Marxism as one of the most important frameworks for studying the exercise of power. In the wake of the World War II, however, elite theory was overshadowed by Marxist class theory. The pursuit of elite theory was undermined by it being linked with fascism and a leadership cult. This explains why German social scientists, for instance, rather than speaking of elites, preferred to use terms such as "leadership groups," "occupants of top positions," and the "political class" (Hoffman-Lange 2001, 201). In the 1970s, the gulf between the elite-centered and the class-centered approach was still just as wide as it was in the early 1900s when Mosca, Pareto, and Michels set out to develop elite research as an alternative and antidote to Marxism. In part this gulf reflected the global conflict between liberal capitalism and state socialism (Higley and Moore 2001, 175–76).

In the 2000s, the balance of power between these theories has been reversed. The popularity of elite theory is explained by two main trends. Firstly, commentators have referred to the third wave of democratization, the start of which coincided more or less exactly with the publication in 1976 of Robert D. Putnam's seminal work *The Comparative Study of Political Elites*. The third wave of democratization prompted an extensive research literature on the pivotal role of elites in the transition to and consolidation of democracy (see Moyser and Wagstaffe 1987; Etzioni-Halevy 1993). Interest in elite research was also stoked by the Phoenix-like resurgence of nomenclature elites in former Eastern Europe from the ashes of the state-centered power structures to the core of competitive capitalism (Higley and Moore 2001, 175–76; see also Dogan and Higley 1998a; Higley and Lengyel 2000; cf. Higley and Pakulski 2000, 236–38).

A third factor contributing to the growing popularity of elite research is the process of European integration, whose impacts on national and supranational (the so-called Euro elite) power structures have also generated growing interest in elite research in Finland (see Westlake 1994; Murto et al. 1996; Ruostetsaari 2003b). In this context of European integration, there have been some comparative research projects focusing on elite groups in different countries (Best and Cotta 2000; Cotta and Best 2007; Best et al. 2012; Conti et al. 2012; Kauppi and Rask Madsen 2013).

Systematic comparative studies of elite structures in different countries are still conspicuous in their absence, however. National elite studies have been carried out in the Nordic countries in the 2000s (Munk Christiansen et al. 2001; Gulbrandsen et al. 2002; Lindvall and Rothstein 2006; Ruostetsaari 2003a; 2010; Ruuskanen et al. 2010; Togeby et al. 2003; Østerud et al. 2004). However, it is very difficult to compare national elite structures on the basis of these studies because the methods, data sets, and variables used differ considerably (see Ruostetsaari 2007b).

In his pioneering synthesis of elite research, Robert D. Putnam (1976, ix) observed that this field of scholarship had produced "copious, but disparate, findings," and that there was an unusually wide gap between abstract, general theories and masses of unorganized empirical evidence (see also Best and Cotta 2000, 2). This gap between the scarcity of theory building about elites and an extensive body of empirical work still persists, to some degree at least, to the present day.

One of the factors that has hindered the growth of a wider interest in elite theory is its connotation with elitism or "superiority," in the same way as interest in Marxism as a theoretical approach has been diluted by it being identified with real socialism. Indeed, it has often been thought that since elite theory is concerned with elites, it must itself be elitist. And in some instances this is true. However, elitism is not a necessary trait of elite theory. Just as elite theory is not irrevocably tied to a dichotomous conception of power structures (power is concentrated in the hands of the elite, while the "mass" is excluded from power), so it is not inexorably tied to an elitist conception of these power structures. Elite theory is focused on the fact that all societies have particularly influential minorities. Elite theory itself is ideologically neutral, insofar as it is not tainted by elite theorists' own ideological bents (Etzioni-Halevy 1993, 30).

Although the concept of elite is derived from the Latin words *eligere* (to choose or select) and *electa* (the chosen or elected), and in many languages "elite" has the meaning of the select few, the very best (Zannoni 1978, 7), elite theory does not mean approving the power of the elite, any more than Marxism means approving class rule. Although some elite theorists have expressed elitist views and praised elites, others have taken the opposite view. The best known example of the latter attitude is the American, C. Wright Mills (1956), who thoroughly vilified his country's power elite. Indeed, modern elite research has largely abandoned such meanings of celebratory praise. On the other hand, elite research is equally averse to praise and condemn elites. Instead, it is interested to explore the actions of elites in their context as well as their positive or negative ramifications for democracy (Etzioni-Halevy 1993, 31). In this current work elites are not seen *a priori* as the "cream" of society, any more than they are seen as an illegitimate club of people in power.

This book is divided into six chapters. The first chapter discusses the reciprocal linkages between changes in elite structures and societal changes and examines the changes that have taken place in Finnish society since the early 1990s. The second chapter sets up the theoretical framework for the work and compares elite theory with rival approaches to the study of power. Furthermore, drawing on classical elite theory and democratic elitism, it proposes a typology of elite structures, which provides the basis on which the research tasks for this work are defined. This typology is used in the concluding chapter to analyze and interpret the changes that have occurred in the Finnish elite structure.

The third chapter presents the research setting and describes the methods commonly used in elite research. This provides the basis for defining the research method and data sets used in this work. In addition, the third chapter offers a definition of power and especially the power wielded by the elites.

The analysis of the changes in elite structures is divided across two chapters. The fourth chapter addresses vertical social mobility, in other words, recruitment into elites. The purpose here is to identify the routes via which people in Finland have moved to the highest echelons of the power structure. The chapter begins with an examination of the social background of those who have moved into elite positions and the changes seen in this regard since the early 1990s. The social background factors in focus are generation, gender, native language, education and educational inheritance, regional mobility, income levels, parental social class, and class identification. Changes in the social background of elites are compared with changes in the general population. Secondly, the fourth chapter studies the career mobility of elites, that is, the impact of home background on the career choices and career advancement of those rising to an elite position, the impact of cultural capital brought from home on career advancement, and more generally factors impacting career development.

The fifth chapter moves on to examine the horizontal mobility of elites, which provides a useful lens for studying changes in the coherence of the elite structure. Firstly, we analyze the lifestyle and informal personal relations of elites in order to gain an insight into their leisure interests, both past and present; their membership in informal contact groups; and the exploitation of the power of media in social engagement. Secondly, the chapter discusses networks of power, that is, the changes in elites' national network of interaction and international contacts. Furthermore, the analysis extends to changes in the attitudinal distance between different elites, and between elites and the citizenry. In this same connection the views of elites and the citizenry on how power relations between institutions in the Finnish political system have changed are compared with interpretations offered in the research literature. Thirdly, the chapter searches for "the elite of elites," in other words, the accumulation of elite positions to individuals; explores the ability of elites to retain their positions; and examines individual mobility between different elites.

The sixth chapter draws together the results of the analyses and discusses how the Finnish elite structure has changed since the early 1990s with respect to vertical and horizontal mobility, and what these changes mean to Finnish democracy. The results for Finland are compared with findings from other Nordic elite studies. The interpretation of the results makes use of the typology of elite structure developed in the second chapter.

INTERRELATION BETWEEN CHANGES
IN ELITES AND CHANGES IN SOCIETY

It is far from straightforward to explain fundamental changes occurring in society by reference to changes in elites. This is because in democracy, it is thought that politics reflects the general structure of societies, their variable historical experiences and heritage, economic success and failure, political cultures, ethnic identities, religious views, and specific political institutions. Indeed, it is a point of much debate whether politics is shaped more by elites than by wider structural forces and institutions in society, and whether elites therefore are primarily an expression and reflection of these kinds of forces and institutions (Burton and Higley 2001, 182). In other words, societal crises can be treated as the independent or the dependent variable (Cotta 2014, 58).

Crises or upheavals are an important aspect of any investigation into the exercise of power, since they may be initiated by the actions or inactions of a small group of leaders at the highest level of societal hierarchies. On the other hand, crises may cause both conflicts between elites and changes in the compositions and actions of elites. Especially in the acute stage of a crisis, elites have significant autonomy and latitude of action. The choices they make at such a moment are often decisive for the outcome of the crisis and for the regimes that follow (Dogan and Higley 1998b, 3, 15; see also Burton and Higley 1998). In sharp contrast to this is the observation by Knight, who says that in times of crisis elites become more fluid, open, and unpredictable, whereas the masses gain more room to maneuver as they challenge the power and status of elites, undermining their authority and limiting their autonomy (Knight 1998, 38–39, 42). Crises do not necessarily have equally dramatic effects on all elite groups, however: economic and other elite groups at greater distance from the corridors of governmental power may often escape dramatic changes (Dogan and Higley 1998b, 3, 15).

It is often problematic to identify the direction of causation in the relationship between societal changes and elites. On the one hand, actions taken by elites may bring about societal changes, while on the other hand societal changes may cause changes in the elite structure. For purposes of examining the changes that have occurred in Finnish society since the early 1990s, then, one possible perspective could be to identify the actors and factors behind these changes. In the current work this perspective is reversed: our aim here is to see how elite structures have changed in Finland from 1991 to 2011, a period marked by major changes and upheavals.

A societal crisis can be defined as an abrupt and brutal challenge to the survival of a political regime, often consisting of a short chain of events that destroys or drastically weakens the equilibrium and effectiveness of the regime over a period of days or weeks. On the other hand, a crisis may be manifested in a chain of small scattered but cumulating events and power confrontations that unfold over several years (Dogan and Higley 1998b, 7). In the 1990s and first decade of the 2000s, crises in Finland were primarily of the latter type.

A sharp economic downturn may challenge a country's political regime by having an adverse effect on a wide segment of the population, forcing ruling elites to adopt dramatically different policies. These news policies may in turn alienate groups that benefited from previous, failed policies and that supported elites. If the new policies do not quickly turn the economy around, and if the ruling elites are unable to create a new and powerful coalition to support those policies, the elites may lose their position (Ibid., 11).

Societal crises are potentially important turning-points in politics. If a crisis is defined as an abrupt and brutal event that unsettles the existing regime, then there are few crises that leave the composition and functioning of elites unaffected. On the other hand, not all crises, even economic crises, necessarily destroy elite structures. For instance, Anglo-American and Scandinavian elites and democratic regimes survived the 1930s Great Depression, whereas in Germany the depression led to the downfall of the Weimar government. Indeed, crises are closely interwoven with elite change. Understanding the importance of crises requires an understanding of the kinds of elite changes they may induce. These questions are the field of elite theory, and elite theorists such as Gaetano Mosca (1939) and Vilfredo Pareto (1963) and, to a lesser extent, Robert Michels (1986) offered some early answers, although it has been maintained that they neglected the role of crises in generating elite change (Dogan and Higley 1998b, 7–15; cf. Knight 1998, 38–39).

However, an examination of the relationship between crises and regime change must not be limited to assessing the changing compositions of elites, but it is also necessary to consider changes in the unity of elite functioning. Revolutionary crises are likely to cause significant changes to both the composition and the functioning of elites. In less severe crises, there might be significant change in only one or the other respect: for instance, there might be a minor shift in the composition of an elite, but a profound change in its functioning. By contrast, most crisis-generated replacements of authoritarian regimes will lead to a significant change in elite composition, but no basic change in elite functioning: authoritarian rulers are replaced by cliques or factions that persist with the same disunited policy that caused the crisis in the first place (Dogan and Higley 1998b, 19). Even a major crisis will not necessarily lead to the exclusion of elite members from the elite structure. In many former Eastern European countries, members of the political elite were often involved in privatizing state-owned corporations, and then later became owners and managers of these enterprises and subsequently known as oligarchs of a new business elite.

The premise here is that societal institutions and the elites running these institutions possess great significance because they make important decisions, sometimes against public opinion, that affect citizens' everyday life. According to Ilkka Heiskanen (2001, 20), the powerful and surprising external factors of change to which institutions are exposed can be examined in three different ways. Firstly, they can be seen as "shocks," as sudden changes in circumstances that decisively change the conditions for agency, either directly or by changing institutional structures. An example is provided by a political revolution or a real collapse of the national economy, although even in these situations old institutional structures often survive and remain influential for a long time. Secondly, these shocks can be regarded as tests of the institutional structure that reveal its true nature, meaning, and directions of ongoing change. Thirdly, external shocks can be seen as catalysts that directly influence actors and actions by undermining or reinforcing ongoing institutional trends in development.

External changes are not always sudden circumstantial changes, but they can also be external factors with a long-term effect. Like shocks, they can decisively change the resources and opportunity structures available to actors. On the other hand, they can also be systemic factors that within sectors and, to some extent, by cross-sectoral dissemination push actors and their organizations toward more or less shared frameworks of action. Key among these systemic change factors are the effects spreading from society's "power sectors" to more peripheral sectors. Examples of the diffusion of institutional change include the spread of privatization from one sector to another in connection with the "deconstruction" of the welfare state, from pure public production to the areas of health services and culture. On the other hand, there are also elements of outright borrowing, as illustrated by the tendencies of commercialization in cultural and arts institutions and their leaning toward the "experience industry" (Ibid., 20–21). Institutional change in one sector of society is therefore not necessarily determined by some other sector, or a consequence of a deliberate and conscious reaction to changes in some other sector, but rather it might be an imitation-based spillover effect.

UPHEAVALS IN FINNISH SOCIETY

Raimo Väyrynen (2000, 3) identifies three major upheavals in Finland's contemporary socioeconomic history. The first began to unfold with the onset of industrial capitalism and increasing foreign trade activity in the 1860s. This period saw the creation of the first governmental institutions, such as the unicameral Parliament and the Bank of Finland. Finland was a grand duchy under czarist Russia, enjoying considerable autonomy until the turn of the century. Politically, Finland was governed by a civil service, but this was now a society in the process of national awakening.

Independence in 1917 brought significant changes to domestic and foreign policy, but the economic and social effects were less momentous. Finland was and remained an agrarian society, although industry was continuing to gain a stronger foothold. The second major societal transformation only occurred in the aftermath of World War II, in the 1950s and 1960s. Industry was at its peak and laid the foundation for the Finnish welfare state. The two major political parties in the presidential system were the Social Democrats and the Agrarian League, which worked closely to promote industrialization, while disagreements centered around consumer-producer relations. Internationally, Finland was part of the Soviet sphere of interests, but it consistently pursued a policy of neutrality in which it showed a keen awareness of its boundaries, yet at the same time took distance from its eastern neighbor (Ibid., 5).

The third transformation that started in the 1990s has been marked by intense socioeconomic globalization, a growing emphasis on the markets at the expense of the state, and the breakthrough of information technology. Soaring foreign investment has integrated Finland more closely with the globalizing world economy. In terms of domestic policy-making, Finland has become an increasingly pluralistic country where cabinet coalitions change regularly and where politics has declined in importance in people's everyday life. Economically and politically, Finland is clearly part of the Western world. It is militarily nonaligned, but in practice it is ever more closely involved in Western security institutions (Väyrynen 2000, 3).

In connection with the third transformation, Finnish society was thrown into crisis following an economic downturn in the early 1990s. The recession that ensued was the gravest test to date not only of the welfare state, but of postwar Finland in general. The crisis caused several profound and long-term changes in Finnish society. The most significant of these changes, in terms of the number of people affected, was a decade of mass unemployment, which led to the growth of long-term unemployment, a problem that previously was virtually unknown in the country. This in turn added a new urgency to the challenges of poverty and social exclusion in the welfare state (Kiander 2001, 5).

In the 1990s, Finland fell into the deepest economic recession in its history. The effects were even more dramatic than those of the 1930s depression. At the height of recession in 1991–1993, GDP fell by more than 10 percent, the value of the country's currency depreciated by almost 40 percent, unemployment climbed to 18 percent and 130,000 jobs, almost one quarter of all jobs in the country, were lost. Finland was plunged into a banking crisis, and many companies that were thought to be financially sound and healthy went bankrupt (see Kiander 2001).

Apart from the great recession, another megatrend affecting Finnish society in the 1990s was the collapse of the Soviet Union, which brought to an abrupt end Finland's bilateral trade with the Soviet Union and contributed to trigger the recession. The financial markets were subjected to uncontrolled liberalization, and neoliberal practices such as deregulation, competitive tendering, and privatization were adopted in the public sector.

The inner circle of the Cabinet of Esko Aho that took office in 1991 consisted of the Cabinet Committee on Economic Policy, which made the country's most important political decisions. The true inner circle in the field of economic policy-making was even smaller, comprising Prime Minister Esko Aho; Minister of Finance Iiro Viinanen; President of the Republic Mauno Koivisto; and Director General of the Bank of Finland, Rolf Kullberg (Kulha 2000, 101). It has even been suggested that the exclusiveness of this inner circle of decision-makers contributed to the outset of the recession. In the words of one decision-maker interviewed by the Finnish Innovation Fund Sitra, "Finland is a secret society of leading circles. I'm sure it's one of the reasons why we were driven into recession. And when this machinery, I mean it's so monolithic that when it makes a miscalculation, then things go seriously wrong" (Kantola 2002, 218). According to the then Minister of Justice, Hannele Pokka (1995, 43), "for outsiders, for us ministers who were not on the cabinet committee, the most up-to-date source of information was that morning's newspaper."

However, it was not only during the recession that key economic policy-making in Finland was limited to a select circle of decision-makers. The same phenomenon was seen during the period of economic recovery. The revaluation of the currency in 1989 and the associated belt-tightening measures were not even submitted to the Cabinet Committee on Economic Policy, but this critical policy revision was made on a handshake between the prime minister and minister of finance. Even the leaders of the parties in the government were bypassed (Ranki 2000, 196). Indeed, since the 1990s civil servants have had much closer control over the drafting of the state budget, partly at least because of the growing prominence of economic considerations in public policy-making (Pekkarinen and Heinonen 1998, 97–98).

Although the recession was exceptionally deep, credit losses from households were negligible. The banking crisis was caused not by household debt spiraling out of control, but mainly by the problems of savings banks' corporate clients. In Finland the banking crisis did not, however, lead to bankruptcies in the commercial banking sector as it did in Norway (Engelstad 2014, 147), although the Bank of Finland did take over one commercial bank and split it among its four rivals. The financial problems of the two biggest commercial banks in the country led to their merging. Private customers had to pay off their debts. The efforts poured into keeping the banks afloat placed a heavy burden on central government finances at the worst possible time and necessitated cuts in other expenditures. Large numbers of companies went under and countless households were driven into excessive debt despite the taxpayer bailouts for banks, which subsequently came in for some sharp criticism. Social security and public services were being severely cut because the government was short of cash, but at the same time huge sums were being pumped into banks, even though it was clear they were partly to blame for the recession. Banks happily accepted the subsidies they were offered, but refused to let their own indebted clients off the hook. People's sense of justice was sorely tested (Kiander 2001, 42–43).

Commentators spoke of a redistribution of assets as banks sold off people's homes and companies' assets at giveaway prices. Households and companies struggled particularly with foreign currency credits from abroad, which had become possible with the deregulation of the financial markets and which banks were eagerly offering and selling to customers. As a result of the devaluation in 1991 and the consequent floating of the Finnish *markka*, the exchange rate of the national currency depreciated by some 40 percent, increasing the market value of foreign currency credits one and a half times over. Although large numbers of people were affected, directly or indirectly, by the banking crisis, it did not incite visible social unrest (Kulha 2000, 288; Pietilä 2008).

The collapse of the Soviet Union brought to an end the Finnish-Soviet Agreement on Friendship, Cooperation and Mutual Assistance in January 1992. This removed old foreign and security policy obstacles to Finland's membership in the European Community (EC), and Finland promptly filed its membership application in March 1992. Hannele Pokka (1995, 81), Minister of Justice in the Cabinet of Esko Aho, describes in her memoirs how the European Community issue was handled in the government: ". . . the prime minister made it known that a decision has been reached. 'What's been decided?' the ignorant ministers asked. 'The decision to commission an inquiry,' the prime minister replied. 'An inquiry into what?' Well, an inquiry into whether or not we shall apply for EC membership. The final decisions that Finland shall seek accession to the EC were made silently. The National Coalition Party [i.e., the Conservatives] would not have wanted a devaluation of the currency. It did want Finland to become an EC member. The Centre Party [formerly the Agrarian League] was in favor of a devaluation and said it would persuade its supporters to get behind Finland's EC membership. A decision was reached in the corridors that both the National Coalition Party and the Centre Party should have it their own way."

Things were moving fast indeed. Just 10 months earlier, President of the Republic Koivisto had given a foreign policy address to the Cabinet of Esko Aho in which he had stressed that Finland was looking to become a member of the European Economic Area (EEA), which effectively excluded the option of EC membership. Following a referendum, Finland joined the European Community in 1995 and the third stage of Economic and Monetary Union when it was launched in 1999. Finland introduced the euro currency in 2002, even though the majority of the Finnish people had never been in favor of joining the euro zone (Karttunen 2009).

The great recession was tackled by putting in place a rigorous savings policy to reduce governmental expenditure. This effectively halted the expansion of the welfare state, which had just been brought up to Nordic standards. Primarily, the savings were achieved through cuts in welfare services for disadvantaged groups. Although Finnish society was still struggling to recover from the great recession one decade later, the economic collapse and the worst years of recession (1991–1993) were to be followed by a robust, seven-year economic rebound that was driven not only by an improving international economy, but largely by governmental investments in research and development and a booming electronics industry, spearheaded by Nokia Corporation (Kiander 2001, 62–65). On the reverse side of the coin of rapid economic growth, however, there were deepening social divisions. Although the welfare state system as such remained intact, Finland's social expenditure growth has been slower than in any other EU country since 1990 (Heiskala and Kantola 2010; Julkunen 2001).

Finland continues to have relatively low income disparities, but they started to rise sharply in the wake of economic growth, even by international comparison (Statistics Finland 2014). However, income disparities do not tell the whole truth about the distribution of welfare. In Finland, inequalities such as low education, poverty, and health differentials are inherited in families. In a European comparison, Finland has exceptionally high socioeconomic differences in mortality and life expectancy (Tarkiainen et al. 2011).

Finnish economic growth came to a halt with the international financial crisis which erupted in September 2008 with the collapse of the Lehman Brothers investment bank, the largest bankruptcy in history, and the Bush administration's decision to let it go under (Best and Higley 2014, 8). Economic growth in Finland was also curtailed by the eurozone debt crisis that started in 2009, which meant that the government had to commit to massive bailout packages for stricken euro countries. This was the first major crisis to hit not just European states, but the European Union as a system (Cotta 2014, 61). The Finnish economy's heavy dependence on exports meant that GDP fell by 8 percent from 2008 to 2009. Although the new recession was only half as deep as that in the early 1990s, GDP in Finland declined more than in other euro countries and in the so-called old EU member states (Pohjola 2010).

As a result of the recession started in late 2008 Finland's economic performance fell sharply, even though economic growth was still in positive territory in 2010–2011. Whereas the great recession of the 1990s was mainly self-inflicted, resulting from the uncontrolled deregulation of the financial markets which caused overheating in the domestic markets, the recession in the 2010s was mainly triggered by exogenous factors. The financial crisis that started in the United States and then spread to other countries brought world trade to a virtual standstill and at the same time paralyzed the export markets for Finnish businesses, particularly in the electronics and forest industries. In 2009 Finnish industrial output fell by 18 percent. Output contracted for two consecutive years (2012–2013) for the first time since the 1990s recession. For ordinary people, however, the effects of the 2010s recession have been less dramatic than those of the great recession. In the early 1990s, unemployment soared to 18 percent, but in the current recession the unemployment rate has remained fairly steady (7.8 percent in 2011), and real estate prices have not slumped. Companies had buffers on their balance sheets at the onset of the recession, banks were in good shape, and interest rates were at historically low levels. Indeed, the international financial crisis and the euro zone debt crisis did not lead to a banking crisis in Finland. Norway and Sweden have likewise avoided a banking crisis (Engelstad 2014, 149).

However, by 2014 the new recession has lasted longer than the great recession of the early 1990s. Furthermore, recovery from the economic crisis that started in autumn 2008 has been much slower than from the recession of the early 1990s, when it took six years for output to recover to pre-recession levels. At the time of writing in 2015, we are in the sixth year post economic crisis, but forecasts are that output will still remain some 5 percent lower than in 2008. The Ministry of Finance predicts that Finnish GDP will not exceed 2008 levels until 10 years on, in 2018. The difference compared to the rebound in the wake of the 1990s recession is huge, when after 10 years GDP was more than one-fifth higher than before the recession. It is possible then that the new recession of the 2010s may last even longer than the economic crisis during the World War I, the longest recession in Finnish economic history when output did not recover to its prewar peak (1913) until nine years later in 1922 (Heikkinen 2014).

However, if comparisons are made between 2007, the year before the international financial crisis, and 2011, the last year of the current research, Finland's economic performance has been quite strong. Finland's GDP growth rate in 2007 stood at 5.3 percent, compared with 3.2 percent in EU-27, 4.5 percent in the USA 4.5; the figures for 2011 were 2.8 percent, 1.6 percent, and 1.8 percent, respectively. The 2007 unemployment figures were: Finland 6.9 percent, EU-27 7.2 percent, and USA 4.6 percent;

and for 2011 Finland 7.8 percent, EU-27 9.7 percent, and USA 8.9 percent. Finally, the general government budget deficit in 2007 stood at +5.3 percent in Finland, compared with –0.9 percent in EU-27, and –1.1 percent in the USA and in 2011 –0.6 percent, –4.4 percent, and –8.7 percent, respectively (Cotta 2014, 60–61).

According to a 2011 postal survey conducted for the present work, Finnish elites reported mainly adverse effects from the international financial crisis and the eurozone debt crisis in their respective branches. One-fifth said the crises had reduced the resources available. One-seventh felt that the crises had added to a sense of uncertainty, while more than one in ten felt they had caused structural and internal changes within their branch. Likewise, one in ten believed there was a stronger sense of caution. Less than one in ten thought the crises had given greater importance and power to the economy.

However, a significant proportion, one in five of elites felt that these crises had not affected their own branch in any way. One in four of the cultural elite and one in five of the business, organizational, and scientific elites had seen no effects in their respective branches. Indeed, the political elite were more sensitive to the effects of the financial crisis and the debt crisis than other elite groups. One in five of the political elite felt that the crises had caused a scarcity of resources and increasing insecurity, and one in eight thought they had given greater importance and power to the economy. The administrative elite mainly reported an increase in resource scarcity as well as structural and functional changes. Almost one in three of the business elite felt that the crises had added to the general sense of caution in their branch, while the mass media elite mainly referred to the growing sense of uncertainty and the science elite to the increasing scarcity of resources. The main effects reported by the cultural elite were an increasing sense of uncertainty and a greater scarcity of resources. The organizational elite reported multiple effects, but more often than other elite groups said they thought the importance and power of the economy had grown.

The international financial crisis and eurozone debt crisis have also led to cutbacks in local and government spending, tax hikes, and redundancies, and via these pathways affected citizens' everyday life and prompted increased grassroots criticism against political decision-makers. The evidence from earlier research indicates that the gulf between elites and the people has grown wider. While individualistic values have persisted or even strengthened among elites since the 1990s, ordinary citizens have wanted to dispense with the competition discourse and instead achieve a greater sense of security and togetherness (Heiskala 2006a, 39). "Competitiveness society" or "the competition state" and the changes implemented in society have made business managers very rich and fulfilled the dreams of leading technocrats, but poor local authorities and the poor long-term unemployed have had no cause for satisfaction (Heiskala 2006b, 212).

It is possible that the increasing frequency of well-publicized political scandals has also contributed to erode the relationship between elites and the citizenry. Political scandals can be divided into four categories based on their subject: sex, espionage and intelligence, negligence, or finances (Paastela 1995, 64). In Finland most scandals involving elites have surrounded the relationship between the elites of politics and business. In the 1970s there were four such scandals, in the 1980s 10, in the 1990s 21, and in the 2000s 37. Increasingly, the individuals at the center of scandals have had to resign their position (Kantola and Vesa 2011, 43).

Since 2008 the political elite in Finland has been shaken above all by the electoral funding scandal, perhaps the most serious political scandal in Finnish history in terms of the publicity given to the issue. The scandal revealed abuses within the inner core of political power. The media disclosed a network of real estate investors and other business magnates who had paid out huge amounts in campaign contributions to candidates running for Parliament from different political parties. Not all of the individuals who received funding made the required statutory declaration (Kantola 2011a, 165). In recent years the media have given critical coverage not only of politicians, but also business leaders. Their stories have described existing reward mechanisms, old boy networks, tax havens, and the poor performance of companies and the economy in general (Pentikäinen 2014, 274).

The international financial crisis and the eurozone debt crisis weakened the position of the political elite in many EU countries. In 30 elections held by 23 EU countries between October 2008 and August 2013 (the three smallest states Cyprus, Luxembourg, and Malta are excluded, as is Austria, where no elections were held during that period), the average win/loss for governing parties/coalitions was 12.9 percent compared with an average –5.1 percent in pre-crisis elections between 2005 and October 2008. However the variation was huge: from –2.1 percent in Poland's 2011 elections to –45.4 percent in Greece's May 2012 elections (Best and Cotta 2014, 3). The combined losses of the coalition in power before Finland's 2011 parliamentary elections in 2011—the conservative Coalition Party, Centre Party, Green Party, and Swedish People's Party—amounted to –10.7 percentage points.

Between October 2008 and August 2013, wholly different government majorities took over in 17 of the 30 European elections, partly different majorities in four elections, while the compositions of governing majorities remained unchanged in only nine elections (Best and Cotta 2014, 3). Between 2011 and mid-2013, previously governing elites were replaced in Cyprus, Denmark, France, Greece, Ireland, Portugal, Romania, Spain, and Slovakia. Except for the common feature of incumbent governments being defeated, not all these changes have had the same meaning and crisis relevance. In Denmark, for instance, the change in political elites took place at a regular election and without major defeat of the previous incumbents. Likewise in France, the Sarkozy-led government was defeated in a regularly scheduled election and the main opposition party, the Socialists, won with promises to change EU policies. In all other countries changes were clearly the consequence of crisis (Cotta 2014, 76).

In Finland, the 2011 elections brought some changes to the composition of the four-party government coalition, and a new six-party coalition was formed in its place. This was the widest coalition since the exceptional circumstances during World War II. Apart from the international financial crisis and the eurozone crisis, there were also specific national factors that contributed to the changes in government. The legitimacy of most political parties had been dented by the electoral funding scandal, and consequently in the 2011 parliamentary elections the True Finns (now known as the Finns Party) achieved a landslide victory (Borg 2012). As a populist political party (see Wiberg 2011) it succeeded in mobilizing public criticism against the political elite, not only on the back of the campaign funding scandal but also the international financial crisis and the Greek and Portuguese bailout packages in connection with the eurozone debt crisis. The popular support for the True Finns soared from 4.1 percent to 19.1 percent and the party's number of seats in Parliament went up from 5 to 39. With the exception of the Swedish People's Party, every other party lost seats in the new Parliament. Nevertheless the resounding winner in the election, the True Finns, decided to stay in opposition.

According to Maurizio Cotta, national elites in the northern countries have under German guidance sailed through the crisis without major internal upheavals, and they have strengthened their influence on European policy-making. A "Berlin consensus," which has enjoyed strong support from Finland, based on principles of austerity and budgetary discipline, has shaped the most important EU decisions during later phases of the crisis. National elites in the southern countries and those in countries like Hungary and Ireland with similar financial problems have been buffeted badly and have had to accept, however reluctantly, the Berlin consensus (Cotta 2014, 76).

However, in the wake of the 2011 parliamentary elections, Finland transformed from a "model pupil" into a "prefect," and according to some foreign commentators even into a "troublemaker": Finland was now the only EU member state to demand collateral for its contribution to the Greek and Spanish bailout packages. This insistence was motivated by the concerns of the then Social Democratic minister of finance about the growing popular support for the True Finns, to which the Social Democrats had lost most of its support in parliamentary elections.

Nowadays elites are given a rougher ride in the media than they were in the 1970s, when political and economic decision-makers enjoyed a more revered public status. The moral demands placed on elites have gotten tougher as well (Kantola et al. 2011, 88). It is this contravening of general moral expectations that turns an indiscretion into a scandal (Paastela 1995, 62). Indeed, the increased attention given to elite behavior and the willingness of the public and the media to report on their behavior may be more a symptom of the underlying changes in public sentiments rather than a cause. If this is true, then, what has changed most of all over time is not the behavior of politicians, but rather the willingness of the public and the media to hold them accountable for their actions—whether personal or political. The performance of politicians and political institutions therefore falls short of citizens' expectations, even if that performance *de facto* has improved. Thus, the gap between citizens' expectations and politicians' and political institutions' performance has widened because expectations have risen faster than performance (Dalton 2011, 197–99).

Elite members caught up in a scandal can no longer rest assured that "old boys" will turn up and bail them out (Ruostetsaari 2003a). This may well have eroded the mutual trust among elites. Indeed, scandals may pave the way for new entrants into the elite, especially when a scandal ousts more established holders of power (Kantola et al. 2011, 88). Indeed, it is thought that revealed scandals have undermined the position of elites and strengthened democracy (Kantola 2011b, 31; Kantola and Vesa 2011, 51).

Elite interactions at national level may have been eroded not only by scandals, but also by the shift to competition economy that has reduced governmental regulation of business; the debate about political decision-makers' private interests; and the increasing controls to which decision-makers are subjected (the duty of disclosure imposed upon ministers and senior civil servants, tighter obligations to report campaign financing following the campaign funding scandal).

However, the EU Commission is not entirely satisfied with the state of the relationship between politics, administration, and economic decision-makers in Finland. Finland is ranked among the top EU performers in combating corruption: one in four Europeans compared to only 9 percent of people in Finland say they have encountered corruption in their daily life. In Europe on average 4 percent but in Finland only less than 1 percent say they have been required to pay bribes within the past year. The Commission's report concludes that corruption among Finland's lower civil servants has decreased in recent years, but the number of cases of bribery reported among high-level politicians, civil servants, and businesspeople has increased (*Helsingin Sanomat*, Feb. 4, 2014).

According to the Commission's report, Finland's main problem lies in its old boy networks, most particularly in connection with public acquisitions and electoral funding. It is thought that old boy networks, that is, the exchange of favors, information, and other benefits could potentially distort public acquisitions. In recent years local authorities have increasingly outsourced public services to private firms, but legislation on transparency has not kept up with these developments. Monitoring of public acquisitions has become more difficult because the publicity requirements do not apply to private firms in the same way as they do to the public sector. The EU Commission concludes that Finland has made welcome improvements to the conditions for campaign financing and its transparency. However, the difficulty is that the relevant authority (the National Audit Office) has no way to ascertain the accuracy of the information supplied by political parties and individual candidates about the funding they have received (Ibid.).

It is impossible to analyze the changes taking place in elite structures by looking only at the changes occurring in society. We must also consider the impacts of the changes at national, European, and global levels on the power relations between national institutions. In recent decades constitutional changes have parliamentarized the Finnish political system, increasing the power of the government and Parliament at the expense of the president of the republic's powers. Having said that, elites can themselves contribute to the changing balance of power between institutions, but on the other hand these changes also shape and influence the environment in which elites operate. Furthermore, not all elites are on a par in terms of the influence they wield: whereas the political elite can exercise significant influence over constitutional changes and thus over the balance of power among various institutions, the cultural elite, for instance, has no such influence.

2

Theoretical Premises

RIVAL APPROACHES TO ELITE THEORY

Elite theory ranks alongside pluralism and Marxism as one of the principal frameworks for studying the exercise of power. It is impossible to understand the true essence of elite theory without considering how it has been influenced by Marxism. The classical elite theorists Vilfredo Pareto (1848–1923) and Gaetano Mosca (1858–1941) devoted just as much effort to refute Marx as they did to explore an ethically neutral political science. Later elite theorists such as James Burnham and to some extent C. Wright Mills sought to synthesize elements of Marx with elements from the originally antagonistic elitist position (Parry 1969, 27).

Elite theorists reject the Marxist assumption that political power is solely economically grounded, and offer instead a political interpretation of history in terms of the conflict of economic classes. They do not, with the exception of Burnham, see politics as a mere reflection of the economic class structure. According to Pareto and Mosca, the power structure of every society is determined by the character and abilities of its political leadership. It is political skill—or the lack of it—which determines who will rule and how power may change hands. Marx, by contrast, argues that the political leader, whatever his class background, is merely the "representative" of the dominant economic class. Elite theorists do not deny the importance of economic factors, but maintain that by political means an elite can control and even counteract economic forces. Marxism asserts that the most significant social tensions are between the class that owns the means of production and the class or classes whose economic position forces them to organize against the ruling class. Elite theorists, on the other hand, take the view that the tension is between the dominant political elite and any rival elite that can arise to challenge for power. In other words, a prime effect of Marx's theory was that it stimulated a rival doctrine which sought to rescue

17

politics and political leadership from the subordinate position to which Marx had relegated them (Parry 1969, 28).

Elite theorists thus attacked Marxism on three points. Firstly, they had the polemical intention of showing that Marx's theory was a time-bound ideology for the working class in capitalist societies rather than the science of society and the guide for action that it claimed to be. Secondly, they rejected Marx's prediction of a future classless, egalitarian society, finding no justification for his belief that the hierarchical structure of society was not inevitable. Thirdly, they challenged the view that economics rather than politics was the determining force in history and the bond that held societies together (Ibid.).

The controversy between pluralism and elite theory can be traced back to the debate in the middle of the twentieth century around representative democracy. Historically and politically, the disagreement had and has to do with the actual distribution of power in society. Pluralists maintain that power in society is relatively diffused and fragmented, whereas elite theory contends that power is concentrated in the hands of elites. At the same time, there were also methodological differences and disagreements in power research. Pluralists took the view that the research focus should be on the actual exercise of power, whereas elite theory stressed the importance of charting the resources of power (Kunelius et al. 2009, 22–23).

A key premise of pluralism is its assumption that the power structure is scattered and dispersed and that power has a tendency to move toward balance. When there are several competing centers of power in society, power is not concentrated in the hands of any particular group. Not all groups in society necessarily have the same amount of power, but wield different amounts of power in different domains. This prevents power from accumulating to any single cohesive group. Pluralism sees the politics of liberal democracies as a process of choice and competition where there is no dominant ideology and where the state appears as a neutral arbiter between societal groups (Schwarzmantel 1987, 17–27).

Methodologically, the pluralist view emphasizes that there is no justification *a priori* to exclude the possibility of a complex and potentially more or less equitable and legitimate distribution of power in society. Conclusions about power should not be based exclusively on how resources are divided, but rather on an exploration of how they are used in concrete contexts. This might involve, for instance, identifying the actors contributing to different stages of the decision-making process, namely initiation, preparation, adoption, and implementation. By working from the assumption that society is fragmented into diverse interest groups with different power resources and partly overlapping memberships, pluralism maintains that it can carve out a more nuanced and complex empirical understanding of decision-making and the exercise of power than elite theory. At the same time, it is liable to change from being a means of description into a description of reality and—from an elite theory point of view—to become part of the legitimization of the prevailing system. There are at least two important things about the pluralist approach: firstly, that power is approached empirically at the level of action and decision-making and secondly, that it keeps open the possibility of the diffusion of power (Kunelius et al. 2009, 25). As we will see later on, modern elite research likewise does not exclude the possibility of the dispersion of power. Even in classical elite theory, the concentration of power to a small group of decision-makers was not considered sufficient evidence to establish the existence of an elite.

Forming in a sense an intermediary approach between pluralism and elite theory, corporatism is nowadays generally considered a more relevant approach than pluralism to studying power relations in the political system. Corporatism works from the assumption that interest groups are unable to compete on equal terms for the favor of government, but they are vertically integrated with the state, which has a tendency to concentrate opportunities for participation and influencing to a limited number of groups with the monopoly of interest representation in their respective fields (e.g., Cawson 1985).

CLASSICAL ELITE THEORY

The essence of classical elite theory[1] can be reduced to Gaetano Mosca's (1939, 50) claim that there are in all societies two classes of people: a class that rules and a class that is ruled. The classical elitist view of polarization in society is therefore not very far from the Marxist maxim, criticized by elitists, which says that capitalist societies are fundamentally divided between the exploiters and the exploited. In other words, there is in every society a small majority who makes all the important decisions. Since these decisions are far-reaching and affect most sectors of society, they are usually regarded as political decisions, even though the minority making these decisions consists not only of politicians in the government or a legislative body. Mosca's "political class," for example, comprises both those who formally make political decisions and those who have an influence on their content.

The mere fact that power is concentrated in the hands of a small group of people who are responsible for all day-to-day decision-making is not, however, enough to justify the existence of an elite. This is the case in virtually all organized societies in the modern world (e.g., Birch 2001, 186). A key criterion for the existence of an elite is that it constitutes a *cohesive, connected, and self-conscious group*. These characteristics are featured in practically all definitions of elite. Indeed, in James Meisel's (1958, 4) words, the three Cs—group consciousness, coherence, and conspiracy—are necessary features of the concept of elite. The latter term refers not to "secret machinations," but rather to a "common will to action" (Parry 1969; Burton and Higley 1987).

An elite has to act together as a group, with some shared purpose. If the elite is based on wealth or private education, its members must act together as the wealthy or as the defenders of private education in order to count as an elite group. If the group does not act as a unified body, it is less an elite than a category of "top persons" in the sphere in question, for instance the category of "most wealthy people" in the

United States or the category of "public school products" in Britain. The unity of the elite is sometimes seen as the outcome of the elite's social background and sometimes the product of the very organization of the elite itself. Power breeds consciousness of power. One of the chief strengths of the elite is its cohesiveness (Parry 1969, 32).

These qualities of self-consciousness, coherence, and unity are thought to reinforce the elite's advantageous position in relation to other groups in society. Elite theorists regard power as cumulative: power gives access to more power. This argument is at fundamental variance with pluralism's basic assumption. Elite theorists' conception of power comes close to Hobbes's definition of power as a present means to some future apparent good. Power is a means to obtain other social goods such as wealth, economic influence, social status, education for children, etc. According to Hobbes, these in turn become themselves power: wealth makes for greater wealth and political power, a group's social prestige adds weight to its political activities. Both wealth and educational opportunities will maintain the elite's domination from generation to generation, converting it into a hereditary caste (Ibid.).

Elite research has been criticized for working with an overly simplistic division between elites and the mass, with the former thought to hold power and the latter thought to be excluded from power. Although elements of such thinking can be detected in the best-known works of elite theory, the elite position is not a black-and-white, either-or proposition. Elite theory can equally well work with a more complex and multilayered conception of power (Etzioni-Halevy 1993, 29).

While the mass, the opposite of the elite, is usually described as lacking power, several elite theorists distinguish between two levels or strata of power within the elite. Such a distinction appears in Mosca (1939), Pareto (1963), and Mills (1956), although with some variation. This represents an attempt to take account of differences in the degree and the type of influence wielded by elite members. In some cases the lower stratum of the elite serves as a bridge between the core of decision-makers and the rest of society. It mediates between the rulers and the ruled, transmitting information in either direction and providing explanations and justifications for elite policy. Furthermore, it may be the source from which the higher elite is recruited as well as the level at which outsiders first enter elite circles from below (Parry 1969, 33).

C. Wright Mills (1956, 288–90), for example, makes a distinction within the power elite between an inner circle and outer fringes. The inner circle consists of those who interchange leading roles at the top of various institutions in politics, business, and the military, for instance. During their career, they move from one leading position to another, transcending the narrower milieu of any one institution and so performing the role of a link between different institutions. These people form the inner circle of the power elite. The outer fringes of the power elite—which are more liable to change than the inner circle—consist of "those who count," even though they are not involved in making decisions, nor do they move from one role to another between institutions. Not all members of the power elite have to be personally involved in making every decision, because their views and interests are taken into account even when they take no direct part in decision-making. In his studies of the political role of large business corporations in the United States and the UK, Michael Useem (1984, 61) has likewise identified among top executives an inner circle that "constitutes a distinct, politicized business segment, if a segment is defined as a subset of class members sharing a specific social location with partially distinct interests."

DEMOCRATIC ELITISM

Elites (and, by implication, elite theory) have been described as the antithesis of democracy (e.g., Etzioni-Halevy 1993, 216). According to Mosca and Pareto, a prime aim of their work was to demolish the myths of democracy (Parry 1969, 141). But there are other interpretations, too. The view that the existence of several elites or leadership groups is compatible with democracy is called democratic elitism or democratic elite theory. A key principle of this theory is that elites cannot be defined *a priori* as compatible or incompatible with democracy, but this compatibility depends on the characteristics of the elite (see Ruostetsaari 2007a). Democratic elitism can be seen as a combination that reconciles classical elite theory (the hypothesis of the concentration of power among elites) and pluralism (the hypothesis of competition among elites).

Democratic elitism is associated not only with Max Weber (1864–1920), but also Joseph Schumpeter (1883–1946). Schumpeter's model of society affords considerable autonomy to political leaders. Once the people have elected their leaders, the leaders must be left alone to get on with implementing their policies. The electorate must exercise "democratic self-restraint": this a necessary precondition for a stable and effective political system. It follows from Schumpeter's concept of democratic self-restraint that political leaders have freedom of maneuver when they are in power: they should not be confined by tight controls of accountability. This touches on one of the most important issues of democracy. There is the danger, on the one hand, that leaders might be freed from any accountability, and on the other hand, that they are so closely bound that they have no flexibility to respond to changing events or situations. Democratic elitism has a built-in tendency toward strong leadership. However, this must not be understood as an authoritarian leadership totally free from democratic control. Both Schumpeter and Giovanni Sartori say that open and competitive elections are a necessary element of democracy so that political leaders are subjected to control by the masses. In between elections, however, democratic self-restraint must prevail (Schwarzmantel 1987; Parry 1969).

In this perspective elections fulfill the functions of a plebiscite, in which the electorate express their approval or rejection of a certain team of leaders. Plebiscitary democracy has its origin in Max Weber's political thought and his ideas of "leadership democracy." The same ideas are found in Schumpeter's work, though in a rather more veiled form. According to Weber, it was necessary for a leadership to gain legitimacy through elections. This much the democratization of societies had achieved, although it had not changed the necessity of leadership. In other words, despite the birth of mass democracy, there was no change in the relationship between the rulers and the ruled: the few continued to dominate the many (Schwarzmantel 1987, 99).

For Schumpeter, democracy is a political method, a certain type of institutional arrangement for arriving at political decisions. For this reason it cannot be an end in itself, irrespective of what decisions it will produce under given historical conditions. That end is the election of competent leaders. The principal function of elections is to produce a strong, authoritative government: democracy simply means that people have the opportunity to accept or reject the people who are supposed to govern them (Schumpeter 1959, 242, 285; see also Bachrach 1967). Sartori stresses the role of the elite at the core of democratic theory and observes in the same vein that the purpose of elections is not to make democracy more democratic, but to elect the best possible leadership. Democracy, he says, is a procedure with which leaders compete in elections for power to govern (Sartori 1962, 124–27, 194).

Democratic elitism, then, is grounded in the premise that the existence of competing elites guarantees democracy. Peter Bachrach (1967, 102), a prominent critic of democratic elitism, says it is true that the political elite has to regularly subject itself to re-election, but the theory fails to recognize that this does not apply to other elites. The civil service elite has significant influence on the legislative process, but its accountability to the electorate is indirect at best. The business elite makes decisions that can have a greater and more tangible impact on citizens' lives than the decisions made by the political elite. These key groups do not have to subject themselves to control in elections. Pluralists can counter this by arguing that different and rival elites control one another. The business elite is controlled and countered by the trade union elite and the civil service elite by ministers, who are politically accountable to parliament and thereby to the people. C. Wright Mills (1956), on the other hand, maintains that elites do not in reality compete with one another, but constitute a single cohesive power elite within which there is close interaction and communication. The main criticism against democratic elitism is the argument that it cuts out of democracy its most crucial element, the involvement of citizens in decisions that concern themselves (Bachrach 1967). For democratic elitism, the key value threatened by democratic citizen participation is the stability of the existing society (see Schwarzmantel 1987).

Eva Etzioni-Halevy's *demo-elite perspective* is one of the most significant attempts to develop elite theory in the 1990s. Etzioni-Halevy's (1993, 29–30, 94–95) description of the structures of power and influence makes a distinction between three echelons: elites, sub-elites, and the public. Elites are those people who occupy the highest echelons of power and influence structures. Next, the middle ranks of power structures are occupied by sub-elites. Finally, the lowest rank is occupied by the public, but even this stratum is not completely powerless. Like classes, each category within the elite structure can be further divided into sub-groups. This categorization is based on Etzioni-Halevy's definition of elite, according to which elites consist of those "who wield power and influence on the basis of their active control of a disproportionate share of society's resources." Resources refer to scarce utilities or factors that affect people's lives, that at least some people require or want, and the demand for which exceeds supply. Since the distribution of resources is a matter of degree, in other words, some people have more and others have less resources, the elite structure or the distribution of power and influence is not a matter of either-or. As resources are not equally divided in any society, elite and power structures are best described in terms of gradations rather than dichotomies (Etzioni-Halevy 1993, 29–30, 94–95; see also 1997; 1999).

Etzioni-Halevy offers little reasoning for her trichotomous model of elites. In the end, it remains unclear what exactly separates the elite from the sub-elite, especially as there can be various sub-categories within them that she does not discuss at all. In any event sub-elites have less power and influence than elites. In the political sphere, sub-elites include backbench or rank-and-file members of legislatures and leaders of sizeable, but not the largest, interest groups. In the economic sphere, sub-elites include the middle management of major corporations and the owners and top executives of smaller companies. Furthermore, they include the middle echelons of the bureaucracy, the military and the police, leaders of smaller social movements, holders of middle-level or even junior judicial, media, and academic positions, as well as officials or activists in labor unions and social movements. Those excluded from these strata constitute Etzioni-Halevy's third stratum, the public (Etzioni-Halevy 1993, 95–96).

According to Etzioni-Halevy, "elites are not only some of the most advantaged, or those who champion the interests of the disadvantaged. Elites therefore include those who are the most active in preserving inegalitarian, elitist structures, that is, the status quo, but also those who are anti-elitist and struggle for change towards greater equality." Even the central leadership of social and protest movements belongs to the elite. By definition, "elites and sub-elites are not only those who sit atop established organizational power structures," but also "those who challenge and wish to challenge them" (Ibid., 95, 201).

Etzioni-Halevy's definition of elite is thus a broad and sweeping one. Indeed, it may well be asked that if the elite is characterized by the exercise of power based on the resources it controls, how can the elite also include the disadvantaged? Etzioni-Halevy herself admits that the elites of most social movements and interest groups may not be very powerful, although they can sometimes be quite significant (Ibid., 202). Etzioni-Halevy's definition of elite is in fact distinctly Paretian: the elite, in this definition, refers to the "very best" or the "crème de la crème" of any branch of activity, which means that it has necessarily nothing to do with the key premise of elite theory, the exercise of power (see Pareto 1963, 1423–30). Thus defined, the concept of elite becomes almost all-inclusive, causing it to lose much of its analytic power.

However, the term "elite," in its Paretian sense, is in common everyday use. For example, Finland's biggest daily *Helsingin Sanomat* (Oct. 25, 2014) interviewed a former criminal who had been caught in a vicious circle of theft from his early teens. His career didn't really take off until his first bank robbery: "It wasn't so much the money, it was what I'd done. That I'd achieved my goal and I was moving up in the hierarchy. I'd done something that hadn't been experienced before. I realized I'd moved up to the elite." In the eyes of common car thieves and drug dealers, the bank robber was a criminal genius.

Indeed, it makes sense to exclude social movements from the category of elite, unless they have significant power resources (assets, personnel, etc.) or well-established channels of interaction with those in established positions of power. However, this does not mean it is impossible for activists and lobbyists of social movements to rise to the elite, even to its inner circle. A Finnish example is provided by two Green League ministers in the second cabinet of Paavo Lipponen (1999–2003), Satu Hassi, and Osmo Soininvaara, who were involved in the well-publicized Koijärvi demonstrations of 1979, which marked the beginning of the environmental movement in Finland.

Another example dates from the early 1970s. Jukka Tarkka (2002, 59–60) describes how a "Social Democratic youth elite," formed around the Committee of 100 in Finland and its *Ydin* magazine, launched a critical campaign against official foreign policy. They advocated unilateral disarmament, a more active peace policy, a stronger emphasis on the Treaty on Friendship, Cooperation and Mutual Assistance with the Soviet Union to discourage inclinations to the west, the diplomatic recognition of the German Democratic Republic, the infusion of younger blood into the Ministry for Foreign Affairs, and opposition to the EEC Treaty. The group included Paavo Lipponen, SDP's secretary for international affairs; Tarja Halonen, a lawyer for the Central Organization of Finnish Trade Unions SAK; Erkki Tuomioja, MP; Jaakko Kalela, director of the Finnish Institute of International Affairs; Jaakko Blomberg, head of bureau at the Ministry of Education; and Osmo Apunen, head of bureau at the Ministry for Foreign Affairs. Urho Kekkonen, the President of the Republic, silenced the criticisms of the young elite in January 1973 by pledging to the most vociferous group members that the doors to the Ministry for Foreign Affairs would eventually open to the Social Democrats. And indeed this is what happened. Since the mid-1990s, these 1970s' foreign policy critics have formed the very core of foreign policy power in Finland: Tarja Halonen became minister for foreign affairs (1995–2000) and president of the republic (2000–2012); Paavo Lipponen became prime minister (1995–2007); Erkki Tuomioja minister for foreign affairs (2000–2007, 2011–2015); Jaakko Kalela became the president's long-standing permanent secretary; Jaakko Blomberg director general of the Political Department at the Ministry for Foreign Affairs and ambassador; and Osmo Apunen became professor of international relations.

Dogan and Higley have a more workable definition of elite. Political elites, they say, refer to holders of strategic positions in powerful organizations and movements, including dissident ones, who are able to affect national political outcomes regularly and significantly (Dogan and Higley 1998b, 15; see also Burton and Higley 2001, 182). However, rather than political elites, it is more appropriate to talk about elites in general; and rather than national political outcomes, it is better to talk about significant societal outcomes. In addition to political outcomes, the latter term comprises decisions that are taken in business and industry and at the international level, but that impact nation-states and citizens. "Political" may give the misleading impression that elites are simply about the exercise of power in the context of political parties or institutions, which clearly is not what these authors have in mind. The advantage of this definition is that it does not necessarily consider the power of elites to depend on the occupancy of some leading official position, but "strategic positions" may include the exercise of influence by virtue of expertise and informal positions, for instance.

In this study, elite refers to people who by virtue of their strategic position in influential organizations or in formally non-organized groups are capable of regularly exercising influence on significant societal outcomes. For conceptual clarity, the political elite at the center of political decision-making is distinguished from the concept of political class: the political class is taken to consist not only of the ministers and MPs who form the inner circle of the political elite, but all the people who live "off" politics, that is, make a living out of politics regardless of whether they exercise power (Burdeau 1975).

There is no compelling reason to view the structures of elites and power as dichotomous or even trichotomous. Society's power structures can be described by the metaphor of a dartboard, in which the inner bulls-eye or the "inner circle of power" is surrounded by progressively weaker rings of influence. The radial sectors of the dartboard describe the sectors of society, which are divided between different strata of power and influence (Ruostetsaari 1992, 70). Drawing the line where the "elite" ends and "the people" begins in each radial sector is an empirical question that has to be separately addressed in each research. Elite theory cannot provide an exhaustive solution for delimitation (see, e.g., Etzioni-Halevy 1993, 95; Putnam 1976).

Classical elite theory posits the mass as the opposite of the elite. The members of the mass have not organized themselves for collective political activity. All individuals live their own private lives, concentrating on their own interests at work and in leisure. Their contacts are limited to family members, neighbors, and colleagues at work. So restricted is such a life that the individual's understanding of public affairs is bound to be limited. In contrast to elite members, these individuals lack the kind of wide view of society that is necessary for ruling. An atomized mass in unable even to see the purpose of their own activities because they cannot see what part they play in the bigger picture (Parry 1969, 54; see, e.g., Mills 1956, 321–22; Giddens 1979; Hewitt 1974).

The mass is able to act as a single coherent group only when it is integrated from outside by the elite. The mass has no desire for leadership, but on the contrary has a psychological need for guidance and direction. Lacking political ambition, the individuals in the mass are glad to have the responsibility of decision-making taken off their shoulders. The elite cultivates its coherence and consciousness while adopting toward the mass a policy of divide and rule. Horizontal contacts between members of society break down and are replaced by vertical contacts between atomized individuals and the elite (Parry 1969, 55).

It follows from the conception of elite and power adopted in this work, that is, the view of an "inner core of power" surrounded by progressively weaker circles of influence, that the mass, designated by classical elite theory as the counterpart of the elite, is not completely deprived of power and influence. For this reason the concept of mass is here discarded in favor of the citizenry.

One key principle of Etzioni-Halevy's demo-elite perspective concerns the autonomy of elites. Non-democratic and democratic elites are separated from each other by the relative autonomy of elites as advocated by liberal philosophy and democratic elite theory, which works in two directions. For the elite to enjoy relative autonomy, it needs to show independence not only in relation to other elite groups and the state, but also in relation to the groups or classes that it represents. Some degree of elite coherence is a necessary component of relative elite autonomy, but on the other hand it is also necessary to have some degree of elite separation. The existence of a representative relationship requires that elites are relatively autonomous vis-à-vis the groups they represent (Etzioni-Halevy 1993, 101).

In fact, Etzioni-Halevy's meta-principle of democracy which emphasizes elite autonomy creates a dilemma: the very principle that should uphold democracy—the combination of elite cooperation and autonomy—actually works against it, because part of elite autonomy is based on the detachment of elites from their foundations, that is, the people they represent (cf. Bang and Dyrberg 2001, 30–31). A workable democracy is indeed inconceivable without a responsiveness on the part of decision-makers to citizens. Etzioni-Halevy herself admits that the ultimate test of the importance of the public in a democracy is its ability to get elites to listen to what it wants. If elites are closely interconnected, that will lead to their isolation from the underprivileged. This rejection of the underprivileged adds to socioeconomic inequality and detracts from the quality of democracy. Hence, the autonomy of elites and the role of the public are closely intertwined. However, the autonomy of elites cannot ensure such responsiveness. The competition among elites, an integral part of their autonomy, increases the likelihood that elites will need the support of the public to maintain their position and to achieve their goals. It increases the likelihood that public opinion will have at least some impact on what the elites do or do not do (Etzioni-Halevy 1993, 101, 108, 242).

An elite or sub-elite can be considered relatively autonomous if, despite some of its resources being controlled from the outside, it has significant resources that cannot be controlled, or can only marginally be controlled from outside its own boundaries. Relative elite autonomy is manifested in separate and often opposing interests with respect to those resources. Employing resources and acting in a manner that does not promote or that even works against others' interests thus reflects the relative autonomy of an elite vis-à-vis other elites. For instance, an elite may demonstrate its independence from other elites by creating and using symbolic resources. It may do so by developing conceptions or ideologies that do not further its subservience to other elites or that detract from the legitimacy of other elites. An elite may demonstrate its independence by revealing damaging information about other elites, or by publicly criticizing and vilifying them. Examples can even be found in 1990s' Finland, where political scandals have been sparked by a member of one elite making revelations about a member of another elite. To sum up then, the relative autonomy of elites is usually manifested in the lack of symbolic subservience to others, and often, but not always, in disagreement and friction with others. Elite confrontations may thus serve as a useful, though not the sole indicator of elite autonomy. For Etzioni-Halevy, this mutual autonomy of elites is a major requirement for democracy (Etzioni-Halevy 1993, 99–101). Etzioni-Halevy's theory has, however, been criticized for its failure to provide hardly any explanation of the origin and foundation of the relative autonomy of elites (Burton and Higley 2001, 184).

The autonomy of elites, which is never complete but always relative and imperfect, is an important precondition of democracy. Without this autonomy, the principles of democracy cannot exist or persist. If elites are closely interconnected, that will lead to their isolation from the underprivileged. This rejection of the underprivileged adds to socioeconomic inequality and detracts the quality of democracy (Etzioni-Halevy 1993, 101, 242).

The ultimate test of the importance of the public in a democracy is its ability to make elites responsive to its own wishes. Here, too, the autonomy of elites and the role of the public are closely intertwined. The autonomy of elites cannot ensure such responsiveness. However, the rivalry between elites, an integral part of their autonomy, increases the likelihood that elites will need the support of the public for the maintenance of their elite positions and for the achievement of their goals. It increases the likelihood that public opinion will have at least some impact on what the elites do or do not do (Ibid., 108).

Some scholars take the view that elite coherence and consensus about the rules of the political game are just as important conditions of democracy as elite autonomy. Eisenstadt, for instance, assumes that conflict among elites contributes to the effectiveness of the democratic political system, provided that it is balanced by elite solidarity and consensus on some basic values and "rules of the game." Etzioni-Halevy maintains that a similar distinction must be made between elite cooperation, on the one hand, and elite solidarity and consensus, on the other, as Dahrendorf makes between social integration and social harmony: the proper functioning of any political system and democracy requires elite cooperation rather than elite consensus and solidarity over the rules of game. According to Etzioni-Halevy, democracy cannot exist without elite cooperation, but nor can it exist without elite autonomy (Ibid., 64, 99–101, 109–110).

Etzioni-Halevy admits that the relationship between elite cooperation and elite autonomy is problematic, but insists it is not necessarily contradictory. In a democracy, she says, elite cooperation that does not encroach on the relative autonomy of elites contributes to the functioning of the political system, and hence to democracy. On the other hand, elite cooperation that breaks or jeopardizes elite autonomy (the subjugation or collusion of elites and sub-elites) jeopardizes democracy. Eliminating or minimizing cooperation of this latter type is thus essential to the survival of a democracy (Ibid., 113).

This study starts from the assumption that elite collaboration is necessary for democracy. Although democracy requires some basic consensus about the rules of the game concerning the political system's procedures, elite collaboration does not equate with consensus. Elites may collaborate without sharing a consensus about the goals and objectives of developing society. On the other hand, it is apparent that there can be no consensus without interaction and cooperation between elites. Coming as they do from similar social backgrounds and careers, members of elite groups may find themselves sharing similar opinions, attitudes, and values, which in turn may promote interaction within and among elite groups. Thus the existence of a power elite—if indeed it is possible to talk about its existence—is based on a triangle whose vertices are the similar social background and career of elites, their close interaction, and shared attitudes. This is why the focus of this study is on the changes that have taken place in the openness and coherence of Finnish elites.

TYPOLOGY OF ELITE STRUCTURES AND RESEARCH TASK

Mobility, in the sense of reproduction, replacement, elite circulation, or convergence, has played a pivotal role in classical elite theories. The replacement of one elite by another occurs in one of two ways: either through a gradual process of infiltration as described by Mosca, or as Pareto had it, "the circulation of elites"; or through a violent revolution in which one group of elites is replaced by another. According to Pareto, the most obvious and most common obstacle to free elite circulation is the aristocratic principle: descendants of the elite are promoted to elite positions regardless of their abilities, at the same time as the most talented descendants of non-elite parents are excluded. Taken to an extreme, this process leads to elite inbreeding and ultimately to the degeneration of the elite. For this reason relatively unhindered elite circulation in the social hierarchy, both upward and down, is a precondition for a healthy and strong society. Mosca, likewise, argues that recruitment into the ruling class occurs in accordance with the aristocratic tendency when new elite members are recruited from amongst the descendants of the existing ruling class. Society degenerates as a result of the loss of contact with the needs and interests of the rest of society. By contrast, the democratic tendency prevails when the ruling class is regenerated through a process of gradual infiltration from below (Parry 1969, 39, 45–50, 60–63).

C. Wright Mills referred to horizontal circulation as a source of the coherence of the power elite. According to his theory, the degree of elite coherence is determined by the density of interplay between institutions. If institutions share several contacts and interests in common, the elites of those institutions will have a tendency to form a coherent group. "Institutional closeness" is highest when individuals move frequently from one leading position to another across institutions. By way of an example, Mills mentions top executives of major American corporations who have held significant public offices, but who have returned to leading business roles or top positions in foundations. The ease with these kinds of roles are exchanged indicates the degree of group cohesiveness within the power elite, that is, the political directorate and occupants of leading positions in major corporations and the military: the more frequently roles are exchanged and the higher the degree of institutional closeness, the greater the cohesiveness of the power elite (Mills 1956, 10–11, 19, 287–88). In other words, a monolithic elite originates as a result of increasing interpenetration and overlapping between elite groups. If, on the other hand, mobility between the various elite groups is relatively weak, and if the separation generated by specialization and expertise is significant, then the pluralist interpretation of elite structure gains support (Dogan 2003, 5).

However, Mills's conception of the elite is not based exclusively on the interrelations between elite members in dominant institutions, but also on their social and psychological similarity and their position in the highest social stratum. The coherence of the power elite can be understood against the origin, career, and lifestyles of elite members. The mutual connections among elite members lead to a common lifestyle and to a sense of unity. Self-consciousness, awareness of one's membership in the elite, furthers the cohesion of the power elite. Most elite members come from a similar social background: they have been recruited into the elite from the highest social stratum in society. Factors that often open the door to power include such demographic traits as old family ties, proper marriage, a fine residence in the right area, the right church and club, and well-respected schools. Education is particularly important to the reproduction of the highest social stratum: exclusive education creates and reproduces the traditions of the highest social stratum and controls the access of new, affluent, and talented individuals into the elite (Mills 1956, 10–11, 63–66, 287–89).

This study combines different elite theory perspectives and integrates vertical and horizontal elite circulation into the same model. Classical elite theory maintains that different elite groups, such as the political, administrative, and business elite, are characterized by exclusivity, coherence, and unanimity (Meisel 1958), which can be cross-tabulated by a typology (table 2.1) (c.f. Scott 1991, 119). The first variable in the typology is the degree of openness of the elite structure, which refers to vertical elite circulation. With respect to openness, recruitment into elites can vary from low (which means that elites have a much higher socioeconomic background than the citizenry) to high (which means that elites have a similar socioeconomic background to the general population).

Table 2.1. Typology of Elite Structures

		DEGREE OF COHERENCE	
		high	low
DEGREE OF OPENNESS	low	Exclusive	Segmented
	high	Inclusive	Fragmented

The second variable of horizontal circulation refers to the degree of elite coherence, combining the variables of cohesion and unanimity. Elite coherence is high if members of the elite groups have close interaction with one another, similar patterns of career mobility, and if they share similar opinions, attitudes, and values. The coherence of the elite structure is also reinforced by high mobility—in other words, frequent exchanges of roles between different elite groups and a sense of shared interests. Weak vertical links with the citizenry have the same reinforcing effect: this will protect the elite against any erosive effects caused by demands and control by the citizenry, which have the potential to create discord by pitting elite members against one another. According to Etzioni-Halevy (1993, 101; see also Bang and Dyrberg 2001), the autonomy of elites requires independence not only vis-à-vis other elite groups and the state, but also the groups or classes they represent. According to Pakulski and Körösényi (2012, 24–25), the political elite, for instance, needs authorization from the electorate—the trust and confidence of voters—but also considerable autonomy, insulation from the immediate pressures that come with mass authorization. Under such conditions of autonomy, politicians can accept public responsibility, the latter discharged to both parliaments and mass electorates.

The elite structure can be described as *exclusive* when elites come from a more privileged socioeconomic background than the citizenry and when they are recruited from society's highest strata, when they have very close mutual contact and they share similar values and attitudes. By contrast there is a wide gulf between the attitudes of elites and the citizenry. At the other end of the typology, a *fragmented* elite structure is characterized by a broad socioeconomic recruitment base, limited interplay between elites, and a wide gulf in attitudes. Elites might share certain societal rules of the game in common, for instance a consensus about the democratic process, but they differ in their views about many societal objectives. On the other hand, there are close links between citizen groups and elites, and they share similar attitudes (Ruostetsaari 2003, 293; see also Higley and Moore, 1981; 2001; cf. Etzioni-Halevy 1993; Bang and Dyrberg 2001; Higley 2007).

In an exclusive elite structure, consensus among the various elite groups is so strong that we can talk about the existence of a single power elite. In a fragmented elite structure, by contrast, the consensus among elites is so weak that it is not justified to talk about a single power elite.

Elite theorists argue that only democratic regimes are subject to regular, systematic elite competition and ascent (Schumpeter), mobility (Weber), and circulation (Pareto) (Pakulski and Körösényi 2012, 16). The importance of elite competition as a necessary precondition for democracy has been stressed above all by democratic elitism (see Etzioni-Halevy 1993; Higley 2007; Engelstad 2010). According to the critics of democratic elitism, however, the classical criteria of democracy are not satisfied by the citizenry exercising its control, primarily through elections, on the political elite only (Bachrach 1967). Competing elites may even be internally oligarchic when they are closed to citizen participation.

We argue in this work is that the degree of democracy in a society depends, firstly, on active vertical circulation, as pointed out by Pareto and Mosca, in other words, on the openness of elites. This means it must be possible for individuals coming from different socioeconomic backgrounds to be recruited into elite positions. However, a very high degree of vertical circulation causes excessive turnover among elite members and therefore does not contribute to the functioning of democracy, because it may undermine both the stability of decision-making processes, the expertise of leaders and executives, and the attractiveness of leadership positions (Pakulski and Körösényi 2012, 153).

Secondly, the degree of democracy depends on slight horizontal elite circulation, as stressed by Mills and democratic elitism, that is, on the separation of elites rather than on elite competition as such. John Higley et al. (1991) have suggested that integrated national elites are not enemies of democracy, but on the contrary are a necessary condition for democracy. This argument, however, can only be accepted on condition that a consensual relationship among the elite groups involves only formally and informally agreed rules and norms of policy-making. Consensus among elites must not be allowed to go so far that they are connected by close interaction and mobility and by agreement about the goals for the development of society. A closely integrated elite structure reduces elite competition and the responsiveness of elites toward the citizenry. For this reason elite autonomy, as stressed by Etzioni-Halevy (1993, 99–101), is an important condition for democracy. In the terms of the elite typology adopted here (table 2.1), an exclusive elite structure is inadequate, whereas a fragmented elite structure best meets the criteria of classical democracy (Ruostetsaari 2006).

The purpose of this study is to analyze the changes that have occurred, firstly, in vertical mobility, that is, in elite recruitment; and secondly, in horizontal mobility, that is, in the coherence of the elite structure in Finnish society in 1991–2011. Based on these analyses, the aim is to find out how the elite structure has changed over the past two decades, a period of great change and upheaval in Finnish society. Finally, the work discusses what these changes mean to the functioning of democracy. The changes seen in the Finnish elite structure are also compared with the results of power studies in other Nordic countries.

NOTE

1. Classical elite theories include Vilfredo Pareto's (1848–1923) *The Mind and Society*, Gaetano Mosca's (1858–1941) *The Ruling Class*; and Robert Michels's (1876–1936) *Political Parties*. The best-known followers of the tradition include James Burnham's *The Managerial Revolution* (1941), C. Wright Mills's *The Power Elite* (1956), and Floyd Hunter's *Community Power Structure* (1963).

3

Approach of the Study

METHODS OF ELITE RESEARCH

Empirical studies of elites have been inspired by classical elite theories. These theories, however, are no longer recognized as the universal scientific truth. Rather, they serve as a source of hypotheses for research on societal power structures. This "neoelitism" is not the exact same approach as that taken by its classical elite theorists, however, because it has been influenced by both pluralism and Marxism. The key difference stems from views on the degree of autonomy exercised by elites in decision-making. It is nowadays widely thought that elites are to some extent constrained by external circumstances such as economic factors and public opinion (Moyser and Wagstaffe 1987b, 5). The study of power structures, an area of research concerned with the distribution and exercise of power in society, dates to the mid-1950s and the publication of the seminal works of Floyd Hunter and C. Wright Mills (Domhoff 1980).

Empirical elite studies have ranged from analyzing the nature of specific elites or the degree of national elite integration, to testing the hypotheses put forward by elite theorists. The approaches and methods used in these studies can be grouped into four categories (see, e.g., Moyser and Wagstaffe 1987a; Parry 1969): 1) The social backgrounds and recruitment patterns of elites, 2) the positional approach, 3) the decisional approach, and 4) the reputational approach.

The approach focusing on the social backgrounds and recruitment patterns of elites is based on a premise that attitudes and political opinions are to a significant extent shaped by social class, descent, education, and other such factors. It is widely thought that sharing a common social and educational background significantly promotes the cohesion of any elite group. For example, the City of London has often been described as a community where everyone who counts knows everyone else who counts. Personal contacts are central to the City's way of business, which is facilitated not only by a common class and educational background, but also by overlapping memberships in boards of directors and family-based connections between companies (Parry 1969, 99–100).

On the other hand, this approach has been used to investigate to what extent elites are a representative sample of the population in terms of education, incomes, and other factors. In other words, based on the representativeness of elites, the aim has been to describe the distribution of opportunities in society. Changes in the criteria of elite recruitment and therefore in the social characteristics of elites are taken as indicators of social changes, and vice versa (Hoffman-Lange 1987, 27).

The positional approach is one of the most widely used perspectives for defining national elites in complex industrial societies. Typically the researcher identifies the most important institutions or organizations in different sectors of society, or in the sectors singled out for study, through which individuals can gain access to power resources. Next, the researcher will define the key positions for the exercise of power within each institution or organization. The incumbents of these positions will then be considered as members of the elite (e.g., Hoffman-Lange 1987, 30).

The decisional approach is the purest manifestation of the pluralist conception of power. The existence of elites—or as pluralists would have it, the category of top leaders—must be ascertained by studying how major concrete decisions are reached and by identifying the actors involved in and influencing decision-making processes. The decisional approach sums up the pluralist criticism against elite theorists, who are said to fail to specify the field in which elite members wield their power and influence. An individual may be influential in one field, but lack influence in another. For this reason it is necessary to focus on "key decisions" in society (see Dahl 1958).

In the reputational method, elites are identified by asking experts to single out the individuals who have the most power and influence in the community in focus. It has even been found that an individual's reputation as someone with power may in reality be more important that the actual exercise of power (see, e.g., Crenson 1971, 80, 130). This approach has mainly been used to study the power structures of small communities, especially municipalities.

The best-known application of this method is Floyd Hunter's study *Community Power Structure* (1963), which analyzed the power structure of "Regional City." The research method comprised several stages, each of which was designed to check on the previous results. In the first stage, Hunter drew up a preliminary list of community leaders that was based primarily on formal positions in politics, business, and certain other organizations. Experts were also consulted in this stage. In the second stage, Hunter selected a panel of experts or "judges" that was to be as representative as possible, both with respect to the different sectors and the community's social characteristics. The panel was asked to name the top leaders from lists describing different sectors of the community. At this stage the definition of power was based on the persons' reputation among panel members. Finally, Hunter interviewed some of the leaders identified, who in turn were asked to identify a group of top leaders from amongst the persons named by the panel. In order to establish the degree of cohesiveness among the leaders, the interviewees were asked how well they knew other leaders and how often they interacted with them.

The current study uses two of the above mentioned approaches, that is, the approach of social background and recruitment patterns of elites, and the positional approach. In addition, shifts in the distribution of power are examined by using the reputational method, with elite members asked to provide assessments of how the power structure of Finnish society has changed. All approaches to elite research have their own strengths and weaknesses (see Ruostetsaari 1992): there is no single approach that is universally applicable to all research tasks and areas of study. Furthermore, different approaches lead not only to different methodological solutions, but they also reflect different conceptions of power.

HOW TO DEFINE POWER AND INFLUENCE?

Viewing power in terms of resources embedded in institutional positions resonates well with Max Weber's definition of power as capital owned or controlled in one way or another by actors. Although power resources are always jointly produced, they are first and foremost unevenly divided. In other words, the constant unequal distribution of different kinds of resources—and the way this is viewed by different actors in society—is power. If power were evenly distributed, it would be hard or impossible to exercise. Power depends crucially on an institutionalized asymmetry of resources and capabilities, and on an acceptance of the structure thus created. Michael Mann (1986, 7) describes this legitimation of power by noting that the few at the top can keep the masses at the bottom compliant, provided their control is institutionalized in the laws and the norms of the social group in which both operate. In other words, the constant control of society's institutionalized resources lies at the very core of power (Kunelius et al. 2009, 18–19).

Another major question of power research concerns the relationship of power with the resources on which it is based. Talcott Parsons (1986) defines power as an independent and concrete means of exchange. It is true that power is based on multiple resources (authority, money, threat of violence, symbolic persuasion), but in its institutional form it is not reducible to any single one of them. From the standpoint of those wielding power, power is a general and abstract resource that can help to achieve the desired actions of others. However, when viewed as a general resource, power refers to the potential embedded in a certain position in society rather than to the actual use of resources (Ibid. 2009, 19–20).

The amount of power held by an actor depends not only on the resources available to that actor, but also on others' perceptions of that power, their abstract assessments of the distribution of power. Power is first and foremost a medium of the political system, because the political system and decision-making are based on the respective parties' mutual assessments of each other's power. The effectiveness of power also ties in with the question of its legitimacy and acceptability. Power can thus be seen as a relationship, since the opportunity of the power holder to exercise power is limited by the consent of those subjected to power. Holders of power can lean on their general power potential so long as there is no objection on the part of those who are subjected to power. If, on the other hand, the latter challenge the power position of those in power, the holders of power will have to resort to their power resources, such as money or sanctions, which will put their effectiveness to the test (Kunelius et al. 2009, 19–20).

New institutionalism, an approach that is interested in the way institutions operate, can easily be interpreted as being at variance with the approach that emphasizes agency and discourses, which is most prominently represented by Michel Foucault. Although it is commonly thought that Foucault rejects conceptions that view power as an essentially hierarchic, constant structure, or as an institutional order (Helén 1994, 276), Anu Kantola (2002, 27, 37–44) has shown that structures and institutions figure prominently in Foucault's work on power. In fact, Foucault writes in different ways about power and has different meanings for power at different periods of his production.

Foucault criticizes traditional power theory, which emphasizes juridical rules, rights and laws, rulers and institutions. His central argument is that understanding power in terms of laws or a ruler's prerogatives is based on juridico-monarchic power, which is not relevant to understanding the forms of power in modern society. Foucault's perspective turns the focus from constitutional paragraphs to non-juridical practices of power, to how the exercise of power is legitimized and justified (Kantola 2002, 27; see Foucault 1992, 67).

This Foucaldian understanding of modern power and control has attracted some criticism, mainly from the side of critical theory. According to Jürgen Habermas (1990), Foucault fails to anchor discourses to their contexts and society's structures. Discourses, he says, emerge and pop like glittering bubbles from a swamp of anonymous processes of subjugation. For Foucault, power is not located in structures or institutions, but it becomes more a force that operates autonomously and that is detached from its societal context. Foucault's followers have come in for their share of this criticism, mainly because their analyses remain at the level of speech and knowledge, because they fail to connect control to socioeconomic changes in society, for instance to income distribution in different regimes (Kantola 2002, 7–38).

However, Foucault's texts from different periods give rise to different interpretations of what he means by power. His later works in particular include elements that can counter at least some of the criticism from critical theory. It seems that during this period, Foucault does not address power as the subject's self-discipline and as a form of all-pervasive knowledge that normalizes individuals, but instead he emphasizes the role of societal structures and institutions. This concept of power is most forcefully put forward in *The Subject and Power*, which was first published in English in 1982 (Kantola 2002, 41–42; see Foucault 2000).

Foucault says that he does not consider power only to be a discursive force embodied in the individual. Language itself does not exercise power. "It is necessary also to distinguish power relations from relationships of communications which transmit information by means of a language, a system of signs, or any other symbolic medium." Power relations, for Foucault, are not the same thing as the structures of communication and language use: speaking subjects do not automatically have power over those who are listening. It is also not true that power is simply the use of language, but economic sanctioning, for instance, belongs to the sanctions of modern societies (Foucault 2000, 337; Kantola 2002, 42).

Foucault writes that "the exercise of power is not a naked fact, an institutional right, nor is it a structure which holds out or is smashed: it is elaborated, transformed, organized; it endows itself with processes which are more or less adjusted to the situation. . . . Power relations are rooted in the system of social networks" (Foucault 2000, 345).

Foucault identifies a number of concrete areas of investigation for the study of power relations. Firstly, he urges investigation of various systems of differentiations that permit one to act upon the actions of others (e.g., economic, linguistic, and cultural differences). Secondly, he is interested to know about the types of objectives pursued by the holders of power, such as the maintenance of privileges, the accumulation of profits, and the exercise of legislative power. Thirdly, it is necessary to analyze the means of exercising power: is power exercised by the threat of arms, the effects of words, or by means of economic disparities? Fourth, Foucault says it is important to analyze the institutionalization of power: what kinds of institutions, statutes, customs, or practices contribute to maintaining power? Institutions must be analyzed from the vantage point of power relations rather than the other way round. Fifth, he draws attention to the techniques of rationalization employed by those in power, that is, the techniques of creating and maintaining power relations. The concept of power, for Foucault, is not just about commitment to language, nor is it individual, but he also views power relations as societal struggles that are connected with institutions and structures (Foucault 2000, 343–45; Kantola 2002, 43).

There are, then, some elements in Foucault's production that approximate Anthony Giddens's (1979) theory of power. According to Giddens, one key problem with power research has had to do precisely with the separation of action and structure. He says there are two versions of how power structures are constituted, and two versions of domination. The first tends to treat domination as a network of decision-making, operating against an unexamined institutional backdrop. The latter considers domination as itself an institutional phenomenon, either disregarding power as relating to the active actions and accomplishments of actors, or treating it as in some way determined by institutions.

Giddens says that the concept of action is logically tied to the concept of power. Power can be related to interaction in a dual sense: as involved institutionally in processes of interaction, and as used to accomplish outcomes in strategic conduct. Actors make use of these structures in their interaction and at once reproduce them. In the context of strategic conduct, the relation between the concepts of action and power can be set out as follows. Action involves intervention in events in the world, thus producing definite outcomes, with intended action being one category of an actor's doings or his refraining from doing. Power as transformative capacity can then be taken to refer to actors' capabilities of reaching such outcomes. Giddens thus defines power both as a transformative capacity (which is how power is seen by pluralists, who view it from the perspective of actors' action) and as domination (which is how power is seen by elite theorists, who are concerned to examine it as a structural characteristic). Both aspects require each other (Giddens 1984, 145–46). The need for this kind of dualist approach is well captured by Ilkka Heiskanen's (2001, 18) observation that "power is always exercised over and above established institutional structures."

The view taken in this study is that an actor (a person or an organization) has influence to the extent that said actor has the capacity to intentionally influence the behavior or attitudes of another actor, regardless of whether the actor being influenced is aware of being a target of influence, and regardless of the means or procedures on which this capacity is based. Influence, as a special case of power, may be based either on positions in formal hierarchies and the authority vested in those positions, or on informal factors (e.g., skills, abilities, and charisma) that are not reducible to formal positions (Ruostetsaari 2003, 49; see also Lasswell and Kaplan 1950, 23; Wrong 1979, 23; Petersson 1987, 17).

POWER AND INFLUENCE OF ELITES

As we have seen, the different approaches taken in elite research reflect the interdependence of theory and method. Different conceptions of elites and power lead to the use of different methods, which will also impact the results and conclusions drawn (Moyser and Wagstaffe 1987a; see also Dahl 1958, 59).

Ursula Hoffman-Lange (1987, 31) has classified approaches of elite research according to the degree to which they take into consideration two dimensions of power, that is, formal and informal power, and direct participation in decision-making and indirect influence on decisions (table 3.1). Her classification additionally includes the codified rules of political decision-making, although this cannot be considered a research approach proper. These are the formal rules that define the formal power structure of a given community (e.g., a state). In Hoffman-Lange's classification, the codified rules represent that extreme with the narrowest conception of power. At the opposite extreme is the reputational method, which can take account of both the exercise of power based on formal and informal resources, and direct and indirect influence on political decision-making.

In practice, the approaches discussed above have gradually become reduced to ideal types: more and more often, they are now combined with one another. Research may start out with an analysis of decision-making processes (e.g., Presthus 1964) or an institutional approach (e.g., Hoffman-Lange 1987), and then proceed to use the reputational method to give more depth to the analysis. On the other hand,

Table 3.1. Relationship of Power to Participation in Decision-making in Various Elite Research Approaches.

POWER RESOURCES	PARTICIPATION IN DECISION-MAKING	
	Direct participation	Direct participation and indirect influence
Formal power	Codified rules of decision-making	Positional approach
Formal and informal power	Decisional approach	Reputational approach

Source: Hoffman-Lange 1987, 31.

research may start out with the reputational method, using a panel to study the formation of the decision-making process (e.g., Agger et al. 1964). Snowball sampling is a method used to interview a population retrieved by means of the positional approach. These people will be asked to identify others who in one way or another have been important in connection with their own use of power. These people will typically be interviewed in the second stage. Interview rounds can be continued until saturation is reached and no new names come up in the interviews. The snowball method differs from the standard reputational method in that the latter involves asking experts directly about the exercise of power, whereas the snowball method is indirect and specific. Experts are consulted as a source of information only insofar as questions concern their own activity. Forming the bigger picture is left to the researcher (see, e.g., SOU 1990: 44, 308–9).

In addition to the approaches mentioned above, elite studies have used some other, less common methods. For example, content analysis has been used to find out how elites use and manipulate symbols (Moyser and Wagstaffe 1987, 19). Some studies have used participatory observation to study the behavior and performance of company directors (e.g., Winkler 1987). Another less common method is the network analysis based on the method of interlocking directors (Ruostetsaari 1989).

Elite research has traditionally relied on quantitative methods, which can be explained by the mainstream role of recruitment studies in this field. One noteworthy quantitative research project spanning an exceptionally long time period is the study by Olli-Pekka Ruuskanen et al. (2010), which traces the changing position of the nobility and the characteristics of people in leading positions in Finnish society over two centuries, from 1809 to 2009. The data for this research have included calendars of nobility and the *Who's Who*.

The use of qualitative methods has gradually increased in elite research, too. Qualitative studies are often either anthropological (e.g., Shore and Nugent 2002; Aguiar and Schneider 2012; Abbink and Salverda 2013) or sociological (e.g., Daloz 2010; 2013), and based on interview methods. Guides are available on how to use different interview methods in elite research (e.g., Hertz and Imber 1995; Dexter 2006). One of the most extensive, if not the most extensive elite study using the interview method is D. Michael Lindsay's *View from the Top* (2014), for which he personally interviewed, over a period of ten years, 550 senior leaders in the United States. Half of the leaders he interviewed worked in business, one-quarter in government, and one-quarter in the nonprofit sector (including higher education). Lindsay calls his interview technique the "leapfrog method": he asked the leaders to recommend others who might be worth including in the study.

In this research, the study of elites' social backgrounds and recruitment patterns is combined with the positional approach and the reputational method. This means that the analysis is concerned with both formal power (leading positions in powerful institutions) and informal power (elite members' expert assessments of the distribution of influence and their informal networking). In other words, the approach takes account of both the actual and potential use of power and influence, both in the context of action and structure.

FINNISH ELITE STRUCTURE IN 1991–2011

This study uses the positional approach to determine and describe the Finnish elite structure. The 1991 elite structure is constructed by analyzing power structures and the roles of organizations in different policy sectors based on earlier studies and various register sources (Ruostetsaari 1992; 1993). Elites are defined as those people who by virtue of their key strategic positions (in practice, senior leadership roles) in influential organizations can regularly influence the formation of significant policy decisions in different sectors of society. The elite structures in 2001 (Ruostetsaari 2003; 2006) and 2011 (Ruostetsaari 2012) are constructed in the same way by analyzing changes in power and organizational structures and in Finnish society more generally.

Organizational changes in 1991–2011 have also brought changes to the lists of elite positions. The figures in table 3.2 describe the number of elite positions in different elite groups (i.e., senior leadership positions in influential organizations, not the number of people holding such positions, because one person may hold more than one elite position). For instance, a member of Parliament who is chair of a parliamentary committee and chair of a significant NGO is included in both the political elite and the organizational elite. For reasons of simplicity, the different elite groups, taken together, are henceforth described as constituting the "power elite" (Mills 1956). Whether or not this description is theoretically justified will be discussed in the concluding chapter.

People holding the following positions are counted as belonging to an elite group. In all three years under study, the political elite includes all cabinet ministers and political state secretaries, as well as the current president and former presidents of the republic. From Parliament, only the most influential positions are included in the political elite: these are the Speaker and deputy Speakers, the leaders of parliamentary groups, and the chairs of parliamentary committees. In 1991 the political elite additionally included the vice-chairs of parliamentary committees, and in 2001

Table 3.2. Finnish Elite Structure in 1991–2011 (the Number of Elite Positions)

Elites and Sub-elites	1991	2001	2011
The Government	18	20	22
Parliament	46	59	59
Party organizations	61	59	60
Political state secretaries	1	1	13
Municipal councils and boards	18	18	20
Regional councils		20	19
MEPs and commissioner		17	14
POLITICAL ELITE TOTAL	144	194	207
Ministries	78	90	79
Central government agencies	37	30	39
Judiciary	18	23	27
Defence Forces	20	16	22
Church	20	22	24
State regional administration	22	21	21
Municipalities	18	18	20
Regional councils' administration		19	19
EU officials		29	39
ADMINISTRATIVE ELITE TOTAL	213	268	290
State-owned companies and public utilities	46	48	51
Cooperatives	40	33	25
Private business	98	137	158
Property	15	15	16
BUSINESS ELITE TOTAL	199	233	250
Employee associations	54	69	64
Business associations	50	69	78
Other NGOs	54	71	79
Organizations in local and regional administration	46		
ORGANIZATIONAL ELITE TOTAL	204	209	221
Daily press	41	45	42
Other press	29	29	30
TV, radio	50	61	79
MASS MEDIA ELITE TOTAL	120	135	151
Universities	22	21	31
Government research institutes	19	18	28
Private research institutes	16	14	15
Foundations	14	14	16
Associations	15	9	16
Academy of Finland	41	53	51
SCIENTIFIC ELITE TOTAL	127	129	157
Art administration	13	16	16
Art forms	63	63	63
Influential persons	27	27	26
Honorary art professors and academicians	11	11	28
CULTURAL ELITE TOTAL	114	117	133
ELITES TOTAL	1121	1285	1409

and 2011 it included all members of the Grand Committee, that is, the so-called EU Committee and secretary generals of parliamentary groups. From the political party organization, the political elite includes the leaders and deputy leaders of parliamentary parties, party secretaries, and the leaders of youth, student, and women's organizations. Local government is represented by the chairs of municipal councils (1991) and the chairs of municipal boards (2001–2011) in larger towns. At the regional level, the political elite includes the chairs of regional councils from 2001 onward. At the European Union level it includes Finnish members of the European Parliament and the commissioner.

The administrative elite is defined as comprising ministerial permanent secretaries, heads of departments, and permanent under-secretaries, as well as the highest-ranking civil servants at central government agencies. The judiciary is represented by the chancellor of justice, the parliamentary ombudsman, and the presidents of the Supreme Court, the Supreme Administrative Court, and Courts of Appeal, as well as the highest-ranking judges of other courts of law. From 2001 on, the administrative elite also includes the chief justices of Administrative Courts. Included in the elite from the Defence Forces are the commanders in chief of the Defence Forces and their various arms, the chiefs of key defense command departments, and the commanders of military provinces (1991, 2011) and defense areas (2001). Furthermore, the administrative elite includes the bishops and deans of the Evangelical-Lutheran Church, and the bishops of the Orthodox Church. Finland does not have an officially established state church, although the state and the church do work closely together in the context of the military, for instance. Both the Evangelical-Lutheran and the Orthodox Church have the power to levy taxes on their members. Regional state administration is represented by governors (i.e., civil servants appointed by the government) (1991, 2001), permanent secretaries of State Provincial Offices (1991), directors general of Regional State Administrative Agencies (2011), directors of Employment and Economic Centres (2001), and directors general of Centres for Economic Development, Transport, and the Environment (2011). Municipal government is represented in the administrative elite by the chief executives of the biggest towns and cities, while the level of regional government is represented by the directors of regional councils (2001–2011). From 2001 onward the administrative elite is also defined as including Finnish European Union officials at director general level or higher, as well as Finnish members of the Committee of the Regions.

The business elite includes the CEOs, the chairs of the boards of directors, and the chairs of the supervisory boards of all state-owned and cooperative companies, and of the highest-turnover private companies. In addition, it includes individuals of the highest personal worth as measured by property taxes paid (1991–2001) or combined earned income and capital income (2011).

The organizational elite is defined as comprising all elective leaders of central employee confederations, and the chairs, first vice-chairs, and the highest-ranking hired officials of the biggest trade unions. Representing the employer's side are the managing directors, chairs, and first vice-chairs of the largest employer confederations and industry policy organizations. The data for the organizational elite in 1991 additionally includes the directors and the chairs of regional council executive committees. Regional Councils have only been part of the public sector since 1991. Finally, the organizational elite was defined as including the chairs and highest-ranking paid managers of the most established NGOs. The mass media elite comprises the editors in chief of dailies (newspapers published three to seven times a week) and the biggest magazines, as well as managing editors at the Finnish News Agency STT. Included from the electronic media field are the management and managing editors of the Finnish Broadcasting Company YLE, MTV3, Nelonen Media, and the biggest local radio stations.

The scientific elite consists of university rectors and chancellors and, in 2011, chairs of the boards recruited from outside universities. Prior to the new University Act of 2010, the board was chaired by a professor elected from the university. Furthermore, the scientific elite includes the highest-ranking executives of governmental research institutes, and for 2011 also their elective chairs of the boards of directors. In the case of private research institutes, the senior executives and chairs of the boards of governors are included from 1991 onward. In addition, the scientific elite is counted as including the chairs of major foundations and scientific societies that provide funding for science and research, as well as their highest-ranking paid officials. Finally, the scientific elite includes the president of the Academy of Finland, the elective members of the Science Policy Council (1991) and the Academy of Finland board (2001–2011), honorary academicians, research professors (1991), and academy professors (2001–2011).

The cultural elite is defined as comprising the secretary general and members of the Arts Council of Finland, as well as the chairs and highest-ranking paid employees of organizations representing different art forms. Furthermore, the cultural elite includes publicly recognized influential persons representing different arts, all art professors, and for 2011 all honorary academicians of art.

THE FOUNDATION OF THE INFLUENCE OF ELITES

Whereas classical elite theories are fairly unanimous about the nature of the mass, the same cannot be said about their views of the foundations of elite power. Although they do share some features in common—such as an emphasis on the irrationality of human behavior—elite theories differ most notably in their assessments of what characteristics and social opportunities are necessary for the achievement of an elite position. For some elite theorists, the explanation for the power of the elite lies more in structural and organizational factors, while others believe the explanation is to be found in the psychological aspects associated with human behavior. According to Mosca and his disciple Michels, the elite owes its power mainly to its organizational abilities. Pareto, by contrast, explained the elite's position by reference to the psychological make-up of the elite and non-elite. Burnham, for his part, in his attempts to marry elite theory and Marxism, argued that the power of the elite was a consequence of its control of economic resources. Mills explained the power of the elite not as a product of its members' personal qualities, but of the positions they held in key institutions in society (Parry 1969). In other words, contrary to a common misperception nowadays, elite theorists did not believe that elite power was grounded only in societal structures.

The idea of the differentiation of species of power goes at least as far back as modern social theory. Ever since Montesqieu's doctrine of the separation of powers and eighteenth-century revolutions, the theory of democracy has embraced the notion that power can and should be divided into different species, both within the state (legislative, executive, and judicial powers) and between the public, private, and third sectors. In the context of work to develop democratic theory and models, scholars have proposed the separation of power in the spirit of pluralism, with the achievement of a balance of power in mind. In the Marxist tradition, on the other hand, the ultimate power resource is capital. Antonio Gramsci drew a distinction between repressive state apparatuses (i.e., those based on violence or the threat of violence) and hegemonic state apparatuses (i.e., those based on persuasion), which have different resources. The Marxist tradition was aimed at understanding how different institutions, such as religion, science, and politics ultimately serve the aims of an unequal distribution of economic power (Kunelius et al. 2009, 32).

In traditional sociology, theorists concerned with trends of differentiation in modern society took the view that different types of organizations deal with specific types of problems and have specialized functions. The theory of functional differentiation also includes the idea that specialized actors have at least relative autonomy. Given the increasing complexity of society and the associated requirements of differentiation, organizations have at their disposal such specialized skills, knowledge, and positions that guarantee them power and influence. This opens up the perspective of institutional pluralism on the distribution of power. The focus here is not so much on how power is divided between groups or social classes, but rather on how resources and capabilities tend to accumulate to form a system of different positions that is built into the organization of society (Ibid., 32–33).

Although the influence wielded by Finnish elites, according to the view taken in this study, stems from their leading positions at the top of the most influential organizations in society, there are differences between the various elites' sources of influence. Table 3.3 describes the forms of Finnish elites' influence and their power resources (cf. Kunelius et al. 2009, 33).

The political elite clearly wields political power. The power of political decision-makers is based on the authority and legitimation coming from the electorate. Ultimately the right of political institutions such as Parliament, the government, the president of the republic, municipal councils, and municipal boards to prescribe binding norms upon citizens is set out in the Constitution.

The power and influence of the administrative elite comes from the same source, that is, the authority of political decision-makers and the laws they have made.

Table 3.3. Sources of Elite Groups' Influence

Elite Group	Type of Influence	Resources	Example
Political elite	political	elections, authority	parliament, the government, local council
Administrative elite	administrative	physical force, authority, expertise	army, police, judiciary, ministries
Business elite	economic	material and economic	business companies, property
Organizational elite	corporatist	economic, collective power	labor market organizations, NGOs
Mass media elite	symbolic	opinion leadership	mass media
Scientific elite	symbolic	expertise, knowledge	universities, research institutes
Cultural elite	symbolic	influence on intellectual climate in society	art, cultural institutions

However, the foundation of the administrative elite's power and influence is more fragmented than the political elite's. The power resources of the administrative elite may be based on physical power (military, police, and judiciary) and regulation of the citizenry, but also on expertise. In the process of drafting laws that will eventually be submitted to Parliament and in implementing these laws, ministries and civil servants exercise influence based on expertise over political decision-makers.

The business elite wields economic power, which is based on the material and financial resources managed by companies. Public finances—and other elites in society—are dependent on the outputs of companies, which contribute to employment and to finance the welfare state. Large masses of property also constitute part of the foundation of the business elite's influence. The organizational elite exercises corporatist influence when it seeks to affect other institutions and elite groups in society, especially the political and the administrative elite. The power resources of employer organizations are mainly of an economic nature, as they represent the interests of companies, whereas the power resources of employee organizations and NGOs derive from the mass power of their memberships.

The mass media, scientific, and cultural elites wield mainly symbolic influence, although there are some differences between their respective power resources. The influence of the mass media elite is based on its ability through the media to affect the views and opinions of other elite groups and the citizenry. In relation to political decision-makers, the role of the mass media can range from a lapdog to a watchdog of power to a yapping mutt. Given its knowledge and expertise capital and educational function, the scientific elite in universities and research institutes can wield far-reaching influence over other institutions in society and their elites. Innovations coming out of universities serve as factors of production in business and industry. Through its creative input, the cultural elite formed by art and culture institutions can influence the intellectual climate in society as a whole.

DATA OF THE STUDY

The main body of data for this research consists of three virtually identical postal surveys I conducted among people included in seven elite groups. I conducted the first postal surveys in November–December 1991 (response rate 66.9 percent), the second in September–October 2001 (53.5 percent), and the third (both a postal and an Internet survey) in September–October 2011 (34.3 percent). The response rates for the various elite groups were as follows: political elite 60 percent (1991), 52 percent (2001), and 25 percent (2011); administrative elite 62 percent, 62 percent, and 47 percent; business elite 55 percent, 46 percent, and 21 percent; organizational elite 70 percent, 55 percent, and 35 percent; mass media elite 67 percent, 44 percent, and 31 percent; scientific elite 64 percent, 61 percent, and 34 percent; and the cultural elite 63 percent, 53 percent, and 35 percent. All these surveys were funded by the Academy of Finland.

The decline in response rates at roughly the same degree across all elite groups reflects a wider trend in postal surveys. Since the respondents in the surveys here were guaranteed anonymity, it was not possible to conduct a detailed analysis of the loss of respondents in the various groups. The respondents were, however, asked to indicate their principal occupation, which provides at least some insight into the loss. Having said that, the elite membership of a large portion of respondents is based not on their principal occupation, but it can also be based on occupancy of an elected office. Therefore the results of the loss analysis are indicative only. The response rate for political elite members active in political party organizations actually increased from 1991 to 2001, but then declined. In the business elite, the response rate for people involved in cooperatives increased to 2001, whereas the response rate for people working in private companies in 2011 was lower than in previous years. In the organizational elite, the response rate for people working in NGOs or holding an elected office in NGOs was lowest in 2011.

Although the response rate in 2011 was markedly lower than in earlier years, the response rates have fallen quite steadily across the various elite groups since 1991— notwithstanding the fact that a lower loss rate was recorded for the administrative and the cultural elite. Although the response rate dropped more sharply in some groups than in others, the whole data set for 1991–2011 is not significantly or systematically biased to such a degree as to make comparisons invalid. It is important to stress that the elite surveys in this research are not based on random samples, but instead on total populations. It follows that loss is not as critical an issue as in sample surveys: all the people who responded to the questionnaire occupy positions of influence, that is, belong to the elite.

There is no single reason for the loss of respondents. It is possible that the electoral funding scandal contributed to the lower response rates in the political and business elites in 2011. That scandal has been constantly in the news since 2008, drawing the public's attention to the close ties between decision-makers in politics and business.

In connection with each elite survey, I conducted identical surveys among the citizenry. The first two citizen surveys (Nov. 15–19, 1991, and Sept. 7–13, 2001) were collected on Gallup Finland's "Finland Channel," and they represent the population aged 15–65.[1] The third survey was conducted as part of a Statistics Finland survey on health and general health care, which was carried out at the same time as the 2011 elite survey in the form of a postal and Internet survey from Aug. 28 to Dec. 9, 2011 (N=2,500, response rate 53.6 percent). This material is used to compare the views of elites and the citizenry about the distribution of influence in society and the intensity of conflicts and contradictions in society.

Furthermore, citizens' attitudes to statements were studied using three data sets. These are, firstly, a survey conducted by the Finnish Business and Policy Forum (EVA), the first of which (EVA 1991) was carried out from Sept. 6 to Nov. 9, 1990 (N= 4,500, response rate 53.9 percent), and the second (EVA 2001) from Nov. 21, 2000, to Jan. 18, 2001 (N= 4,500, 49.2 percent). In other words, the surveys among elites and the citizenry were not conducted at the exact same time, and therefore the comparisons between these two groups for 1991 and 2001 are indicative only. Nonetheless the questions used in all these surveys were identical. The third survey concerning attitudinal statements was conducted as part of the above mentioned Statistics Finland survey, so in 2011 the elite and citizen questionnaires were conducted with identical questions at the exact same time. All five surveys for the citizenry were based on random samples. The response rates in all these surveys have been at a reasonable level since the early 1990s.

NOTE

1. Launched in 1990, Finland Channel is a survey system designed to collect data from a set panel of respondents. The data for the 1991 survey were collected with PCs only, but in 2001 data were also collected via the Internet. Internet terminals have been set up for this purpose in 1,000 Finnish households, and in addition 300 households answer questions on their own PC. Household members have received instructions on how to use the equipment in connection with PC installation. Completing the survey forms requires no special ICT skills. The weekly household response rate is maintained at over 80 percent of all contactable households. Response rates are not calculated at the individual level due to the nature of the survey system. The sample is regionally and demographically representative of all households in the country. Sampling was a stratified three-stage design, yielding a fixed sample. The sample structure is constantly monitored and maintained.

4

Recruitment into Elites

RESEARCHING THE SOCIAL
BACKGROUND OF PEOPLE IN POWER

Recruitment into elites and changing recruitment patterns were a major focus for classical elite theorists, and they continue to remain a major focus in present-day empirical research, both in Finland and internationally. Although the connections between shifting elite configurations and wider developments in society are highly complex, most scholars agree that changes in the makeup of elites provide an important tool of historical analysis. Since the composition of elites is more easily observable than the exercise of power per se, the analysis of these compositions can serve as a kind of seismometer for detecting shifts in politics and the system of governance more generally (Putnam 1976, 166).

The concept of social background (makeup, composition, or structure) is used in two senses. In its narrower sense, it usually refers simply to the individual's social status and origin, although sometimes demographic and regional characteristics are included as well. In its broader sense, social background additionally comprises the individual's education and participation in various elective offices before recruitment into an elite. As this broader understanding takes account of people's active participation in society before recruitment into an elite, it also allows us to explore the various avenues of elite recruitment (Noponen 1989, 117). This is the path chosen in the present study.

There are many good reasons to analyze the social background of elites. Firstly, social background may influence people's decision-making: elite members will want to further their own and their background groups' interests. People's behavior and decision-making may also be influenced by their socialization in childhood and youth. For instance, it may be assumed that a civil servant or company director who

49

has grown up in the countryside will have a better grasp of living conditions in rural areas, which again will influence their decisions (Uusitalo 1980, 16).

It is clear, however, that actual decisions cannot be directly extrapolated from information about social background. Elite members' social attributes such as age, gender, and education have little value in predicting the decisions they make. Parental social class and factors describing the individual's growth environment have even less predictive value (Ibid.). According to C. Wright Mills (1956, 280), the direction of policy cannot be inferred merely from policy-makers' social origins and careers. The social and economic backgrounds of people in power do not tell us all we need to know to understand the distribution of power in society. This is because (1) people in high positions may be ideological representatives of the poor and humble. (2) People of humble origin may effectively serve the most vested and inherited interests. (3) Not all people who effectively represent the interests of a certain stratum need to belong to it or personally benefit from the policies that further its interests. Finally (4), among top decision-makers are people who have been chosen for their positions by virtue of their expert knowledge.

These four reasons, Mills argues, explain why the social origins and careers of the power elite do not allow us to infer the policy directions of a modern system of power. Suleiman (1978, 10) notes that although the French administrative elite is not a representative sample of the population either at the regional level or in terms of education and social class, its behavior is directed more by its official position than by social background. However, Mills (1956, 280) says this does not mean that the social background of elite members is irrelevant to the understanding of the policies pursued. It's just that we must be careful not to draw simple and direct inferences from the origins and careers of elite members to policy contents. When conclusions are drawn about the origins and careers of political actors, it is imperative to understand the institutional landscape in which they operate.

Secondly, research into the social background of elites serves to advance the study of social mobility. This area of study is important to the achievement of equal opportunities, a principle advocated in both liberal and socialist thinking. Research on social mobility and the analysis of elites' social background sheds important light on the *de facto* distribution of opportunities for upward mobility and on how those opportunities have changed (Uusitalo 1980, 17).

The third reason for studying the social background of elites also has to do with social classes and strata. Elites' social background presumably reflects the relative balance of power between classes and strata in society. The larger the share of people from a certain stratum within the elite, the stronger the position of that stratum in society. The power of classes or strata is reflected, among other things, in their influence over recruitment criteria. Different social classes or strata will aim to emphasize such criteria that favor their own members (Ibid., 17–18).

Fourthly, research into the social background of elites allows us to analyze to what extent differences and changes in elite members' background reflect past or ongoing political, social, and economic changes (Noponen 1989, 117). Elite recruitment can serve as a revealing indicator of the regime and its policies (Eulau 1976, 25). This assumption is based on the idea that higher social classes are better placed than others to choose their life careers. Given this freedom of choice, they are more likely to gravitate toward fields with great or increasing significance. If one elite group moves away from the prevailing trend and becomes more upper class in its social background, we need to ask whether this group is gaining in importance. If, on the other hand, its social background is converging with the general population, then we need to ask whether the elite group is losing power. For instance, the exceptional tendencies of convergence that were seen in the clergy from the nineteenth to the early twentieth century coincided with a decline in the role of the church in society (Uusitalo 1980, 18).

Not forgetting the reasons set out above, the single main reason why this study addresses the social background of elites is that a uniform social background is one of the principal factors strengthening the coherence of the power elite. A shared social background, say in terms of origin and education, can facilitate communication through the same language, and also harmonize values, attitudes, and opinions. This, in turn, may promote the mobility of individuals between institutions, further adding to elite cohesiveness. Clearly, then, we must answer in the affirmative Robert D. Putnam's question as to whether the social background of elites matters. But it would be false to assume that there is a direct correlation between the social origin of decision-makers and the content of their decisions (Best and Cotta 2000, 18).

SOCIAL MOBILITY

The study of social mobility can be described as an exercise in studying how society is changing. The more mobility there is, the more open the society. High social mobility offers individuals equal opportunities to gain access to a social group that is not dependent on their home background, that is, their parental social class. Indeed, mobility research is grounded in the notion of an ideal meritocratic society that is based on equality of opportunity. In a meritocratic society, children's motivation and talent are not dependent on their parents' social class. The more obstacles there are to intergenerational mobility, the more clearly social class is not determined directly by the individual's skills, talents, and merits, but also by traits inherited from previous generations, such as financial resources, family background, or social skills (Sirniö 2010, 7).

The importance of social mobility can be justified not only on grounds of justice and equality of opportunity, but also based on its broader benefits to society and the maintenance of social harmony: the social cohesion of society is undermined by social inequality as the gulf between the privileged and the disadvantaged grows wider (Ibid., 7–8).

Traditionally, sociological studies of social mobility have used the concept of social class. Class theories are often premised on the assumption that social classes are hierarchic, that people in higher social classes are in a better position and have more power than people in lower social classes. In Finland, however, recent research on social mobility has increasingly moved away from the concept of class in favor of socioeconomic status or social group. These terms are intended to refer both to the individual's economic and social status in society, but without the automatic implication of a hierarchy of classes (Sirniö 2010, 6). In this study, however, a different approach is taken. One of the main tasks here is to explore the changes that have taken place in the openness of the elite structure, and therefore social classes are interpreted from an elite theory perspective as hierarchic so that the upper class is considered more privileged in terms of its economic, cultural, and social capital than the middle class, not to mention those recruited into the elite from a working-class or farming background. The concept of class, as typically employed in class research, is only used here for examining the class identification of elite members, when social classes are presented as targets of identification comparable to other divisions in society. Otherwise, without taking any stance on class theorists' views on the content of "class," the concept of social class is here translated into social stratum, which lends itself more readily to the study of social mobility.

Sociological research routinely makes a distinction between absolute and relative mobility. Absolute or generational mobility refers to children moving up or down from the class position held by their parents. Relative mobility, then, refers to the association between parents' and their children's class position after controlling for generational differences over time in class structures. It is important that this distinction is made, especially if our research interest is in equality of opportunity. Career mobility, then, refers to the movement of individuals from one occupation or occupational position to another during the course of their employment careers (Härkönen 2010, 53; Blom et al. 2012, 14). In this study, however, the concept of career mobility is used in a broader sense and understood as comprising the individual's career trajectory from childhood home through to the elite as well as the factors contributing to elite recruitment.

Assessments of absolute mobility give an indication of how many individuals have changed their social class since leaving their childhood home. But absolute mobility does not yet tell us anything about the causal connections between parents' and children's class positions. Absolute mobility is the sum of broader structural changes in society and relative mobility. Like other industrial countries, Finland saw very high levels of absolute mobility during the era of industrialization since the late 1960s when people moved from rural areas to cities and from small farms to factories, because the structure of society was changing (Härkönen 2010, 53–54).

Relative mobility or circulation is considered a more accurate measure of equality of opportunity than absolute mobility. Relative mobility measures how parental class position impacts on children's class position regardless of society's class structure at any given time. Increased relative mobility can be seen as an indication of improved equality of opportunity (Ibid., 54).

From the 1950s onward, with the advance of industrial restructuring, educational expansion, and the growth of white-collar employment, there was a growing belief in the positive effects of education. But upward mobility on a larger scale was ultimately made possible by the rapid transformation of agrarian society into a service and information society, which opened up for younger people not only new educational opportunities, but also new positions in the occupational structure. In other words, this was largely exogenous or forced social mobility that is due to social and occupational restructuring (Naumanen and Silvennoinen 2010, 70).

Earlier comparative studies have shown that rates of social mobility in Finland are relatively high. The picture in Finland is quite similar to the other Nordic countries, although the late onset of industrialization means that Finnish rates of social mobility have been even slightly higher (e.g., Pöntinen 1983; Erikson and Pöntinen 1985; Erikson and Goldthorpe 1992; Breen 2004). Indeed, compared with other industrial countries, Finland appears as a relatively open country where associations between parents' and children's social stratum are relatively weak. Some 70–80 percent of Finnish children have a different social stratum than their parents, and relative mobility is quite high in international comparison. However, some concern has been voiced that due to the growth of inequalities from the 1990s onward, Finnish society may be headed toward stagnation and reduced social mobility (Härkönen 2010, 65).

A 2009 survey on intergenerational mobility in Finland compared the respondents' and their parents' occupational status. Mobility was measured by asking the respondents to compare their current job with their father's job at the time that the respondents were 15 years of age. Almost half of the respondents thought they were in much higher (11 percent) or higher (34 percent) position than their fathers had been, and around one-third thought their positions were more or less the same. Less than one in five (17 percent) thought their occupational status was lower than their fathers'. Among the respondents whose father had been in a leading position, the occupational status for 19 percent was the same, while 45 percent became upper functionaries, 29 percent lower functionaries, and 16 percent manual workers (Blom et al. 2012, 14–16).

The survey results revealed no differences in the experiences of men and women. Respondents in younger age groups, however, felt more often than others that their fathers had had a better occupational status than they had; in the age group under 30 the proportion was 30 percent. This is in part explained by young people still making their careers, but even in the age group 31–40 one in four thought they were in a lower position than their fathers. This probably reflects in part the decline in social mobility in the wake of 1960s restructuring, but perhaps first and foremost the effects of the 1990s recession, including the growth of uncertainty and short-term job contracts. People in the age band 31–40 were the first to enter the restructured job market when they graduated from school (Ibid., 15).

In 2000, 68 percent of men and 78 percent of women in Finland occupied a different class position than their father. The rate of absolute mobility in Finland is just above the European average, and has remained fairly stable. Along with its Nordic neighbors, Finland ranks among the most open societies in the world. However, the mobility of Finnish men to higher class positions than those occupied by their fathers has declined, and their downward social mobility has increased. Among women, upward social mobility has increased somewhat, whereas the probability of downward social mobility has remained more or less unchanged (Härkönen 2010, 53–57).

Finnish society was hard hit by the 1990s recession: unemployment was persistently high, and income disparities increased. It has been suggested that the long shadow of the recession and so-called neoliberal economic policy both contributed to a marked decrease in social mobility (e.g., Jokinen and Saaristo 2002, 107). However, the evidence for solidification and closure in Finnish society is far from conclusive. Quite the contrary, Sirniö (2010, 48, 51) reports that relative mobility has increased somewhat since the mid-1980s, and the inheritance of parental socioeconomic status has decreased. Having said that, it is possible that the effects of the recession on social mobility will only become visible in the longer term (Ibid., 58–59).

Earlier research predicting a tendency toward reduced mobility and closure of the social structure refers mainly to the impermeability of the middle classes. The argument is that movement into middle-class (that is, usually white-collar) positions from other backgrounds is becoming increasingly difficult, and that most people recruited into these positions are offspring of white-collar parents. Sirniö, however, has shown that social mobility has in fact increased in Finland in 1985–2005. The extent of relative mobility has increased clearly. This kind of "voluntary" mobility that is independent of structural changes in society has increased in both genders, rising to around 58 percent among men and to 44 percent among women in 2005. In other words, it seems that structural changes in Finnish society have slowed to a point where ever fewer people have to move to some specific group dictated by structural change. Both women and men are now less at risk of arriving in a social class that is different from their class of origin, and the dependence between original social class and class in adulthood has decreased. In the early 2000s, socioeconomic status can no longer be as straightforwardly predicted as before based on parental socioeconomic positions or the prevailing social structure, but there is more social mobility that is independent of these factors than there was in the 1980s and 1990s. These results contrast with earlier forecasts predicting a decrease in relative mobility. In other words, social groups have opened up in 1985–2005 so that it has become easier to move into these positions—either upwards or downwards (Sirniö 2010, 62–63).

Finnish studies have reported a significant increase in women's social mobility from the 1970s to the 1990s, but there have been only minor changes in men's mobility. From the early 1990s to 2000, there has been hardly any change at all. Family background showed a slightly stronger association than earlier with the class position of early-career-stage women born in 1966–1975 and entering the labor market during the recession. As the impact of family background usually subsides in later career stages, it has not yet been possible to form a clear and complete picture of social mobility in this age group (Härkönen 2010, 58).

Results from Finnish and international studies on the associations between childhood home, education, and social position can be summed up as follows: 1) Childhood class background impacts the length of the young person's educational career and level of education obtained. The higher the class background, the higher the degree completed. 2) Childhood class background impacts employment, job placement, and career advancement. On average, young people from a higher class background tend to have a higher class in adulthood than age peers from a lower class background, but from the same educational level. 3) There is a clear association between class position of origin in childhood and social class in adulthood. Offspring from the highest social classes have a much higher likelihood of arriving in the highest classes in adulthood than descendants of the lowest classes. It is easier to retain a position in the highest social classes than to move up to such a position. Young people coming from the lowest social classes are accordingly most likely to remain in the lowest class positions (Naumanen and Silvennoinen 2010, 87).

The following discusses the social background of Finnish elites, factors impacting the career trajectories of people recruited to elite positions, and changes in these factors since the major upheavals of the early 1990s. The journey to positions of leadership is a journey to power (Pentikäinen 2014). Although this study describes the changes that have taken place at the very highest echelons of Finnish power over a period of two decades, the data available do not allow us to make any predictions about how the exercise of power will change in Finland over the coming decades. There were very few people who foresaw the changes that began to unfold in the early 1990s and that were to have a profound impact on Finnish society, such as the collapse of the Soviet Union, Finland's accession to the European Union, the international financial crisis, and the eurozone debt crisis.

DISTRIBUTION OF THE POWER ELITE BY GENERATION

The concept of generation has two main uses in the research literature. Firstly, generation can refer to a group of people who share experiences of certain life stages. Their relationship to certain sociohistorical processes that have affected their socialization is determined by biological age and date of birth (Roos 1987, 51–52). Pierre Bourdieu (1996), on the other hand, points out that generation has nothing to do with biological age: the division of people into generations is based on how their activity is determined within a certain field, say art or science. He insists that the criteria of appreciation and distinction shared in common by a generation have little to do with age. People are categorized as belonging to a certain generation based on their position within the field concerned. In this study the concept of generation is used in the former sense, because in order to compare different elites it is necessary to have a consistent criterion of generation.

However, just being the same age does not yet create a bond of togetherness among a generation. That sense only comes with shared experiences and their culmination in a "key experience." Intense key experiences are brought about by dramatic transitions and upheavals, such as war, rapid urbanization (rural flight), or deep recession. Their effect will be most strongly felt by the age group who at the time are at their most impressionable age for personality development, that is, around 16–18 years. When the time is right, the young person matures into an adult: this is when the fundamental nature of the self is established that will remain with the individual for the rest of his or her life. This individual-level mechanism provides the foundation for the generation's shared experiences: the age group experiences its childhood, youth, and impressionable age through the same period of history. This, at once, lies at the root of generational differences: as different generations have reached their impressionable age at different points in time, they will also occupy a different position in society's temporal history of experiences. Therefore the same time will be a different time for different people, because they have experienced it at different stages of the development of the self. Even people of the same generation will have a different view of the exact same event or upheaval: they are involved in the unfolding "play" either on stage, seated in the lower or the upper circle, or (most relevantly from the point of view of elite research), in a box seat. Depending on their position, the same upheaval produces different experiences, even though the source of the experience is the same. The temporal distance of generations from one another is not tied in advance to anything. They may be separated by one, five or thirty years, or any number of years, depending on the rate of upheavals producing key experiences (Virtanen 2001, 20–35, 357).

A shared world of experiences shapes in many ways the tastes, preferences, and behavior of a generation, creating a habitus that unites and binds it together. It is at this level that people often unconsciously participate in changing society. Indeed, generations may differ in their preferences and values, but this does not mean they are necessarily involved in an organized cultural struggle (Ibid., 23).

In his studies of Finnish lifestyles, J.P. Roos (1987, 53–56) has divided Finnish people into four generations whose birth year ranges I have earlier (Ruostetsaari 1992) specified as follows: the generation of war and depression 1910–1926, the generation of postwar reconstruction 1927–1939, the generation of the great upheaval 1940–1949, and the generation of suburbs 1950–1972. The last year of birth for the suburban generation was set at 1972 for the simple reason that the youngest person in the power elite was born that year (Ruostetsaari 2003). Now, in hindsight, it seems that 1972 was indeed a theoretically justified choice for the end-point of one generation. The great recession created such a powerful key experience that people born in 1973 and later can with good reason be identified as a fifth generation, that is, the generation of recession. Wass and Torsti (2011, 174) reported that as many as one in three of the people born in 1975–1984 mentioned the recession as their most important key experience. They consider this to reflect the high intensity with which this generation was affected by the early 1990s recession.

When the national economy collapsed in the early 1990s, even the oldest members of the generation of recession were at an age susceptible to the experiences and conditions that came with the recession. Matti Virtanen (2001) has described how most people born in the 1970s have grown up in cities, and those born in the 1980s in an almost fully-developed welfare state. "Then suddenly, the foundation of welfare and security caved in: those who had not personally experienced unemployment, bankruptcy, or insolvency, at least knew someone in their immediate circle who had been affected. The key experience of the generation of recession was one of profound uncertainty and injustice—the exact opposite of what they were looking for, an equitable, safe, and just society."

In the early 1990s, Finnish society was clearly dominated by two equally strong generations: the generation of postwar reconstruction and the generation of the great upheaval. By the early 2000s, power had changed hands: the generation of the great upheaval had risen to ascendancy, with its share increasing from two-fifths to three-fifths, at the same time as the previous generation had seen its share drop from two-fifths to just one-tenth of all power elite positions. Even the suburban generation was growing strongly, doubling its share in the space of a decade. In the early 2000s, just a few early representatives of the generation of recession had risen to elite positions. This is natural in view of the fact that the "power stage" of life is said to come relatively late, that is, at ages 41–65, in the years following the "active stage" of life (ages 18–40) (Jääsaari 1986). The generations born in 1927–1939 and 1940–1949 were heavily overrepresented in the power elite, while the other generations were underrepresented. By the early 2000s, however, the 1927–1939 generation was already underrepresented in the power elite (table 4.1).

By 2011, power has once again swung from one generation to another. The generation of war and the generation of postwar reconstruction have effectively been ousted from the power elite. The 1950–1972 suburban generation now occupies two-thirds of all elite positions, while the 1940–1949 generation has seen its share decline to just over one-fifth. In the business and scientific elites, however, the generation of the great upheaval still accounts for around one-third of all elite positions. In all elite groups the suburban generation accounts for the largest share of all positions. The generation of recession still accounts for no more than a marginal (6 percent) share of the power elite, but in the political elite its share has risen rapidly to one-fifth. This is largely explained by the fact that the leaders of political youth and student associations are included as members of the political elite.

However, this generational analysis hides from view a significant increase in the average age of the power elite. While in 1991 the average age of various elite groups was 51 years and in 2001 54 years, by 2011 it had risen to 55 years. The youngest elite group is the political elite, where the average age rose from 43 years in 1991 through 48 years in 2001 to 50 years in 2011. In 2011, the second youngest group was the cultural elite (50 years in 1991, 56 years in 2001, and 52 years in 2011), followed by the organizational elite (51, 54, 53), the administrative elite (54, 55, 57), the business elite (54, 55, 58), and the scientific elite (54, 59, 60). With the

Table 4.1. Elite Groups by Generation (%)

Year of Birth	Political Elite 1991	2001	2011	Administrative Elite 1991	2001	2011	Business Elite 1991	2001	2011	Organizational Elite 1991	2001	2011	Mass Media Elite 1991	2001	2011	Scientific Elite 1991	2001	2011	Cultural Elite 1991	2001	2011	Power Elite Total 1991	2001	2011
1910–1926	4	1	0	6	1	0	7	0	0	4	0	0	4	0	0	16	9	2	4	7	0	6	2	0
1927–1939	18	7	0	55	9	0	55	11	2	40	10	0	40	2	1	40	20	6	35	15	7	41	10	2
1940–1949	34	41	24	35	71	29	37	60	35	48	66	18	48	55	4	39	55	37	42	49	9	40	59	23
1950–1972	45	41	57	4	20	71	2	29	63	9	24	73	9	41	87	5	16	55	18	29	76	13	27	69
1973–1989	0	9	19	0	0	1	0	0	0	0	0	9	0	2	9	0	0	0	0	0	9	0	2	6
N	85	87	46	127	166	132	108	91	46	141	111	71	80	58	46	80	75	49	71	59	45	692	607	424

exception of the cultural and scientific elites, the average age has increased in all elite groups. In these elite groups the average age is now higher than in the early 1990s, but lower than in the early 2000s.

Since it is often argued that power rests with the "baby boom generation," the following looks more closely at the share of elite positions held by people born in 1945–1950. A total of more than 95,000 people were born in these age cohorts after World War II.

It is clear that during its youth in the late 1950s and 1960s, this age cohort was exposed to influences that were more conducive to strong political and ideological views than is the case in the present-day political climate. Many sociopolitical dividing lines and antagonisms, such as the division between the left wing and right wing or bourgeois and socialist goals, were very prominent throughout the presidency of Urho Kekkonen from the 1950s to the late 1970s (Borg and Ruostetsaari 2002).

The baby boom generation's occupancy of elite positions doubled from 18 percent in 1991 to 39 percent in 2001. By 2011, the figure has dropped back to 23 percent, but still remains higher than in the early 1990s. In other words, the baby boom generation no longer occupies a dominant position, nor has it completely moved out of the inner circle of power.

The influence of the baby boom generation in society has been based not only on its overrepresentation in elite groups, but this age group is more actively involved in politics than the population at large. It is estimated that around four-fifths of baby boomers voted in parliamentary elections even during their years of youth. Studies of the 1987 and 1999 parliamentary elections indicate that voter turnout had dropped in all age cohorts, but more sharply in the youngest age groups. By contrast, the turnout rate for the baby boom generation did not fall to the same extent, but remained over 75 percent, clearly exceeding the 70 percent average for the whole population (Martikainen 1988; Martikainen and Wass 2001).

The baby boom generation has also been more active than other age groups in party politics. It can be estimated that the baby boomers' proportion of most political parties' memberships has been almost twice as high as in the adult population of that age cohort (Borg 1998; Ruostetsaari and Borg 2002). More recent electoral studies confirm that voter turnout is generationally dependent: the younger the generation, the lower the turnout rate (e.g., Wass and Torsti 2011). It has also been shown that political participation is dependent on generation in the sense that turnout does not increase with advancing age, but it may remain at the low level established in youth. This may mean that when the generation of recession eventually steps up to occupy a dominant position in the political elite, its relationship with the electorate of the same age may remain thin and tentative.

WOMEN'S REPRESENTATION AMONG THE ELITES

Women's share of elite positions increased from 12 percent in 1991 to 19 percent in 2001 and further to 26 percent in 2011. These figures are calculated for all elite members (table 3.1) and not only for survey respondents. As women have accounted for around 51 percent of the total population since the early 1990s, they continue to remain substantially underrepresented in the power elite (OSF 2012). In the United States, for instance, just 12 percent of the 550 elite members interviewed by Michael Lindsay (2014, 23) were women, even though they make up half the population.

There are quite marked differences between elite groups in the share of women's representation. In 2011, women's share of elite positions was highest in the political elite (43 percent), followed by the cultural elite (41 percent), mass media elite (33 percent), organizational elite (25 percent), scientific elite (23 percent), administrative elite (22 percent), and business elite (6 percent). Since the early 1990s, women's share has increased most in the administrative elite, where it has quadrupled. In the mass media and scientific elites, the share of women has increased three times over, while in the organizational and cultural elites it has doubled. In the business elite, that is, among CEOs of major corporations and chairs of boards of directors and supervisory boards, women remain in a marginal role, even though their share has doubled since the early 1990s.

Among the companies listed in the Helsinki stock exchange in 2011, not a single one had a female CEO. Four women served as chairs of boards of directors. However, the share of seats held by women on the boards of listed companies increased from 7 percent in 2003 to 18 percent in 2011. Women's rise to the highest business leadership roles has been very slow in Finland. In 2007, Finland ranked 25th among the 27 EU countries: just 17 percent of all CEOs in Finland were women compared with an average of one in three women CEOs in all EU countries. In the United States, there are not many women in CEO roles in major corporations, but nonetheless more than in Finland. In 2011 there were just 12 female CEOs in the biggest Fortune 500 companies (Central Chamber of Commerce 2011).

Women's representation has increased the least in the political elite, which is explained by the high baseline level in the early 1990s. In the 1991 parliamentary election women accounted for 38.5 percent of all MPs, falling back to 36.5 percent in 1999, and then edging up to 42.5 percent in the 2011 parliamentary election. Indeed, the share of female MPs in Finland, as in the other Nordic countries, has been among the highest in the world since the early 1900s (e.g., Christmas-Best and Kjær 2007, 86). According to data compiled by the European Commission, Finland was the only one of the EU's 28 member states that at the beginning of 2015 had the government in which women outnumbered men (10–7). Women accounted for 40 percent or more of the governments of six member states. There were no female cabinet ministers at all in the Greek, Hungarian, and Slovakian cabinets (*Helsingin Sanomat*, Jan. 30, 2015).

An examination of marital status shows quite noticeable differences between the power elite and the general population. In 2011, 8 percent of the power elite (6 percent in 1991 and 5 percent in 2001) were unmarried, 84 percent (88 percent, 89 percent) were married, living together or in a registered partnership, 6 percent (4 percent, 5 percent) divorced, and 2 percent (1 percent, 2 percent) widowed. In

Table 4.2. Elite Positions Held by Women (%)

Sub-elite	1991	2001	2011
The government, presidents	39	40	46
Parliament	28	46	40
Political party organizations	48	46	50
Political state secretaries	0	0	39
Municipal councils and boards	6	6	30
Regional councils		10	32
MEPs and commissioner		41	57
POLITICAL ELITE TOTAL	35	37	43
Ministries	4	10	25
Central government agencies	5	20	33
Judiciary	11	13	26
Defence Forces	0	6	9
Church	0	0	4
State regional administration	9	33	33
Municipalities	6	11	5
Regional administration		0	5
EU officials		31	31
ADMINISTRATIVE ELITE TOTAL	5	14	22
State-owned companies and public utilities	0	4	10
Cooperatives	3	6	4
Private business	0	2	4
Property	33	20	13
BUSINESS ELITE TOTAL	3	4	6
Employee associations	17	19	28
Business associations	4	4	15
Other NGOs	24	23	33
Organizations in local and regional administration	0	*	*
ORGANIZATIONAL ELITE TOTAL	12	15	25
Daily press	2	7	14
Other press	17	41	50
TV, radio	14	34	37
MASS MEDIA ELITE TOTAL	11	27	33
Universities	0	14	16
Government research institutes	5	11	21
Private research institutes	19	7	14
Foundations	0	0	25
Associations	13	11	25
Academy of Finland	10	26	29
SCIENTIFIC ELITE TOTAL	8	16	23
Art administration	46	44	50
Art forms	24	29	37
Influential persons	15	41	39
Honorary art professors and academicians	9	55	50
CULTURAL ELITE TOTAL	23	36	41
POWER ELITE TOTAL	12	19	26

*not included in elite structure

the population of the same age (55–59 years) at year-end 2012, the proportion of unmarried people (18 percent), divorcees (21 percent), and widowed persons (3 percent) was higher, whereas the figure for those married (58 percent) was lower. The figure for registered partnerships was 0.1 percent (OSF 2013).

One indication that it has become easier for female elite members to reconcile career and family life is provided by the statistic that the share of unmarried women has fallen from 18 percent in 1991 to 13 percent in 2011. On the other hand, the share of divorced women has increased at the same time from 13 percent to 16 percent, although in 2001 the figure was lower at 10 percent. Also, the share of unmarried men has slightly increased from 4 percent to 6 percent, and the share of divorcees from 2 percent to 3 percent. Since the early 1990s, nine in ten men in the power elite as compared with just seven in ten women in the power elite are married or living together. The marital status difference between men and women in Finland is similar to that in the US elite. According to the study by Michael Lindsay (2014, 104–5), 96 percent of men as opposed to just 64 percent of women were or had been married. Women were nearly three times as likely as men to have been divorced.

It seems that women have greater difficulties in reconciling positions of power with family life than men do. Women who manage to break the glass ceiling in the corner office can still find themselves trapped by traditional gender assignments at home (Ibid.). This can be tested with a structured item in which members of the power elite are asked directly about the effect of their gender on their career advancement.

Among men, the most common answer to this question since the early 1990s has been "no effect": the proportion choosing this response option has risen from 37 percent to 62 percent in 2011. However, the benefit that men feel they have gained from their male gender has all the time decreased. Among men the proportion of those who feel their gender has (clearly or to some extent) advanced their career has fallen from 58 percent in 1991 to 27 percent in 2011. At the same time, the proportion of those saying their male gender has (to some extent or considerably) hampered their career has increased from 2 percent to 6 percent.

Women's assessments of the effects of their gender on their career have not changed as straightforwardly as men's. In addition, women are divided by this issue. Among women, too, the proportion of those saying that their gender has had no effect on their career has increased from 28 percent in 1991 to 33 percent in 2011. Among women the proportion of those who thought their gender had advanced their career initially increased from 28 percent in 1991 to 38 percent in 2001, but in 2011 returned to the same level as in the early 1990s. The proportion of women saying that their gender had hampered their career fell sharply from 39 percent in 1991 to 26 percent in 2001, but then bounced back to 33 percent. In other words, the assessments of female elite members regarding the career effects of their gender took a negative turn in the early 2000s. On the other hand, only very few woman thought that their gender has severely hampered their career (6 percent, 7 percent, and 2 percent). In 2001, the number of women who believed their gender had adversely affected their career was highest in the cultural elite and lowest in the political elite.

NATIVE TONGUE

Finland was part of Sweden for more than six centuries before it was annexed to Russia in 1809. Under Russian rule, Finland nonetheless retained its political and economic autonomy, and the Swedish Constitution remained in force. In fact, Finland's long shared history with Sweden goes a long way toward explaining Finnish society's western European and Nordic character. In 1863, the Russian czar ordained that Finnish, the language spoken by the vast majority of people, was to attain equal status with Swedish over a transitional period of twenty years. This decision gave a boost to the Fennomanian movement, whose goal it was to make Finnish the predominant official language of Finland (Karvonen 2014, 11–12). However, during both Swedish and Russian rule in Finland, Swedish speakers occupied a dominant position in Finnish elites. In the nineteenth century, the Finnish elite structure was internally cohesive because Swedish-speaking senior civil servants in central government had no serious rivals either in the university, the church, or in business and industry (Alapuro 1990, 214–49).

Industrialization from the late nineteenth century onward only reinforced the position of Swedish speakers within elites. In the 1880s, there were very few Finnish speakers in leadership positions in business and industry. Industry, wholesale, the insurance sector, and especially the banking sector were all dominated by Swedish speakers and foreign nationals. The language balance was finally restored when Finland gained independence in 1917 and Swedish-speaking capital, mainly represented by commercial banks and the forest industry, was challenged by Finnish-speaking, "blue-and-white" capital (Kuisma and Keskisarja 2012, 48). The Constitution of Finland, which was passed in 1919, recognizes two national languages, Finnish and Swedish. However, the relative position of these languages was a matter of intense political contestation well into the post-World War II period.

In the early 1900s, Finnish elites and the citizenry were still speaking different languages. Native Swedish speakers accounted for 12.89 percent of the Finnish population. By 1990, this figure had dropped back to 5.94 percent, falling further to 5.60 percent in 2001 and to 5.39 percent in 2011 (OSF 2012). At the same time, Swedish speakers' share of all elite positions was twice as high as their share of the general population. But Swedish speakers' share of elite positions was also declining. In 1991, Swedish speakers accounted for 13.2 percent of all elite positions, in 2001 for 11.5 percent, and in 2011 for 10.6 percent. These percentages have not been calculated from the survey responses, but from all people classified as elite members based on their first name and family name (table 3.1).

In 1991 and 2001, Swedish speakers had the strongest representation in the business elite. In 2011, their numbers were the highest in the cultural elite. In 1991, Swedish speakers accounted for 19.6 percent of business elite members, in 2001 for 18.0 percent, and in 2011 for 15.2 percent. The corresponding figures for the cultural elite were 13.2 percent, 13.7 percent, and 16.5 percent; for the scientific elite 12.6 percent, 10.1 percent, and 12.7 percent; for the political elite 11.8 percent,

10.8 percent, and 11.6 percent; for the mass media elite 12.5 percent, 9.6 percent, and 7.9 percent; for the organizational elite 11.8 percent, 7.2 percent, and 7.7 percent; and for the administrative elite 10.3 percent, 10.4 percent, and 5.8 percent. Since the early 1990s, then, the share of Swedish speakers has increased consistently only in the cultural elite, although their numbers in the scientific elite in 2011 are also higher than in 1991. In all other elite groups the share of Swedish speakers has declined. In relative terms the shares have declined most sharply in the administrative elite, which had a dominant position in the nineteenth-century elite structure. Despite the trends of Europeanization and globalization, foreign nationals have only a marginal representation in elites: in 1991 they accounted for 0.2 percent of all elite positions, rising to 1.3 percent in 2001 and further to 2.1 percent in 2011.

The survey respondents were also asked about the primary language spoken in their childhood home. Again, the responses confirm the tendency of a declining share of Swedish speakers in the elite structure. Finnish speakers' share of elite positions increased from 84 percent in 1991 to 85 percent in 2001 and to 89 percent in 2011. The figures for Swedish speakers were 9 percent, 10 percent, and 8 percent, respectively. In addition, 5 percent, 4 percent, and 2 percent came from a bilingual background (Finnish and Swedish). A marginal share of elite members came from homes where some other language was spoken (1 percent, 0 percent, and 1 percent).

In the early 1990s, Swedish speakers had the strongest representation in business (14 percent) and political (12 percent) elites, but by 2011 the highest figures were recorded for the scientific (14 percent) and cultural (11 percent) elites. After the early 1990s the proportion of Swedish speakers increased only in the scientific (+2 percentage points), administrative (+2), and cultural (+1) elites, but declined in the business (–5), mass media (–5), and political (–3) elites.

The political party representing the Swedish-speaking population in Finland, that is, the Swedish People's Party in Finland (SWP), was founded in the nineteenth century, and it has been represented in the unicameral Parliament since its inception in 1906. The party has been uninterruptedly represented in every cabinet coalition in 1979–2015. Support for the SWP both in the power elite and in the population as a whole has been highly stable, albeit on a slight downward trend since the early 1990s. Compared with the party's performance in parliamentary elections, however, it has been consistently overrepresented in the elites. In the power elite, support for the SWP has dropped from 9 percent to 8 percent and in parliamentary elections from 6 percent to 4 percent since the early 1990s. In the business elite, the SWP is the second largest political party after the conservative National Coalition Party, although its support has dropped from 15 percent to 7 percent.

Party political preferences are very often inherited in the Finnish power elite. In other words, there is little intergenerational political mobility: elite members tend to support the same party as their fathers and mothers. This inheritance effect is the strongest in the case of the SWP. In 1991, 68 percent of elite members whose father was an SWP supporter said they voted for the same party; the figures for 2001 and 2011 were 66 percent and 81 percent, respectively. These figures are much higher than in the general population, where according to a study of the 2007 parliamentary election around 40 percent of voting preferences were inherited from the father's and mother's side. However these latter findings showed considerable intergenerational variation in the inheritance of political preferences. Half of the people in the oldest generation (born in 1930–1944) as opposed to only 24 percent of those in the youngest generation (1985–1994) said they had voted for the same party as their father. Party inheritance from the mother's side (53 percent, 30 percent) was slightly higher. The reason why political preferences were inherited far less often in the youngest than in the oldest generation probably had to do with the fact that those in the youngest generation did not know their fathers' and mothers' political views as well as those in the oldest generation. In part, the weaker inheritance of political preferences in younger generations may be due to the tendency for families to talk less about politics than before, and to the increased perception that one's political views are a private matter (Wass and Torsti 2011, 176–77).

REGIONAL MOBILITY

More than four in five elite members live in southern Finland. This is because most organizations belonging to the elite structure, including Parliament and the government, are headquartered in the capital city of Helsinki and elsewhere in the region. However, the proportion of elite members living in southern Finland has declined marginally since the early 1990s (83 percent in 1991, 82 percent in 2001, 81 percent in 2011). The proportion of those living in central Finland, on the other hand, has slightly increased (9 percent, 10 percent, 12 percent), while the figures for those living in the north of the country have been falling (7 percent, 6 percent, 5 percent). The proportion of elite members living abroad has also edged up slowly (0 percent, 1 percent, 3 percent).

Finland's regional electoral system that is made up of 13 constituencies explains why the proportion of people living in southern Finland—less than four in five—is lower in the political elite than in any other elite group. The share of people living in southern Finland has increased in the organizational elite (+8 percentage points in 1991–2011), mass media elite (+7), and political elite (+1), while it has decreased in the business (–9), scientific (–8), and administrative elites (–6). The proportion living in central Finland has increased in the scientific (+8), business (+6), and administrative (+4) elites, but decreased in the cultural (–7) and mass media (–4) elites. Finally, the share of those living in northern Finland has slightly increased in the cultural (+4) and business elites (+2), but fallen in the organizational (–7) and administrative elites (–2). Only the administrative, scientific, and cultural elites have members who live abroad. In all these groups the figures have increased somewhat since the early 2000s.

Place of residence in youth has a bearing on elite recruitment. According to Lindsay, people who grow up in large cities have a higher chance of reaching the top than those who grow up in rural areas. Over half or 57 percent of the 550 US elite members he interviewed grew up in one of the 51 metropolitan areas with a population over 2 million in the 2010 census, even though these urban areas represented only 42 percent of the country's population in 1950. Living in cultural, political, and business centers provides them with more opportunities in their rise to prominence. Rurally raised elite members tended to move to the city as young adults. In fact, 34 percent had moved to one of these metropolitan areas (having been outside of them), while only 5 percent moved out of the country's major cities. However, according to Jorma Ollila and Harri Saukkomma (2013, 187–88, 267), CEO, president and chairman of the board (1992–2012) of Finnish ICT company Nokia, "Most directors who succeeded at Nokia grew up, for whatever reason, in smaller places around the country, many of them in western Finland. . . All five of us [members of a key group of Nokia's board of directors in 1994–2004] had a similar background: we were all Finnish, we all came from outside the metropolitan area, and we'd all studied in Helsinki and came to work at Nokia."

More than three-fifths of Finnish elite members have lived in southern Finland *in their youth* (ages 10–18). However, regional mobility has increased among elites since the early 1990s. In 1991, the proportion of those who had lived in southern Finland in their youth was 65 percent, in 2001 67 percent, and in 2011 60 percent. At the same time, the proportion of those recruited to elites from central Finland (21 percent, 18 percent, 24 percent) and northern Finland (14 percent, 15 percent, 16 percent) has slightly increased.

The share of those who lived in southern Finland in their youth has increased only in the political (+3) and the mass media elite (+1). In other elite groups the share of those originating from the south has decreased since the early 1990s, in some cases even significantly. The share of those who had lived in southern Finland has fallen most sharply in the administrative elite (−11 percent), where their share in 2011 is lower than in any other elite group (54 percent). Since the early 1990s the share of people originating from southern Finland has also fallen in the business (−9 percent), cultural (−7 percent), organizational (−4 percent), and scientific (−4 percent) elites. The share of those who lived in southern Finland in their youth increased in the organizational, mass media, and scientific elites significantly from the early 1990s to the early 2000s, but then declined significantly.

The share of those recruited into elite positions from central Finland has increased in the administrative (+9 percent), business (+6 percent), and political (+5 percent) elites, but declined in the mass media (−9 percent), scientific (−2 percent), and cultural elites (−1 percent). In the cultural elite, however, the share increased from the early 1990s to the early 2000s, but then began to fall. The proportion of those who lived their youth in northern Finland has increased in all groups except the political elite (−8 percent).

Regional mobility patterns have changed significantly for the political elite. Whereas in 1991–2001 the political elite recruited a larger share of its members from northern Finland than any other elite group, in 2011 this situation was reversed.

This has brought the political elite's patterns of regional mobility closer to other elite groups. From 1991 to 2011, the proportion of elite members recruited from northern Finland increased in the cultural elite by 7 percentage points, in the mass media elite by 5, in the administrative elite by 4, in the scientific elite by 3, in the business elite by 2, and in the organizational elite by 2 percentage points.

Other than purely economic factors may also be relevant in explaining social inheritance. American scholars in particular have devoted much research to the impact of the social environment beyond the family, for instance the role of residential area characteristics. Although families generally have much greater significance to children's financial success later in life, it has been shown that living in a deprived and troubled residential area has a clear adverse effect on children's cognitive development (Härkönen 2010, 64).

An examination of the type of residential area where people spent their youth lends support to the interpretation of a slight increase in regional mobility. In 2011, the proportion of power elite members who spent their youth in sparsely populated areas has bounced back to 25 percent, having dipped to 23 percent in 2001. By contrast, the share of those who lived in sparsely populated rural areas and in small towns with less than 10,000 inhabitants has fallen slightly from the early 1990s to the 2010s. The proportion of those who lived their youth in medium-sized towns has increased noticeably since the early 2000s, which is probably explained in part by urbanization. In the early 1990s, 40 percent of power elite members came from large towns with a population of over 35,000. This figure edged up to 44 percent in 2001, but then fell back to 37 percent.

The increased recruitment into the political and mass media elites from southern Finland is also reflected in an examination of types of residential area. In these elite groups, the share of those who lived their youth in sparsely populated areas and in medium-sized towns has increased since the early 1990s, whereas the share of those coming from large towns started to decrease after the early 2000s. The increased prominence of southern Finland as a source of recruitment into the administrative, business, cultural, organizational, and scientific elites is reflected in dual trends in an examination by type of area: the share of those coming from sparsely populated areas, on the one hand, and from medium-sized towns, on the other, has increased at the expense of large towns. However, half of the cultural elite still come from large towns, which is a larger proportion than in other elite groups. The share of those who grew up in large towns has increased most of all in the scientific elite, from just over one-third in the early 1990s to one-half in 2011.

The postwar expansion of the university system to cover the whole country has created a much broader regional basis for elite recruitment. New universities have been set up around the country in order to boost regional development. The northernmost university in Finland, the University of Lapland, is located in Rovaniemi, and the southernmost universities are in the capital city of Helsinki. Finland also has two Swedish-speaking universities, the Hanken School of Economics (Helsinki, Vaasa) and Åbo Akademi University (Turku).

INCOME LEVEL OF THE POWER ELITE

Income disparities in Finland decreased from the mid-1960s until the 1980s. The period from the 1980s to the mid-1990s saw only minor changes, but income inequality then began to increase quite rapidly by international comparison. One major factor behind the growth of income disparity was the 1993 tax reform, which established the separation of earned income and capital income taxation. Earned incomes are taxed progressively, whereas capital incomes attract a flat tax rate. Following the international financial crisis that began in 2008 and the euro-zone debt crisis, the growth of income disparities has again been slowing. Today, income inequality in Finland is lower than in Europe on average. Income inequality is measured by the Gini index, which is 0 when everyone has the same income and 100 when one person earns all the income in the country. In 2011, Finland's Gini index was 25.9, compared with a European average of 30.6. The only countries with lower income disparities than Finland were Norway, Slovenia, Iceland, Sweden, the Czech Republic, Slovakia, and the Netherlands. Europe's highest rates of income inequality were recorded in Spain (35.0) and Latvia (35.7). In 2013, Finland's Gini index was 26.9, compared with 40.1 for Russia, 40.8 for the United States, 42.1 for China, 54.7 for Brazil, and 63.1 for South Africa (Statistics Finland 2014; *Helsingin Sanomat,* Oct. 3, 2014).

In the United States, income disparities have grown more sharply than in Finland. In 2010, the US Gini index was 41.1 (World Bank 2014). Since 1970, the share of income going to the top 1 percent of Americans has steadily increased, and in the economic boom from 2002 to 2007 that preceded the most recent recession, incomes in the top 1 percent grew 62 percent, while those in the bottom 90 percent grew only 4 percent. Even with the recent economic downturn, executive compensation has grown by an average of 4 percent per year over the past decade (Lindsay 2014, 109).

The following discusses the income of Finnish elite members based on an open-ended question concerning 2010 total income before tax (gross income), including performance bonuses, options, and similar benefits. Table 4.3 shows the results using a classification into eight income brackets.

One-eighth of the power elite earned 50,000 euros or less, two-fifths earned 100,000 euros or less, and over one-quarter 150,000 euros or less a year. Only three percent had an income of more than 500,000 euros, and one percent an income of over one million. Compared with the general population, the power elite is in a different league altogether. In 2011, 90.1 percent of all people in Finland earned less than 50,000 euros, and just 1.3 percent earned more than 100,000 euros. The average income per employee was 26,555 euros, among men 30,824 euros and among women 22,533 euros (Statistics Finland 2011). In the same year the median income for all Finnish people was 30,514 euros (OSF 2013).

There are substantial income disparities not only between the power elite and the citizenry, but also among elite groups. The lowest income, by a wide margin,

Table 4.3. Annual Incomes of Elite Groups and Power Elite in 2010 (%)

Annual Income €	Political Elite	Administrative Elite	Business Elite	Organizational Elite	Mass Media Elite	Scientific Elite	Cultural Elite	Power Elite Total
≤50 000	31	3	2	10	7	4	58	13
50,001–100,000	52	45	13	44	59	28	28	41
100,001–150,000	10	41	21	23	21	46	5	27
150,001–200,000	5	7	11	7	5	13	5	7
200,001–300,000	2	4	19	9	7	4	0	6
300,001–400,000	0	0	11	1	0	4	0	2
400,001–500,000	0	0	4	0	2	0	0	1
500,001–750,000	0	0	9	1	0	0	0	1
750,001–1,000,000	0	0	9	1	0	0	0	1
1,000,000 ≥	0	0	2	3	0	0	0	1
Total	100	100	100	100	100	100	100	100
N	42	131	47	69	44	46	43	412

is reported by cultural elite members, three-fifths of whom earn 50,000 euros or less. The political elite have the second lowest income: one-third of them are in this income bracket. While 86 percent of the cultural elite earn 100,000 euros or less, the corresponding figure for the political elite is 83 percent, for the mass media elite 66 percent, the organizational elite 54 percent, the administrative elite 48 percent, the scientific elite 36 percent, and the business elite 15 percent. The elite group with far and away the highest income is the business elite: 20 percent of business elite members have an income of over half a million euros, and 2 percent earn a million or more. It is hardly surprising to see the business elite at the top of the income table: in 2010 the average income of CEOs of listed companies in Finland, without bonuses, was 654,106 euros, or 54,500 euros a month (*Taloussanomat*, July 30, 2011).

Income differences within elite groups are the greatest in the organizational elite. In this group one in ten earned 50,000 euros or less and more than half earned 100,000 or less. But 5 percent of organizational elite members had an income of over half a million euros, and 3 percent earned more than one million. These wide disparities are explained by the fact that this elite group includes both managing directors and elective chairmen of business and industry associations whose day-to-day job is to run major corporations, but also hired managers and senior elected officials of employee associations and NGOs.

There is also a sizeable gap between men's and women's incomes in the power elite. In 2010, no more than 10 percent of men as opposed to 25 percent of women earned 50,000 euros or less. One-quarter of men but half of women had an income of 84,000 euros or less. The proportion of men who earned at least 168,000 euros was 18 percent; among women the figure was 9 percent. At the top end of the income scale the gender distribution was more balanced: more than 5 percent of men compared with 2 percent of women reached earnings of at least half a million euros. The US elite women interviewed by Michael Lindsay (2014, 23) earned 66 percent of the salaries earned by men, and even among CEOs the figure was no more than 69 percent. In 2015, female directors of Finland's biggest companies earned 95 percent of the salary of male directors, compared with 91 percent in 2010 (Central Chamber of Commerce 2015).

It is not possible to directly examine how incomes have changed in the different elite groups over the past two decades because in 1991 and 2001, the data were collected using a structured item, and in 2011 using an open-ended question. Finland gave up its own currency, the *markka* (FIM) on 1 January 2002 when the euro was introduced. However, the 1991 markka values can be converted into 2011 euros by taking account of the depreciation of the value of money (Money value converter 2014). The share of elite members earning 250,000 markka or 58,712 euros or less fell from 25 percent in 1991 to 15 percent in 2011. The share of those with an income of over one million markka or more than 234,851 euros more than doubled from 6 percent to 16 percent.

The development of earnings in different elite groups from 1991 to 2011 can be analyzed by examining the shares of those earning 500,000 markka or 117,425 euros or less. In the power elite this share dropped from 77 percent to 62 percent. The proportion of earnings more than this increased accordingly from 23 percent to 38 percent. In other words, the biggest relative increase in incomes—that is, the sharpest relative decrease in the share of those earning 177,425 euros or less—was recorded in the scientific elite (84 percent, 50 percent), followed by the mass media elite (91 percent, 70 percent), administrative elite (84 percent, 64 percent), organizational elite (77 percent, 58 percent), political elite (100 percent, 84 percent), business elite (27 percent, 17 percent), and cultural elite (95 percent, 86 percent). The cultural elite is thus set apart from other elite groups both by the higher proportion of low income earners, and by more modest income growth than in other elite groups. The cultural elite was the only group that saw an increase in the share of those earning less than 100,000 markka or 23,485 euros in 1991–2011.

The above does not yet give a clear enough picture of the development of earnings in the business elite, however. When we turn to examine top earners with incomes of over one million markka or 234,851 euros, it is clear that the business elite has moved into a completely different league than other elite groups. The share of these top earners increased in the business elite from 28 percent in 1991 to 57 percent in 2011. The second largest increase in the proportion of top earners was recorded for the scientific elite (4 percent, 22 percent), and the third largest for the organizational elite (4 percent, 19 percent), followed by the mass media elite (1 percent, 11 percent), the cultural elite (1 percent, 9 percent), and the administrative elite (0 percent, 8 percent). The political elite did not have a single top earner in either of these years. Income trends in the cultural elite have thus become polarized: the share of both low and high income earners has increased.

INHERITANCE OF CULTURAL CAPITAL

Researching the Inheritance of Education

Pierre Bourdieu (1996, 287) emphasizes the role of cultural capital as a criterion for elite recruitment. He says that the rise of cultural capital has increasingly implied a shift from direct reproduction of elites, where power is mainly transmitted within the family via economic property from generation to generation, to school-mediated reproduction, where transfer of power takes place through educational institutions. However, Bourdieu is keen to stress that the growing relative weight of cultural capital does not do away with the significance of economic and social capital.

Education is recognized in international studies as the single most important avenue of social reproduction and mobility. Children whose parents come from a higher class position and a higher educational background usually get a higher education than others, and those with a higher education are in turn much more likely to arrive at a high social class (Härkönen 2010, 59; see also Breen and Jonsson 2005; Hout and DiPrete 2006; Björklund and Jäntti 2009). High parental education often fosters an atmosphere in the family that is conducive to education and that inspires children (Garcia de León et al. 2000, 38). According to a recent study based on an examination of calendars of nobility and *Who's Whos*, education has indeed been a major means of upward mobility in Finnish society over the past two centuries (Ruuskanen et al. 2010, 54).

In an examination of the associations between parental social stratum and children's educational attainment level, it is useful to make a distinction between primary and secondary effects. Primary effect refers to the interdependence between parental social stratum and children's school grades, with children coming from higher social backgrounds performing better at school. Secondary effect, then, means that among children with high school achievement, those coming from a higher social background are more likely than others to continue their education (Härkönen 2010, 59).

Finnish studies have shown that schooling is unable to iron out the differences stemming from students' socioeconomic backgrounds. The highest school achievers are talented learners who come from the highest social backgrounds. Lack of talent is not a barrier for those with a privileged background: even if their school achievement is below average, it is unlikely they will have no success later in life. For children from lower social backgrounds, by contrast, below-average talent will almost certainly be a barrier to success: in order to succeed, they would have to do much better at school than their peers. The higher the family social background, the less likely it is for people to arrive in the lowest social strata, even if they have no education (Naumanen and Silvennoinen 2010, 79, 84).

International studies have found that the primary effects of social stratum explain most of the association between parental social stratum and children's educational attainment level. The secondary effects of social background are probably most readily explained by social strata differences in incomes and assets: people from higher social backgrounds can afford to spend more on education. However, the secondary effects of social background can even be seen in the Nordic countries, where education is free of charge through to university level (Härkönen 2010, 59–60).

In Finland, the connection between family background and education have mostly been studied based on the family provider's socioeconomic status, education, or income level. These studies have repeatedly demonstrated the effect of social background on the educational career of the family's offspring. Longer-term analyses have shown that over time, the effect of family background on recruitment into higher education, for instance, has declined, although the difference in favor of the offspring of upper functionaries and academically educated parents has remained clear. When persons born in 1946 are compared with those born in 1976, the effect of social background on gaining an academic education has decreased by more than one-half (Härkönen 2010, 59). In fact, the Nordic countries usually stand apart in comparative analyses in that here, family background shows a weaker association with children's schooling than in other countries (Naumanen and Silvennoinen 2010, 73).

Different theoretical traditions have slightly different explanations for the persistence of educational differences between social strata. According to *reproduction theory*, the educational system is ultimately a creation of elites wielding economic and political power, and education primarily serves their interests. Education reproduces economic and social inequality, as well as asymmetric power relations. The researchers leaning on the Marxist theory tradition take the view that education first and foremost works to reproduce societal structures. *Theories of rational choice*, then, explain educational differences in the population by reference to individuals' microlevel choices in which they weigh relative benefits and drawbacks. Members of lower social strata have a different assessment of the benefits and risks of education than people in higher social strata: for the former, an extended education does not appear to be worth the investment required or the risks involved (Naumanen and Silvennoinen 2010, 73–74).

One explanation for the educational inequality that has gained increasing popularity in recent years is the theory of *relative risk aversion*. Rational individuals, the theory goes, will seek to maximize their lifelong income. As education is associated with high parental income, children and their parents are keen to invest as much as possible in education. The theory has it that parents' and their children's decisions concerning education are geared to avoid downward social mobility. In other words, families will want to make an investment in their children's education that at the very least will ensure they can attain the same social status as their parents. When families make their decisions about education, they will weigh their children's prospects of success on each educational pathway and at the same time consider the monetary and other investments required by education as well as the lost income due to time spent in education. This theory has been put to the test in several studies over the past decade, and it has gained quite widespread support (Härkönen 2010, 60).

According to the *theory of maximally maintained inequality*, educational inequality between social strata can only be ironed out once the upper strata have exhausted all educational opportunities to the very highest level, so that they can no longer gain relative advantage by means of education. Seen from this point of view, the increasing availability of educational opportunities not only perpetuates educational inequalities between social strata, but actually amplifies them, for it is the higher strata that can best capitalize on these new opportunities (Naumanen and Silvennoinen 2010, 74).

According to the *theory of effectively maintained inequality*, the movement toward universal education effectively reconstitutes the conflict of interests between social strata: as the children of privileged groups gravitate toward higher quality education, programs that purport to offer the same level of education in fact become differentially valued and so maintain the relative inequality between social strata (Ibid., 74).

Cultural explanations have it that the educational differences between social strata stem from their respective cultures. School achievement and educational choices are influenced by the interplay of culture and way of life at home, on the one hand, and culture and practices at school, on the other. Students coming from a lower social origin do not have access to the kind of cultural capital—knowledge, skills, talents, and attitudes—they would need in order to meet the expectations of the school environment and to do well at school. This, in turn, feeds into negative perceptions of themselves, their learning abilities, and future prospects. In higher educated families, the culture at home supports school achievement, which in turn is conducive to an ethos of success (Naumanen and Silvennoinen 2010, 74–75).

In addition to the theories mentioned above, the quest to explain the constant educational differences between social strata has also focused on the role of institutional factors, such as the hierarchical structure of the educational system, welfare policy, and labor market characteristics. Many sociological approaches to education share the view that this is a field of competition. In other words, education is seen as a means of competition by individuals for welfare, wealth, and appreciation (Ibid., 75).

Studies of social mobility have shown that a higher education in particular is to a very large degree inherited in Finland. The higher their parents' level of education, the more likely it is that children will obtain a higher education. Mothers' higher education in particular correlates strongly with children's education. According to an analysis of the period 1980–1995, the probability that children of higher educated fathers will themselves obtain a university degree has been significantly high compared with children of other fathers, even though the inheritance of higher education from fathers to children has decreased somewhat. It follows that in the new labor market environment, education, which used to be seen as the most important channel for upward mobility, no longer guarantees a route to higher positions in society. Following the reform of the comprehensive school system and the expansion of the higher education system, the level of education in Finland has risen significantly in recent decades. Indeed, the comprehensive school reform has clearly reduced the effect of fathers' income on their sons' earnings in adulthood. The availability of higher education has improved significantly with the increased number of student places (Sirniö 2010, 17, 21).

Our analysis here of the cultural capital of elite members in Finland is focused, firstly, on the educational level of elites and, secondly, on the associations of their educational level with their parents' education. Later on, we will also explore the impact of family background on the career choices and career advancement of people recruited into elites.

Educational Level of the Power Elite

In his discussion of the role of cultural capital as a criterion for elite recruitment, Bourdieu divides the concept into three dimensions. Firstly, cultural capital can exist in the form of individuals' long-lasting dispositions such as habits, language, and their relationship to schooling and culture. Secondly, it can exist in the form of cultural goods such as paintings, books, and instruments. It is not yet enough that these goods are transferred to the next generation, but knowledge of how they are used must also be handed down. Thirdly, cultural capital has an institutionalized form, which is based on the certificates awarded by the educational system. This form of cultural capital can be directly converted into economic capital on the labor market. But even academic qualifications do not as such guarantee access into positions of power, but it is also necessary to know how to use them. Educational expansion and unemployment have tightened the competition among people with academic qualifications, and therefore it is necessary to resort to other forms of cultural, social, and economic capital in order to create a strategy for the utilization of this asset. In this respect social inequality regarding career and educational achievement may be a consequence of social inequality in the distribution of cultural capital. To these inequalities must also be added socially constituted individual dispositions and choices. According to Bourdieu, habitus is a principle which shapes the representations and behavior of social actors, thus reflecting the social class or fraction to which the individual belongs (García de León et al. 2000, 37–38).

Bourdieu describes the legitimate exercise of power by the school system using the concept of symbolic power. One of the expressions of this form of power is the belief that school offers equal opportunities to all and that education will ensure the right people will find their way to the right place in society's hierarchy of functions. The selection that takes place in the educational system is "covered up" so that the school transforms social inequality into educational inequality, and the structural and objective differences in opportunities for getting ahead into subjective differences due to individual dispositions. This way, both those who do well and those who struggle to keep up can be persuaded to believe that the reasons for failure lie ultimately in individuals' own problems (Ahola 1995, 28).

Since there exists no direct measure of the sources of family cultural capital, it is here described using the concept of educational capital. Later on, the examination is extended to incorporate lifestyles. Father's or mother's educational capital can be regarded as a kind of proxy for cultural resources (García de León et al. 2000, 49).

The level of education in the Finnish population has risen very rapidly. At the same time, age group differences in education have increased. In 1970, three-quarters of Finnish people of working age had no post-lower secondary education, and only one in four had an upper secondary degree or higher. In the space of three decades, these proportions have been reversed: in 2000 three in four had completed an upper secondary degree. The rise in women's educational level has been faster than men's. In 1970, one in seven men and one in ten women had a university degree, while in 2000 around one-third of both men (31 percent) and women (34 percent) had completed a university degree. In the group of young adults aged 25–34, an upper secondary education became the norm in the mid-1980s, as the proportion with an upper secondary degree climbed to 60 percent. By the mid-1990s the proportion of young adults with a tertiary education exceeded the figure for those with no more than a lower secondary education (Naumanen and Silvennoinen 2010, 68–69).

Finnish elite members have a much higher education than the whole population. The proportion of elite members with a *matriculation examination* increased from 87 percent in 1991 through 90 percent in 2001 to 92 percent in 2011. Not surprisingly, these figures are highest in the scientific elite: since the early 1990s virtually all members of this elite group have had a matriculation certificate. In 1991, the elite group with the lowest share of matriculation graduates was the organizational elite (78 percent), but since then the figure has been lowest in the political elite (77 percent in 2001, 81 percent in 2011).

The proportion of elite members who had completed no more than *secondary school or comprehensive school* edged down from 7 percent in 1991 to 6 percent in 2011. The corresponding figures for the age group 50–54 in the total population was 39 percent in 1999 and 28 percent in 2009 (OSF 2001, 482; 2011, 381). In 1991, 6 percent of elite members had completed no more than the lowest level of education; in 2001 and 2011 that figure was down to 2 percent.

The proportion of elite members with a *university degree* increased from 82 percent in 1991 to 87 percent in 2001 and to 88 percent in 2011. By comparison, virtually all of the US elite members interviewed by Michael Lindsay (2014, 28) had graduated from some college. Only 3 percent of the leaders he interviewed did not graduate, and among this small group, most attended for some amount of time. However, this comparison is complicated by the fact that virtually all Finnish elite members with a matriculation examination have an MA degree. In the early 1990s, the proportion of university degree holders in Finland was lowest in the mass media elite (68 percent), one decade later in the political elite (68 percent), and in 2011 in the cultural elite (76 percent). Since the early 1990s, up to one-quarter of elite members have held a postgraduate degree (licentiate or doctorate)—although this figure is swollen by the fact that in the scientific elite eight in ten and even in the administrative elite three in ten have a postgraduate degree. In the United States one-quarter of elite members had earned a doctorate (Lindsay 2014, 30). The proportion of college or polytechnic degree graduates in Finnish elites has remained quite low (8, 7, 7 percent). In the general population the proportion of university or polytechnic degree holders in the age group 50–54 was 26 percent in 1999 and 30 percent in 2009 (OSF 2001, 482; 2011, 381). Recruitment into the elite is virtually impossible for people with no more than vocational training qualifications: in the early 1990s just 8 percent of the power elite had less than post-secondary level vocational training, and that share subsequently dropped to 5 percent.

Throughout the research period from 1991 to 2011, the most common field of education among those with a university degree has been the social sciences. The proportion of social science graduates has increased from one-fifth in the early 1990s to over one-quarter in 2011. In the early 1990s, the second most popular field of education, almost on a par with the social sciences, was law, followed by the humanities, engineering sciences, and business and commerce, all with roughly equal proportions. One indication of the social sciences' increasing prominence is that since the early 1990s, the figures for both humanities, engineering sciences, and law graduates have slightly fallen in the power elite. In contrast, the share of business and commerce graduates dipped in the early 2000s, but in 2011 recovered to the levels seen in the early 1990s.

However, people are recruited into different elite groups from different educational backgrounds. The following describes the fields of education of elite members with a university degree. Since the early 1990s, the major avenue of recruitment into the political elite has been via the social sciences. The proportion of social science graduates increased from over one-third in the early 1990s to one-half in 2001, and then dropped to two-fifths. Law in particular but also medicine has become a more important channel for recruitment into elites: the proportion of law graduates has risen to one-fifth and that of medical graduates to one-seventh. This is a significant change given that lawyers in Finland—in contrast to the United States, for instance—have had only a small representation (less than 5 percent) in Parliament, ever since the first elections to the unicameral Parliament in 1907 (Ruostetsaari 2000, 65). In the United States, 22 percent of the elite members interviewed by Michael Lindsay (2014) had a law degree. The proportion of theology graduates has also increased in the political elite. The humanities and economics or business administration, on the other hand, have become less significant avenues of recruitment into the political elite.

In the administrative elite, the most common academic qualification is a law degree: one-third of all academic graduates in this group have a law degree. However, it is noteworthy that the predominance of lawyers has clearly waned. While in the early 1990s two-fifths of administrative elite members had a law degree, this proportion dropped to less than one-third by the early 2000s, and further to one-quarter in 2011. The importance of this trend is underscored by the fact that administrative elite members work at the very highest level of the professional hierarchy, and the share of lawyers has traditionally increased toward the higher echelons of that hierarchy (see, e.g., Tirronen 1990; Stenvall 1995).

The role of law as an avenue of recruitment into the administrative elite has decreased mainly at the expense of the social sciences, the share of which has increased consistently from one-tenth in the early 1990s to almost one-quarter in the early 2010s. The figures for other fields of education among university degrees completed are clearly lower, although engineering sciences, economics or business administration and, to a lesser extent, theology and agriculture and forestry have gained increasing prominence.

In the early 1990s, the main avenue of recruitment into the business elite was via an education in economics or business administration (over one-third), followed by engineering sciences (one-quarter) and law (one-seventh). In 2001, the relative weights of these fields of education were more or less unchanged, but by 2011 an engineering education was on a par with education in economics or business administration education (both accounting for one-third), and the social sciences (just under one-fifth) had overtaken law. In fact the share of social sciences doubled by the early 2010s. Likewise, the share of humanities and agriculture and forestry graduates has increased somewhat in the business elite, while the natural sciences have lost even the remnants of what always was a marginal role.

In the early 1990s, the most common field of education in the organizational elite was law (one-quarter), followed by the social sciences and engineering sciences (one-fifth in each). By 2001, the social sciences (one-quarter) had overtaken law, which was followed in third place by economics or business administration. One decade later, the top two fields of education in the organizational elite were the social sciences and economics or business administration, followed by law and agriculture and forestry, which were equally strong. Overall the social sciences and economics or business administration have gained increased prominence in providing the qualifications of the organizational elite, whereas the roles of both engineering sciences and law have dwindled.

In contrast to other elites, recruitment into the mass media elite has been dominated by two fields of education, that is, the social sciences followed by the humanities, while all other disciplines have remained quite marginal. However, the relative shares of these two leading disciplines have moved in completely opposite directions. While the share of social science degree holders increased from two-fifths in the early 1990s to two-thirds in the early 2010s, the proportion of humanities degree holders fell from one-third to one-sixth. The proportion of natural science and economics or business administration degree holders has also increased slightly since the early 1990s, but they continue to remain marginal.

In the scientific elite there is a more balanced representation of different fields of education, which is explained by the fact that Academy Professors represent different disciplines. Nonetheless engineering and natural sciences have a strikingly strong representation in the scientific elite. Throughout the research period the proportion of natural science graduates has been higher in the scientific elite than in other elite groups. Furthermore, this proportion has increased from one-fifth in the early 1990s to just over one-fifth in 2011, following a slight dip in 2001. The share of engineering graduates has risen from one-eighth in the early 1990s to one-fifth in the early 2010s.

The cultural elite's educational profile differs noticeably from other elite groups. In 1991 and 2001, two-fifths of the cultural elite had a higher education in the humanities or arts. By 2011, this share had increased to seven in ten. The second most common field of education is the social sciences, although in 2011 the figure for economics or business administration graduates was equally high. Indeed, economics or business administration is the only field of education whose share in the cultural elite has increased since the early 1990s, while the figure for university graduates in all other disciplines has declined.

The expansion of higher-level white-collar employment in Finland has coincided with a rising level of education and a growing demand for education, possibly contributing to educational inflation. This has changed the association between education and social status, as attaining a certain position requires a greater investment in education than before. A higher education no longer automatically guarantees a certain level of earnings and social status, as it would have done in earlier decades. Indeed, it has been reported that higher education graduates reach upper functionary positions less often than before. In 1970, 90 percent of those with an MA degree reached an upper functionary position, but by 2000 that figure had dropped to 76 percent. The figures for those with a BA degree were 81 percent in 1970 and 55 percent in 2000 (Sirniö 2010, 64–65). It is apparent, then, that the relative benefit of the matriculation examination and an academic education in elite recruitment has decreased since the early 1990s: as the educational level of both the whole population and elites has continued to rise, other factors are needed to promote recruitment into the elite.

It is quite plain and clear that equal access to higher education has contributed to upward social mobility in Finland. There is a fairly high number of universities in the country for its population (21 for a population of 5.3 million), and they are geographically dispersed across the whole country. Furthermore, there are no elite universities in Finland comparable to the Ivy League Schools in the US or Oxbridge in the UK. All universities are funded primarily by the state, and tuition is free of charge, even for foreign nationals. To help with students' living costs, government has guaranteed student loans and given free student grants ever since the 1970s.

Inheritance of Education

The level of basic education among elite members' parents has changed very little since the early 1990s. One-third of elite members' fathers have taken the matriculation examination (31 percent in 1991, 31 percent in 2001, and 33 percent in 2011). However, there are marked and even surprising differences among the elite groups. In 2011, the proportion of fathers with a *matriculation certificate* was highest in the scientific elite (47 percent), followed by the mass media elite (38 percent), cultural elite (37 percent), political elite (37 percent), organizational elite (32 percent), business elite (28 percent), and administrative elite (25 percent). The proportion of fathers with a matriculation certificate increased after the early 1990s in all elite groups except the administrative, business, and cultural elites, where the figures declined. The proportion of mothers with a matriculation certificate was lower than the figure for fathers, but nonetheless rising (22 percent, 26 percent, 29 percent).

The level of *vocational training* among elite members' fathers has also remained stable. Since the early 1990s, 30 percent of fathers have had a university degree. In 2011, the proportion of fathers with a *university degree* was far and away the highest in the scientific elite (45 percent), followed by the cultural elite (34 percent), organizational elite (31 percent), mass media elite (31 percent), administrative elite (24 percent), and business elite (23 percent). The share has increased in the political, organizational, and scientific elites, but declined in other elites. The proportion of university graduates has increased more among the mothers than fathers of elite members (12 percent, 16 percent, 21 percent).

When both basic education and vocational training are taken into account, fathers of scientific elite members have had the highest educational level ever since the 1990s, suggesting a high degree of inheritance of educational capital. On the other hand, the educational level of fathers increased in most elites, but fell in the administrative, business, and cultural elites, which might be expected to represent the highest level of cultural capital. The most significant change has taken place in the political elite: while fathers' educational level in this elite group was lower than in others in

1991 and 2001, it then showed the sharpest rise, even exceeding the level of other elite groups. The same trend has been found among the mothers of elite members. Overall, educational (i.e., cultural) capital in the sense of parental educational level has become more evenly spread among elites since the early 1990s.

One way of studying the inheritance of education between elite members and their parents is to cross-tabulate their educational levels. Almost three-quarters or 71 percent of the 1991 elite members whose fathers had no vocational training were university graduates (including postgraduates). In 2001, the corresponding proportion was 79 percent, and in 2011 85 percent. Among the elite members whose mothers had no vocational training, the figures were even higher (78 percent, 86 percent, 87 percent). In 1991, 90 percent of the elite offspring of university graduated fathers had themselves completed the same or higher postgraduate degree. The corresponding proportions in the 2001 and 2011 elites were 93 percent. In 1991 and 2001, the figures for offspring of university graduated mothers were higher than for offspring of university graduated fathers (94 percent and 94 percent), but in 2011 the figure was lower (89 percent). Since the early 1990s virtually all elite members whose mother or father had a postgraduate degree have had a university-level education.

There is, then, a clear association between elite members' and their parents' level of education (table 4.4): mechanisms of educational inheritance are at work both in the general population and at elite level. Furthermore, the findings from population studies suggesting a reduced level of educational inheritance from fathers to sons, also applies to elites. In other words, the correlation between elite members' and their fathers' educational level has become weaker since the early 1990s (Spearman .175 in 1991, .171 in 2001, and .152 in 2011). On the other hand, while earlier population studies have shown that a higher level of maternal education in particular correlates strongly with children's education (e.g., Sirniö 2010, 17, 21), at elite level this correlation has remained weaker than in the case of fathers. The correlation between elite members' and their mothers' educational level has decreased more rapidly than the correlation with father's education (.126, .074, and .038). In contrast to the situation in the general population, then, education among elites is more readily inherited from the father's than the mother's side. This is at least partly explained by the fact that elite members' fathers have had a much higher level of education than mothers. A 2010 study of academically educated people who had been to university found that father's level and field of education had a slightly greater effect on the son than the daughter, and accordingly mother's level and field of education had a slightly greater effect on the daughter than the son (Ahola and Tolonen 2013). Most elite members are men. Overall, the heritability of education has decreased both on the father's and mother's side, but more so on the mother's side. At elite level, too, the reduced heritability of education is likely due to the reform of comprehensive schooling and the expansion of university education and the consequent rise in the population's educational level.

Table 4.4. Association between Elite Members' and Their Father's Vocational Training (%)

| | Father's Vocational Training | | | | | | | | | | | | | | | | | | | | |
| | No Vocational Training | | | Training Course | | | Vocational School | | | College | | | University | | | Postgraduate Degree | | | All | | |
Elite Member's Vocational Training	1991	2001	2011	1991	2001	2011	1991	2001	2011	1991	2001	2011	1991	2001	2011	1991	2001	2011	1991	2001	2011
No vocational training	5	5	3	2	1	0	3	1	3	3	1	0	1	2	0	0	0	0	2	2	1
Training course	2	1	3	8	1	3	5	0	9	0	1	0	1	1	0	3	0	0	3	1	2
Vocational school	6	7	1	2	1	4	1	1	0	0	1	0	0	0	3	0	0	0	2	2	2
College or polytechnic	13	8	9	10	9	6	7	10	10	7	6	8	5	5	3	0	0	0	8	7	6
University	51	60	66	51	60	67	63	66	50	69	63	70	61	65	67	53	46	48	57	62	64
Postgraduate degree	20	19	19	26	25	21	20	21	28	20	27	20	29	28	26	43	54	52	25	26	25
Other	3	0	0	1	4	0	1	0	0	0	1	0	3	0	0	0	0	0	2	0	0
N	140	111	79	177	136	81	81	80	58	75	81	74	160	141	100	40	35	29	678	584	425

SOCIAL STRATUM OF THE POWER ELITE

Social mobility has been an important focus for social class research. If there is high social mobility, then class boundaries will become blurred. Individual social mobility may also prevent collective social mobility: it may provide an opportunity for talented members of lower social classes to move up in the social hierarchy, which in turn may make it harder for the lower classes to organize themselves. Studies of the openness and closure of elites are often interested to measure how common it is for descendants of lower social classes to advance to the highest stratum. On the other hand, the same question can be asked from an elite point of view, turning the focus to the homogeneity or heterogeneity of elites' social background. Following C. Wright Mills (1956), it might be thought that sharing a similar social background is one of the factors contributing to the coherence of elites (Uusitalo 1980, 17).

Elite members were asked identical structured questions in 1991–2011 concerning their parents' occupational status at the time that the respondents themselves were young (table 4.5). Traditionally, the highest social stratum has accounted for a larger share of Finnish elites than of the general population (Ruostetsaari 2003a). The share of offspring whose fathers occupied a leading position and who were manual workers has increased since the early 1990s, whereas the share of upper and lower white-collar functionaries and the share of entrepreneurs and self-employed people has declined. There has been very little change in the proportion of descendants of farmers. However, elite groups differ from one another with respect to father's occupational status.

In the political elite, the proportion of offspring of the highest social groups, that is, functionaries in leading positions and upper functionaries, has increased since the early 1990s, but the same applies to the share of manual workers. On the other hand, the proportion of descendants of lower functionaries, entrepreneurs or self-employed people, and farmers in particular, has decreased. In the administrative elite, by contrast, the proportion of offspring of leaders and upper and lower functionaries has fallen, while the share of offspring of self-employed persons and farmers has increased since the early 1990s. There have been no changes in the proportion of children of manual workers.

Change in the social background of the business elite has been twofold. On the one hand, there has been an increase in the proportion of offspring of leaders at the top end of the occupational hierarchy, but also in the proportion of descendants of manual workers and especially farmers at the lower end of the hierarchy. On the other hand, the proportion of offspring of upper and lower functionaries as well as entrepreneurs and self-employed people has decreased. The picture is much the same in the organizational elite: the proportion of offspring of employees in leading positions in particular, but also of manual workers has increased, while the proportion of offspring of fathers representing other occupational groups has decreased since the early 1990s. The only difference separating the mass media elite from the organizational elite is that the proportion of offspring of entrepreneurs or self-employed

Table 4.5. Occupational Status of Elite Members' Fathers (%)

Father's Occupational Status	Political Elite			Administrative Elite			Business Elite			Organizational Elite			Mass Media Elite			Scientific Elite			Cultural Elite			Power Elite Total		
	1991	2001	2011	1991	2001	2011	1991	2001	2011	1991	2001	2011	1991	2001	2011	1991	2001	2011	1991	2001	2011	1991	2001	2011
Leading position	13	11	15	21	15	16	19	24	26	12	16	23	25	16	20	14	20	29	27	24	23	18	18	20
Upper functionary	11	19	20	25	23	23	18	18	9	19	18	17	16	32	24	28	27	23	25	16	5	20	21	18
Lower functionary	14	11	13	18	15	13	19	14	9	14	21	11	22	13	13	18	8	10	16	12	27	17	14	14
Manual worker	18	19	22	14	14	14	7	12	11	21	19	23	13	18	20	9	10	13	15	16	23	14	15	18
Entrepreneur or self-employed	17	19	13	8	11	11	19	8	9	10	7	9	12	11	13	13	12	4	10	24	16	13	12	11
Farmer	24	22	15	15	22	22	19	23	34	24	19	16	13	11	7	18	23	19	7	9	2	18	19	18
Other	4	0	2	0	0	0	0	0	4	0	0	1	0	0	2	0	0	2	0	0	5	0	0	2
Total	100	100	100	100	100	100	100	100	100	100	100	100	100	100	100	100	100	100	100	100	100	100	100	100
N	84	81	46	126	165	134	108	90	47	137	105	70	77	56	45	78	74	48	68	58	44	678	590	423

people has slightly increased, whereas the proportion of descendants of upper functionaries increased significantly in the early 2000s, and then began to decline, although it did not fall back to the level seen in the early 1990s. In the scientific elite only the share of offspring of fathers who were manual workers or farmers has increased, while the shares for all other occupational groups have declined. A feature that sets the cultural elite apart is that the proportions of offspring of lower functionaries, self-employed people, and manual workers have increased, while the figures for those coming from other occupational backgrounds have declined.

In order to provide a picture of the changes in the openness or closure of the power elite over time, the following describes the social stratification of Finnish elites based on an occupational analysis. This analysis uses the classification of the population into four categories that was first used by Heikki Waris (1948) and later successfully applied by Erik Allardt (1983, 136), that is, the distinction between blue-collar workers, farmers, the middle class, and the top stratum. Functionaries in leading positions and entrepreneurs and self-employed people are combined into the "top stratum." Upper and lower functionaries constitute the middle class.

Although the top stratum thus constructed may also include small entrepreneurs and practitioners who in the Waris classification belong to the middle class, the power elite as a whole is fairly upper class in its social background. Almost one-third of all elite members come from the highest stratum, one-third from the middle class, one-fifth from a farmer background, and over one-seventh from working-class homes (table 4.6). The highest social stratum is also overrepresented in the American elite, but 59 percent of the elite members interviewed by Michael Lindsay (2014, 24) were drawn from the middle class, and a significant minority, 28 percent, grew up in homes where one or both parents worked blue-collar jobs or were near poverty (4 percent).

When functionaries in leading positions and entrepreneurs and self-employed persons are included in the highest social stratum, the proportion of those recruited into the power elite from this stratum has remained highly stable since the early 1990s. The middle class, comprising upper and lower functionaries, was the largest social stratum in the power elite in all three years of study, although its share has been on the decline since the early 1990s. However, the most noteworthy trend is the growing proportion of lower social strata in elites: the proportion of manual workers' offspring has increased since the early 1990s, while the proportion of farmers' offspring was the same in 1991 and 2011, but slightly higher in 2001.

Adding together the proportions of manual workers' and farmers' offspring (32 percent in 1991, 34 percent in 2001, and 36 percent in 2011), it is evident that Finnish elites have become opened up to lower social strata since the early 1990s. In other words, there has been generational mobility at elite level, which has widened the social basis of the power elite.

Social stratification in the power elite differs substantially from the general population. In a study of Finnish men aged 25–63 using the Erikson-Goldthorpe class scheme (see Erikson-Goldthorpe 1992) in 1990 and 2000, the highest social

Table 4.6. Socio-economic Status of Elite Members' Fathers (%)

	Political Elite			Administrative Elite			Business Elite			Organizational Elite			Mass Media Elite			Scientific Elite			Cultural Elite			Power Elite Total		
	1991	2001	2011	1991	2001	2011	1991	2001	2011	1991	2001	2011	1991	2001	2011	1991	2001	2011	1991	2001	2011	1991	2001	2011
Top stratum	30	30	28	29	26	27	38	32	34	22	23	32	36	27	33	27	33	33	37	48	39	31	30	31
Middle class	25	30	33	42	38	37	36	32	17	33	39	29	38	45	38	46	35	33	41	28	32	37	35	32
Farmer	24	22	15	15	22	22	19	23	34	24	19	16	13	11	7	18	23	19	7	9	2	18	19	18
Blue-collar	18	19	22	14	14	14	7	12	11	21	19	23	13	18	20	9	10	13	15	16	23	14	15	18
Other	4	0	2	0	0	0	0	0	4	0	0	1	0	0	2	0	0	2	0	0	5	0	0	2
Total	100	100	100	100	100	100	100	100	100	100	100	100	100	100	100	100	100	100	100	100	100	100	100	100
N	84	81	46	126	165	134	108	90	47	137	105	70	77	56	45	78	74	48	68	58	44	678	590	423

stratum—higher-grade professionals including managers, medical doctors, and judges—accounted for 11 percent and 12 percent, respectively. Lower-grade professionals such as teachers accounted for 21 percent and 23 percent; higher-grade non-manual employees such as bank employees and secretaries accounted for 1 percent and 2 percent; and customer service employees such as nurses and waiting staff for 3 percent and 4 percent. In both years self-employed people accounted for 10 percent, while the share of farmers and smallholders was 8 percent in 1990 and 6 percent in 2000. Both in 1990 and 2000 the single biggest class group was the working class, accounting for 47 percent and 45 percent of the population, respectively (Erola 2010, 31–37).

In an international comparison, Finland was a more working-class country than Sweden (36 percent) in the early 2000s. In fact, Finland has had a larger working class than even the UK (34 percent), traditionally regarded as the class society par excellence. Finland's class structure bears the closest resemblance to Germany's (47 percent). If class positions are understood primarily as clusters based on objective occupational differences, then Finland in the 2000s resembles traditional class society more closely than either the UK or Sweden (Ibid., 38). The social stratification of the power elite and the general population in Finland suggests the conclusion that since the early 1990s, offspring of functionaries in a leading positions, upper functionaries, and farmers have been overrepresented in the power elite, while people from a working-class background and, to a lesser extent, lower functionaries have been underrepresented.

Overall, however, the examination of the power elite fails to capture the major changes that have taken place in the social mobility of different elite groups since the early 1990s. If people coming from farming and working-class backgrounds are defined as the "lowest social stratum," the combined share of this stratum in the early 1990s was highest in the organizational elite (45 percent), followed by the political elite (42 percent). In 2001, it was highest in the political elite (41 percent). In other words, the political elite shows greater openness to recruitment than most other elite groups until the early 2000s, and it has offered to lower social strata a more effective channel for upward social mobility into positions of power. Since the early 2000s, however, this opening up has come to a halt, and the political elite has become emphatically middle-class. The proportion of political elite members of working-class origin has increased somewhat, at the same time as the proportion of those coming from an agricultural background has decreased. In fact, in the early 2010s, the lowest stratum accounted for a smaller share of the political elite than it did of the business elite and the organizational elite. Since the early 1990s the only elite group where the proportion of the lowest stratum has fallen more sharply than in the political elite is the organizational elite. Taken together, these changes suggest that politics has become a less important avenue of upward social mobility, and that social mobility at elite level is becoming detached from social background.

In 2011, the group showing the greatest openness to recruitment from the lowest social stratum, surprisingly, was the business elite (45 percent), where the combined share of people from a working-class and farming background has increased since the early 1990s more than in any other elite group. This change is due to the sharp rise in the share of people from a farming background since the early 2000s, which has occurred at the expense of the middle class. Having said that, the group that in 2011 showed the least openness to recruitment from a working-class background was the business elite. Social stratification in the business elite is twofold in the sense that in 2011, the share of the highest social stratum was the second highest in this group after the cultural elite, although slightly lower than in the early 1990s. The growth of the highest stratum after the early 2000s is explained by the increasing share of offspring of functionaries in leading positions and the declining share of descendants of entrepreneurs.

In 2011, openness to recruitment from the lowest stratum was second highest in the organizational elite, even though it has moved clearly toward greater closure. The share of the top stratum has increased clearly, at the same time as the share of the middle class has declined significantly since the early 2000s. For the lowest social stratum, this change has been twofold: at the same time as the share of those from a farming background has declined, the share of people from a working-class background has grown. Since the early 1990s the share of people from a farming background has fallen more than in any other elite group.

The fourth most open elite group to recruitment from the lowest social stratum has been the administrative elite. This elite group has a distinctly middle-class, partly upper-class social background. Having said that, the share of the middle class has been falling since the early 1990s. The share of the highest stratum was at its highest in the early 1990s. The opening up of the administrative elite to the lowest stratum came to a halt in the early 2000s, since when the share of the lowest stratum has no longer increased. Although the share of people from a farming background is almost twice as high as the share of those of working-class origin, the numbers for the former have no longer increased since the 2000s, whereas the share of people from a working-class background has remained unchanged since the early 1990s.

As early as the 1970s Alestalo and Uusitalo (1972, 205) stressed the impact of education on elite social stratification. They found that elite groups in which an academic education is a key recruitment criterion had a much higher proportion of people originating from the highest and middle strata. These elite groups include public officials, the science elite, and the church elite. The proportion of people coming from the highest and middle strata is considerably smaller in the political, art, and military elites.

By the early 1990s it was apparent that an academic education no longer can explain the elite stratification. The general level of education in Finland is so high that, with the possible exception of the political elite, an academic degree is now required for recruitment into all elite groups. According to the criteria applied by Alestalo and Uusitalo, the administrative and scientific elites should be more upper-class in their social composition than other elites, as these are the only elite groups where an academic degree is an explicit criterion for promotion to most positions. However, this is clearly not the case. As was discussed earlier, the administrative elite does not stand out as a particularly upper-class group. On the contrary, its social structure leans increasingly toward the lower strata.

In the early 2010s, the scientific elite is the fifth most open group to recruitment from the lowest social stratum. The scientific elite has a balanced social stratification structure: the highest stratum, the middle class, and the lowest stratum each account for one-third of this elite group. The share of the highest stratum increased until the early 2000s, whereas the share of the middle class has declined since the early 1990s. The proportions of people from a farming and working-class background are higher today than in the early 1990s. However, with the exception of the business elite, the scientific elite is more closed to people from a working-class background than other elite groups.

The sixth most open, that is, the second most closed elite group to recruitment from the lowest social stratum is the mass media elite. This elite group has seen hardly any change in its openness since the early 1990s. This is because the share of people from an agricultural background has declined and at the same time the share of people from a working-class background has increased. The share of the highest social stratum fell in the early 2000s, but then started to increase again, although it did not return to the level of the early 1990s. In 2011 the share of the middle class fell back to the level of the early 1990s, having been slightly higher in the early 2000s.

The group least open to recruitment from the lowest social stratum throughout the research period is the cultural elite. The highest social stratum accounts for two-fifths of the cultural elite, a larger share than in any other elite group. In the early 2000s, this stratum accounted for as much as one-half of the cultural elite. In the early 2010s, the middle class accounted for one-third, more than in 2001, but clearly less than in 1991. The share of the lowest social stratum in the cultural elite has increased somewhat, which is explained by the growing share of people from a working-class background since the early 2000s. In 2011, the share of people of working-class origin in both the cultural elite and the organizational elite was higher than in other elite groups. For children from a farming background, by contrast, the cultural elite has been the most closed elite group since the early 1990s, just as the scientific elite has been for people from a working-class background; or, in an alternative interpretation, the least attractive avenue for upward social mobility. The picture that emerges of the social background of the cultural elite thus differs essentially from the finding by Kartovaara (1972) that the scientific elite together with the political elite differs from other elite groups in that the share of people coming from the highest social background is considerably smaller than in other elite groups.

Elite members' mothers have had a clearly lower occupational status than fathers. In the early 1990s not a single mother of elite members was in a leading position, and even in 2011 their share was still no more than 3 percent. A much lower proportion of mothers than fathers have worked as upper and lower functionaries, blue-collar workers, farmers, and entrepreneurs. However, the proportion of mothers who have worked white-collar and blue-collar jobs has increased consistently since the early 1990s. In 2011, the share of mothers who had worked blue-collar jobs was close to the corresponding proportion for fathers.

The single largest occupational group among elite members' mothers has been housewife, although the figures have dropped from 45 percent in 1991 to 23 percent in 2011. However, there are marked differences among elite groups. In 2011, one-third of scientific (35 percent), business (34 percent), and cultural (30 percent) elite members were recruited from homes where the mother was a housewife, but the figures for the political (7 percent), mass media (11 percent), organizational (16 percent), and administrative (28 percent) elites are clearly lower. The rapid decline in the proportion of housewives is explained by the Finnish welfare state model, which has required the participation of both parents in the labor market.

CLASS IDENTIFICATION OF THE ELITES

Occupational class position has been found to have a major impact on subjective class identification. However, people's own views of the class they represent cannot be fully reduced to objective class positions. Subjective class identification also depends on other factors such as education, income, and especially the class positions of other family members (Erola 2010, 43).

There is conflicting research evidence on the ability of Finnish people to define their own class position. For instance, no more than one in seven people in the Finland 1999 and Finland 2004 data sets said they did not belong to any social class (Erola 2010, 38). However, 23–27 percent of the respondents to the Finnish Business and Policy Forum (EVA) surveys since 1984 have said they do not identify with any social class. At the same time, though, the proportion of people who have been able or willing to identify with some class group, has consistently increased since the early 1990s (EVA 2011, 130). As a significant proportion of Finnish elites still come from the highest social stratum, the following discusses elite members' subjective class identification: do they themselves feel they belong to the upper class?

Class-based voting has been widespread in Finland, especially since the Second World War. More than in most western democracies, people in Finland have found their political home on a class basis. Popular support for political parties was quite stable from World War II through to the 1990s, primarily perhaps because of so-called transgression, which resulted in a noticeable expansion of the traditional class basis of political parties, especially in the 1960s. The exhaustion of ideologies has led to increasing convergence between political parties as they have sought to win new supporters outside their traditional voter bases (Sänkiaho 1991, 37–38).

In the wake of restructuring of society, the value revolution, and changes in the political system, citizens no longer feel they belong simply to society as the traditional Marxist understanding of class would have it. Therefore, the measurement of class identification has turned to new types of classifications. The classification used in this study draws not only on the work of Marx, but also on Max Weber, who maintains that social identity is determined not according to people's role in production, but rather their status. Weber argues that this status (or in his words, "estate") comprises education, consumption, and other such factors (Sänkiaho 1991, 41).

The Finnish power elite's subjective class identification leans firmly toward the upper middle class. The elite members identify themselves far and way most often with this class: one-third identified with the upper middle class in the early 1990s, and one-half in 2011. In 2011, the second most common target of identification was "high income earners," followed in shared third place by "wage earners" and "middle income earners." Patterns of class identification have changed very little in the past two decades. The only movements worth mentioning are the decrease in the proportion of those identifying mainly with the upper class and with wage earners from 13 percent to 5 percent and from 18 percent to 9 percent, respectively.

Patterns of class identification in the elites can be roughly compared with those in the general population based on surveys conducted by the Finnish Business and Policy Forum EVA, which have had the response options of "working class," "middle class," "upper class," and "no class." Finnish people identify most often, and increasingly, with the middle class: in 1990 the proportion identifying with the middle class was 45 percent, in 2000 54 percent, and in 2011 56 percent. The second most common target of class identification was "no class": the proportion of respondents opting for this choice has dropped from 37 percent in 1990 through 28 percent in 2000 to 23 percent in 2011. The proportions identifying with the working class in 1990 and 2000 were 18 percent and 17 percent, respectively, edging up to 21 percent in 2011. Hardly anyone in Finland identifies with the upper class: the figures for 1990, 2000, and 2011 were 1 percent, 0.5 percent, and 0.3 percent, respectively (EVA 2011, 130). In other words, the proportion identifying with the upper class has fallen since the early 1990s both in the elites and in the citizenry (table 4.7).

It is apparent from the marginal and declining share of people who identify with the upper class that the very notion of such a class carries a strong negative connotation of elitism, both among elite groups and the citizenry. Living in a society that swears by egalitarianism, people in Finland feel it is culturally incorrect to belong to the upper class, even if they do meet the objective criteria of education, occupation, and income, for instance. One illustration of this is provided by the statistic that the proportion of political elite members—who for the most part owe their position to popular election—identifying with the upper class has dropped from 6 percent to 2 percent. In the business elite, who have much higher incomes than other elite groups, the proportion identifying with the upper class has fallen from 29 percent to 9 percent. In the scientific elite, the group with the highest education, the figure has slumped from 15 percent to 2 percent. In the administrative elite, the very pinnacle of the hierarchy of public officials, the proportion identifying with the upper class has fallen from 21 percent in the early 1990s to 9 percent in the early 2010s. However, the negative connotation associated with the upper class in Finland is not internationally unique: in the United States, for instance, the upper class avoids using the class term (Lindsay 2014, 149).

Table 4.7. Elite Members' Primary Class Identification (%)

	Political Elite			Administrative Elite			Business Elite			Organizational Elite			Mass Media Elite			Scientific Elite			Cultural Elite			Power Elite Total		
	1991	2001	2011	1991	2001	2011	1991	2001	2011	1991	2001	2011	1991	2001	2011	1991	2001	2011	1991	2001	2011	1991	2001	2011
Manual workers	6	6	2	1	0	0	1	1	2	2	2	0	0	0	0	0	0	0	0	2	2	2	2	1
Lower middle class	3	3	9	2	1	2	0	0	2	0	3	3	4	0	0	2	0	0	0	7	5	1	2	3
Upper middle class	37	21	20	33	43	57	27	24	35	35	39	45	50	60	65	38	51	63	35	21	42	35	37	49
Upper class	6	5	2	21	14	9	20	6	9	5	3	4	8	2	2	15	14	2	14	7	5	13	8	5
Employers	2	2	4	10	4	8	17	13	9	5	7	7	2	6	2	3	11	2	0	7	5	6	6	6
Wage earners	18	18	20	18	16	4	7	3	0	28	20	17	15	10	11	23	12	6	10	12	5	18	14	9
Entrepreneurs	6	5	7	0	0	0	9	13	13	9	3	4	0	0	0	2	0	4	10	10	15	5	4	5
Low income earners	2	2	4	0	0	0	0	0	0	0	1	0	0	4	0	0	0	0	6	0	2	1	1	1
Middle income earners	10	24	20	5	8	8	3	6	4	8	4	9	13	12	4	5	0	8	10	12	7	7	9	9
High income earners	6	13	7	10	13	10	15	31	24	8	16	9	6	4	15	8	11	13	10	12	7	9	14	11
Don't know	5	2	7	1	1	2	1	3	2	0	1	1	2	2	0	3	2	2	6	10	5	2	3	2
Total	100	100	100	100	100	100	100	100	100	100	100	100	100	100	100	100	100	100	100	100	100	100	100	100
N	63	62	46	95	141	131	75	68	46	100	90	69	48	50	46	60	57	48	51	42	41	492	479	416

CAREER MOBILITY

Researching Career Mobility

Family background impacts on social mobility via school achievement (primary effects), but also in other ways via decisions made about education. In Finland, it is estimated that genetic heritage explains at most some 40 percent of the similarity between parents' and children's social status. Although genetic heritage affects the social status attained by children and contributes to explaining social inheritance effects, environmental factors and childhood growth environment also have a major impact on children's development, socioeconomic status in adulthood, and social inheritance (Härkönen 2010, 61–63).

Sociologists have long stressed the role of expectations, values, and behaviors inherited from the family milieu: these are all crucial for children's subsequent success in life. For instance, parents can encourage their children to value and appreciate education and occupational success. According to Melvin Kohn's (1963) classical argument, working-class parents place greater emphasis on discipline than middle-class parents, who are more inclined to emphasize independence and the development of personal skills and talents. Furthermore, it is often thought that people coming from higher class backgrounds have access to cultural capital that will make it easier for them to adapt to the cultural requirements of the school system and the workplace. Middle-class and higher educated parents are also better placed to create expectations of attaining higher social positions and to support their children's belief that these positions are indeed attainable. Taken together, these factors explain part of the mechanisms of social inheritance (Ibid., 63).

Social background impacts not only on how far children continue their education, and educational attainment in turn impacts on placement in working life, but it also has a direct impact on employment careers. Placement in working life does not always depend on educational qualifications, but both finding a job and advancing a career are often based on factors that have nothing to do with education. The higher the social position of an individual's parents, friends, and family, the more likely it is that this individual will know people who can help with recruitment and placement. Apart from social networks, economic and cultural living conditions will impact the individual's manners and demeanor, language, lifestyle, way of thinking, self-confidence, and various aspects of style. Individuals position themselves most readily into roles and environments that in some way resonate with their cultural background and mold their habitus, that is, the attitudes and structured dispositions that are typical of the individual (Naumanen and Silvennoinen 2010, 83).

The impact of education on the individual's status in society is always contingent on that individual's other traits and qualities—gender, skin color, ethnic group, social stratum, and habitus. A female MA graduate with a working-class background will not reach as high a position as her male counterpart with a middle-class background, unless she has the right kinds of contacts and the right kind of habitus (Ibid.).

Employers are interested not only in the educational qualifications of the people they recruit. Outcomes of socialization outside the school setting, at home and during leisure time, may be more important signals of the applicant's suitability to the job and potential to grow and develop. The value of education in the labor market is adversely affected by an excess supply of qualified labor and intense competition for jobs. The greater the number of formally qualified applicants, the greater the weight of personal attributes and sociocultural skills. People coming from a higher social background have not just the formal qualifications, but also other social and cultural resources, skills and abilities (demeanor, language, style, appearance, and lifestyle) that are considered important assets in the labor market (Naumanen and Silvennoinen 2010, 83–84).

The following looks more closely at the factors that have advanced the careers of people recruited into elite positions. We begin from the impact of the home background on career choices and career advancement. Next, we proceed to discuss the factors that have contributed to elite members' career advancement and life stages that have been important to their careers. Finally, we examine in closer detail people's training for the elites based on the elective positions they have held. The inheritance of active involvement in society is analyzed based on the elective positions held by elite members' parents.

Impact of Home on Career Choice and Career Advancement

Elite members were asked in the 1991–2011 surveys to assess the impact of their childhood and youth home (parents, siblings, family members, upbringing, etc.) on their *career choice*. The response options were very much, rather much, to some extent, rather little, very little, not at all, and don't know.

Home background has had a significant effect on the career choices of people recruited into elites. Nineteen percent of elite members in 1991 and 2001, but 16 percent in power elite said their home background had very much influenced their career choice. The proportion who said their home background had had rather much influence on their career choice increased from 23 percent in the early 1990s to 27 percent in 2011. When those who indicated that their choice had been impacted "to some extent" are taken into account, three-fifths in the early 1990s but two-thirds since the early 2000s thought their career choices had been influenced by their home background. The proportion reporting very little (12 percent, 11 percent, 9 percent) or a non-existent (13 percent, 9 percent, 10 percent) effect has accordingly declined.

In the early 2010s the effect of home background is most clearly evident in the cultural elite: half (52 percent) of the elite members in this group feel that their background has impacted their career choice very much or rather much. The proportion of respondents indicating that their choices had been impacted a lot showed the sharpest increase since the early 1990s in this elite group (+12 percentage points). The figure for the political elite (51 percent) is almost as high, and the increase in this elite group since the early 1990s is also the second highest. The effect of home background has been lowest of all in the business elite, where in 2011 only two-fifths (38 percent) said their home background had very much impacted their career choice. The share has declined most sharply (–12 percentage points) in the business elite, which might be explained by the declining proportion in this group of those coming from a middle-class background, while the proportion of those coming from a working-class and agricultural background has increased.

The effect of childhood and youth home on *career advancement to current position* was assessed using an open-ended question. The factor mentioned most often in 2011 was an appreciative attitude to education, which was mentioned by 26 percent of all elite members. As described by Nokia's former CEO Jorma Ollila (Ollila and Saukkomaa 2013, 25, 39), "I was aware that I was expected to do well, and I wanted to be worthy of that trust. It was my mother. It was she who encouraged me to study, to respect the value of knowledge and education . . . Later on in the business world when I found myself facing situations that seemed impossible, I used the idea I had learned at home. Everything is possible if you just study things through, learn the lessons, and do your job properly."

Other important legacies from the childhood home were application and dedication (23 percent), encouragement and support (16 percent), an appreciation of hard work and learning (16 percent), open-mindedness (15 percent), intellectual climate (15 percent), independence and self-confidence (12 percent), interaction with other people (10 percent), and upbringing and setting an example (10 percent). All these career-enhancing factors are mentioned increasingly often since the early 1990s. It is noteworthy that career inheritance and contacts are thought to have only a minor effect on career advancement: the proportion mentioning this factor fell from 12 percent in the 1990s to 6 percent in 2011.

Overall, recruitment into Finnish elites takes place on the strength of very different kinds of childhood legacies. One extreme might be represented by an orphan who has grown up in a foster home, or the son of a poor single parent who from a very young age has had to learn to hold his own and look after other family members; and the other extreme by an eighth-generation matriculation examination holder who is a descendant of two well-established families who have held leading positions for generations. While for some it has been the most natural of choices to enter an academic education, in keeping with the family tradition, for others, lacking money or landed property, it has been the only possible vehicle for social ascent. For some, the legacies of their childhood home have been decisive to their recruitment into an elite position, a key stage of life that has profoundly affected their social thinking and values, while others feel they got ahead in life despite their childhood home. In 2011, some one in ten elite members felt that their childhood and youth home had had no effect on their career. In line with the earlier examination of parental social stratum, the survey responses to this open-ended question support the observation regarding the relative openness of the Finnish elite structure: in this country it is possible to break into the ranks of the elite from very kinds of different socioeconomic backgrounds.

Different elite groups place somewhat different emphasis on the various career-advancing factors, but all attach the most importance to those that were mentioned earlier as the key common factors for the power elite as a whole. The political elite place more emphasis than other groups on the career-advancing legacy effects of inherited political views and political participation, and interaction with other people. However, the proportion emphasizing the importance of a political view and active participation has clearly declined since the early 1990s. On the other hand, a larger proportion of the political elite as compared with other elite groups felt that their upbringing at home had been only a minor influence. This suggests that a higher than average proportion of people recruited into the political elite come from a background where there is less cultural capital than in other elites.

The administrative elite differs hardly at all from other elite groups. However, members of the administrative elite attach more importance than others to the sense of basic security passed down: the proportion referring to this factor has clearly increased since the early 1990s. The administrative elite also place greater emphasis than average on the impact of the intellectual climate and set of values assimilated in childhood. The business elite, then, emphasize different career-advancing factors than other elite groups. Members of the business elite attach far more importance than other elite groups to the legacy of application and dedication, an appreciation of hard work and learning, and upbringing and the example set by parents. They place less emphasis than other elite groups on the role of encouragement and support, open-mindedness, career inheritance, and contacts. Also, the benefits of a positive attitude to education are clearly stressed less often than in other elite groups.

The organizational elite is set apart from other groups by its emphasis on the career-advancing legacy effects of a positive attitude to education. In fact, an increasing proportion of elite members in this group has emphasized this factor since the early 1990s. However, the group that has most and most consistently stressed the importance of an appreciative attitude to education since the early 1990s is the scientific elite: in this group belief in the career-advancing effects of a positive attitude to education has strengthened. This is only to be expected in the sense that recruitment into the scientific elite requires postgraduate qualifications. Members of this group also emphasize more often than average the importance of open-mindedness as well as the upbringing and example provided by parents as career-advancing factors. Somewhat surprisingly, members of the scientific elite (together with the cultural elite) mention less often than others the role of application and dedication, the appreciation of hard work and learning, independence and self-confidence. The scientific elite also mention less often than average the intellectual climate of the home and the role of career inheritance and contacts.

The cultural elite are most clearly set apart from other elite groups by how they think their childhood and youth home have impacted their career advancement. They attach importance more often than other elite groups to the role of encouragement and support, open-mindedness, career inheritance, contacts, and general education. With the exception of career inheritance and contacts, these factors have been emphasized much more since the early 1990s. Cultural elite members refer less often than others to the legacy effects of a positive attitude to education, the intellectual climate in the home, and a sense of duty and responsibility. In 2011, none of the cultural elite members mentioned a legacy of a political view and political participation as career-advancing factors.

Factors Contributing to Career Advancement

After the early years of childhood and youth socialization, decisions and personal attributes begin to evolve at school, in the workplace, and in networks of social interaction that will eventually influence people's life courses and careers. At every step along this road, people build up capital that can contribute to their career development. In all three years of this study, elite members were asked an identical question about the factors that had favorably impacted their career development. Presented with a list of 29 factors, the respondents were to select a maximum of five that they thought had most advanced their careers.

The factor mentioned most often by all elite members was personal talent and abilities: half (49 percent) of those in the power elite in 2011 said this had contributed to their career development. Other factors mentioned most frequently were the ability to get along with different kinds of people (47 percent), work experience (41 percent), and diligence (40 percent). All these factors have been considered increasingly important to career development since the early 1990s. Of these, the factor that has emerged as the most important of all, that is, the ability to get along with different kinds of people, requires adapting to new kinds of jobs and roles, which is a necessary condition in order to advance to the elite level (see Lindsay 2014, xvii).

Given that a positive attitude to education emerged as the most important career-advancing legacy factor in the open-ended item, it is somewhat surprising that education did not rank among the top factors in the structured responses concerning career advancing factors. In fact, the proportion saying that education has advanced their career has declined from 43 percent in the early 1990s to 36 percent in 2011. The proportion who mentioned the ability to handle pressure and conflicts, on the other hand, has increased from 26 percent to 31 percent in 2011. This is possibly explained by the increased levels of stress and turbulence in the present-day workplace. In other words, later on in the career, even a good education is no longer enough on its own, but in order to break into the elite it's necessary to have other attributes as well.

The third most frequently mentioned cluster of career development factors included passion to progress and ambition (mentioned by 28 percent in 2011), a wide range of expertise (27 percent), and presentation and public speaking skills (27 percent). All these factors have gained in importance since the early 1990s. The fourth cluster of career development factors included courage to take risks (18 percent), ability to take others into account (17 percent), independence (15 percent), cre-

activity (15 percent), negotiation skills (15 percent), extensive contact networks (15 percent), open-mindedness (15 percent), involvement in associations (13 percent), and language skills (12 percent). The only factors that have become more important since the early 1990s are the ability to take others into account, extensive contact networks, and open-mindedness. All other factors have declined in importance. There have been no changes in the perceived value of negotiation skills.

Given the current trends of globalization, it is surprising that no more than 7 percent of the Finnish power elite in 2011 mentioned international contacts as a career-advancing factor. The figure was the same in the early 1990s, but edged up to 11 percent in the early 2000s. In 1991, just 10 percent thought that their political party preference and a political view had advanced their career. In 2011, this figure was down to 8 percent. Even good relationships with superiors are not thought to have an impact on career advancement: the proportion mentioning this factor fell from 6 percent in 1991 to 5 percent in 2011. Good family and friendship relations have in practice had no role to play in career advancement.

As was mentioned earlier when discussing the impact of gender on career, the proportion of men who thought their gender had advanced their career development fell from 58 percent in 1991 to 27 percent in 2011. Among women, the proportion who thought their gender had advanced their career initially increased from 28 percent in 1991 to 38 percent in 2001, but in 2011 dropped back to the same level as in the early 1990s. However, in both genders an increasing proportion felt that their gender had had no bearing on their career development. Against this background it is surprising that in the structured questionnaire, where gender was listed as one of 29 possible career-advancing factors, no more than 1–2 percent of power elite members have mentioned it since the early 1990s. This suggests that although gender may be relevant in terms of career advancement, many other factors are much more important.

A closer examination of distinctive career-advancing factors in each elite group helps to create a profile for them and to see which factors set them apart from one another. However, as these meriting factors are liable to change along with the changes occurring in society more generally, it is unrealistic to offer any forecasts based on these elite group profiles. Having said that, the two-decade time span covered by the surveys is such a long period that the career development factors highlighted now can well be expected to remain relevant over the next decade.

In the political elite, the career-advancing factors that stand out more prominently than in other groups are involvement in associations, the ability to take others into account, party preference and a political view, and pleasant demeanor, which all fit in naturally with the politician's role. With the exception of involvement in associations, which has declined in importance, all these career development factors have gained increasing weight since the early 1990s. The declining role of involvement in associations can be explained not only by the mediatization of politics, but also by the erosion of political party organizations, which has meant that politicians increasingly have to connect with the electorate through the media (see Ruostetsaari 2005).

For this reason it is surprising that fewer political elite members as compared with other elite groups feel that presentation and public speaking skills have contributed to their career advancement. The figure increased from 28 percent in 1991 to 39 percent in 2001, but fell back to 23 percent in 2011. A smaller proportion of the political elite as compared with other elite groups believe that a wide range of expertise and creativity have advanced their careers. Only a marginal proportion of the political elite thought that international contacts had promoted their careers, and the figure has dropped from 4 percent to 2 percent.

The administrative elite hardly differ at all from the power elite as a whole in their views of career-advancing factors. Members of the administrative elite more often emphasize the role of personal talent and abilities, length of service, and education. Nonetheless it is thought that the traditional promotion criterion in public administration, that is, seniority, has only a marginal role: the proportion mentioning this factor has dropped from 10 percent to 7 percent in 2011. This is explained by the fact that over the past two decades, seniority has lost much of its importance both as a promotion criterion and as a salary factor. Even party preference is considered a more important factor than seniority: it was mentioned by 13 percent in 1991–2001, but by 6 percent in 2011. Members of the administrative elite attach less importance than other elite members to the courage to take risks: the proportion mentioning this factor has fallen from 18 percent in the early 1990s to 10 percent.

The business elite's views on career-advancing factors are quite different from those in other elite groups. Members of the business elite attach more importance than others to the ability to getting along with other people, diligence, passion to progress and ambition, independence, and training received on the job (together with the cultural elite). On the other hand, they refer less often than other elite members to personal talent and abilities and to involvement in associations. It is noteworthy that members of the business elite, who work in an environment of increasing globalization and competition, feel less often than others that the courage to take risks has advanced their career. The proportion mentioning this factor has dropped from 29 percent in the early 1990s to 17 percent in 2011. One possible explanation for this finding is that during the economic crises of the early 1990s and 2000s, the business elite have had to learn the hard way that excessive risk-taking can have dire consequences both for one's business and for one's career. Surprisingly, the business elite thought that international contacts have helped to advance their career less often than power elite members as a whole. The proportion who mentioned this factor increased from 6 percent in the early 1990s to 12 percent in 2001, but dropped to 4 percent in 2011.

Members of the organizational elite (together with the mass media elite) believe more often than other elite groups that the ability to handle pressure and conflicts, presentation and public speaking skills, and good relationships with superiors have helped to advance their careers. The organizational elite mention involvement in associations the second most often after the political elite, but the perceived benefits to career development have decreased since the early 2000s. Ever fewer organizational elite members mention negotiation skills and party preferences as career-advancing factors in the 2010s.

The media elite's views of career-advancing factors differ quite noticeably from those of the power elite as a whole. Firstly, a smaller proportion of the mass media elite feels that education has advanced their careers. The proportion mentioning education has declined significantly, from 40 percent in 1991 to 17 percent in 2011. The mass media elite place more weight than other groups on work experience, the ability to handle pressure and conflicts, creativity, extensive contact networks, good relationships with superiors, and a pleasant demeanor. There are several career-advancing factors that members of the mass media elite mentioned less often than other elite groups: independence, involvement in associations, negotiation skills, language skills, and international contacts.

It is not surprising that the scientific elite place more weight than other elite groups on the merits of education. In 2011, members of the scientific elite also mentioned more often than others the career-advancing role of negotiation skills, language skills, open-mindedness, and international contacts, all of which are obviously important to a scientific career. On the other hand, the scientific elite place less emphasis than other elite groups on the ability to get along with other people and on passion to progress and ambition. The cultural elite, then, attach the second least importance after the mass media elite on the role of education as a career-advancing factor. The cultural elite place more weight than other groups on a wide range of expertise, the courage to take risks, and creativity, and less often than others mention presentation and public speaking skills and extensive contact networks. Only the scientific elite attach more importance than the cultural elite to the role of language skills. Virtually no one in these two elite groups has felt that their party preference and political view has contributed to advance their careers at any of the three points of measurement.

Life Stages Critical to Recruitment into Elites

To complement the above picture of career-advancing factors in different elite groups, the following looks at the various life stages that are most critical to elite recruitment. In 1991, 2001, and 2011, elite members were presented with an open-ended question that invited them to describe life events or stages that, in hindsight, seem to have been particularly significant to key life decisions or choices, or that saw them establish contacts that helped them move forward in life.

The open-ended responses about key life stages present a somewhat different picture of career development factors than the structured item. In 2011, members of the power elite said the most important stage of their life was their international activity and personal contacts, both of which were mentioned by 27 percent of the respondents. In the structured item neither of these featured among the most important career development factors. Both international activity and personal contacts have gained increased importance since the early 1990s. However, the proportion of elite members underlining the importance of personal contacts did decline in the early

2000s, but in 2011 bounced back to an even higher level than in 1991. Responses to the structured item also stressed the importance of diverse contacts, whereas international contacts did not gain increasing weight after the early 1990s. International activity refers here both to studies abroad (including time spent as an exchange student) and to overseas job assignments and foreign duties in elective positions, which may also provide a forum for establishing personal relations.

Other life stages that were considered important to career advancement, in order of the number of mentions received, were as follows: appointments and nominations (mentioned by 24 percent in 2011); work experience (17 percent); university studies (17 percent); involvement in associations (17 percent); choices of study fields (16 percent); involvement in politics (14 percent); involvement in student associations (9 percent); family and growth environment (6 percent); crises/difficulties (4 percent), luck/chance events (2 percent); and conscription (national military service is compulsory for all adult males in Finland) (1 percent). Among these factors, work experience and education ranked 3rd and 5th in the structured responses concerning career-advancing factors. While the family and growth environment has gained slightly in importance since the early 1990s, luck or chance events, conscription, and crises/difficulties have become slightly less important. However, according to Jorma Ollila (2013, 43, 91, 103): "Events that seem like mere coincidences can change the course of our lives. When something as momentous as that happens, we don't notice it straightaway. It takes much longer. For me, being admitted to Atlantic College was one such event. . . Deep down, I'm a rationalist, but I still have to admit that without a long chain of random coincidences, I would never have become a business executive. . . Without the army [reserve officer training], I would have known much less about what's really happening in society and what people in Finland think."

For many elite members, their first job and later job changes appear in hindsight as crucial turning points in life. Often, these turning points have also involved building new contact networks. According to Lindsay (2014, 38), the events and decisions made in one's twenties and early thirties have a profound impact on the course of the rest of one's life. Crises and difficulties here refer to problems in family life, for instance, a family member's illness or problems at work. For large numbers of elite members, the 1990s' great recession marked a major turning point either in the shape of job losses or experiences of tough and difficult assignments. For many respondents—probably more often for women than for men—the birth of a child in the family has been an important turning point. Although maternity leave and child care leave have slowed some people's career progress, they will also have strengthened skills needed later on at work. Although conscription is mentioned less often as a key life stage since the early 1990s, some say the leadership training they received in the army improved their self-confidence and presentation skills and provided valuable leadership experience. For some elite members, national defense courses, a highly respected invitation-only series of lectures for influential figures from various sectors of society, have served as important networking forums (see Ekholm 2006). Although luck and chance events are mentioned less often as key life stages on career paths leading to elite positions, they may still have some influence ("one man's death is another man's bread," "in the right place at the right time").

The elite groups differ somewhat in their assessments of the life stages that have been most crucial to their career progress. In 2011, the political elite said the following had been key life stages to them: involvement in politics (mentioned by 52 percent), involvement in associations (27 percent), international activity (24 percent), personal relations (21 percent), and involvement in student associations (21 percent). For this elite group, in other words, the necessary merits required for recruitment into the political elite still come primarily from involvement in associations. The proportion considering this a key stage in life has increased since the early 1990s. In particular, the political elite consider international activity much more important in 2011 than they did two decades earlier. The most important stages of life or events for the administrative elite, then, are personal relations (31 percent), appointments and nominations (31 percent), and international activity (30 percent), all of which have gained in importance since the early 1990s. By contrast, work experience (19 percent), university studies (19 percent), and choices of study fields (14 percent) have become less important, while involvement in associations (14 percent) has become slightly more so.

In the business elite, the most important life stages in 2011 were appointments and nominations (23 percent), international activity (20 percent), involvement in associations (20 percent), work experience (17 percent), and choices of study fields (19 percent). In this elite group the stages of life that had gained increasing importance to career progress were involvement in associations and the family/growth environment, while study choices, personal relations, work experience, university studies, involvement in student associations, and luck and chance events had become less important. For the organizational elite, the most important life stages were personal relations (28 percent), involvement in associations (25 percent), appointments and nominations (19 percent), involvement in politics (17 percent), international activity (17 percent), and work experience (15 percent). Personal relations, international activity, involvement in politics, and crises/difficulties have gained increased importance since the early 1990s, while the importance of appointments and involvement in associations has declined.

For the mass media elite, far and away the most important life stages is appointments and nominations (46 percent), followed by personal relations (27 percent), study choices (15 percent), international activity (15 percent), work experience (15 percent), and involvement in student associations (15 percent). With the single exception of choices of study fields, all these life stages have gained in importance since the early 1990s. Involvement in politics also has less significance than before.

In 2011, the scientific elite rated their international activity (33 percent) as a more important life stage than university studies (30 percent), which was followed by personal relations (27 percent), work experience (21 percent), and study choices (18 percent). The proportion mentioning international activity did increase significantly in the early 2000s, but subsequently declined, although still remaining higher than in the early 1990s. Personal relations, university studies, and work experience, on the other hand, have gained increasing significance since the early 1990s, whereas appointments and involvement in student associations have become less important.

For the cultural elite, too, international activity (43 percent) has been by far the most important stage of life in terms of career advancement. Next in order of importance are personal relations (26 percent), university studies (23 percent), work experience (20 percent), study choices (17 percent), appointments and nominations (17 percent), and involvement in associations (17 percent). While international activity, study choices, university studies, and involvement in associations have gained in importance, personal relations, appointments and nominations, work experience, and involvement in student associations have become less important to elite recruitment. Until the early 2000s one-tenth of cultural elite members felt that conscription was a significant life stage, but in 2011 this share was down to zero. Another difference between the cultural elite and other elite groups is that only 3–4 percent in the cultural elite describe involvement in politics as an important event that has advanced their career progress.

Elective Offices and Their Inheritance

The following discusses the elective offices held by elite members and their parents in order to gain an insight into the inheritance of one specific form of cultural capital, that is, active involvement in society. This is an important subject not only from the point of view of recruitment into elites, but it is also relevant to the coherence of the power elite, because elective offices serve as a glue that holds different elite groups together.

In 2011, the most common elective offices held by power elite members were positions on a company board of directors or supervisory boards (30 percent), a governmental committee, working group, or task force (20 percent), a hobby association (18 percent), a political party (14 percent), an education or science association (13 percent), a cultural association (13 percent), Rotary, Lions, Zonta, etc., clubs (11 percent), and an international association (10 percent). The number of such offices held has decreased in virtually all types of organizations since the early 1990s. The only exceptions to this trend are Rotary clubs etc., veterans' or reservists' associations, the church, and regional councils. In 2011, the numbers holding an elective office in a hobby association were as high as in the early 1990s, having dipped slightly in the early 2000s.

Members of different elite groups obviously hold elective offices in somewhat different types of public organizations and associations (table 4.8). It is no surprise that members of the political elite mainly have elective roles associated with the political party, or that they hold seats on municipal boards or councils. Memberships of company boards of directors or governors, the most common type of elective offices, also figure prominently in an examination focused on individual elite groups. In the business elite and the organizational elite, these positions are the most common type

Table 4.8. Most Common Elective Offices Held by Elite Members in 2011 (%)

	Political Elite	Administrative Elite	Business Elite	Organizational Elite	Mass Media Elite	Scientific Elite	Cultural Elite	Power Elite Total
Parliament	17							
Committee, commission, working group	17	28		27	7	18	15	20
Municipal council or board	70				7			
Municipal committee	32							
Regional council	45							
Company board of directors or board of governors	28	16	70	48	13	29	24	30
Political party	79			10	7	14	9	14
Hobby association	19	17	32	27	11	14	9	18
Sports club	13		13	11	13	10		9
Rotaries, Lions, Zonta clubs, etc.	13	15	26			8		11
Church		13						
European Union		11						
Cultural association		11	15			16	41	13
Employer association			23	14				
Business associations			19	10				
Education or science association			15	21		35		13
Cooperative association			19					
Veterans' and reservists' associations			19					
International association			13	22		8		10
Employee association				19				
Social and health care association				10				
Other occupational association					9		13	

of elective office, in the mass media and cultural elites the second most common type of office, in the administrative elite the third most common, and in the political elite the fifth most common type of elective office.

It is noteworthy, however, that the number of elective offices has fallen most sharply for the most common positions, that is, memberships of company boards of directors or supervisory boards, and governmental committees, working groups, and task forces. In the early 1990s, 54 percent of power elite members held an elective office in a business company, but in 2011 that figure was down to 30 percent. In the political elite, the figure dropped from 53 percent to 28 percent and in the business elite from 94 percent to 70 percent. As almost half of the power elite hold an elective office in some business company, it is fair to say that the economy continues to have significant cohesive force within the power elite.

MPs began to dissociate themselves from businesses in the 1990s. In 1991, MPs still held on average 2.5 elective offices in business companies, either as a CEO, a member of the board of directors or supervisory boards, or a business partner. In 2001, that number was down by almost one-quarter to 1.9. This trend is explained by the increasing number of non-business-involved MPs elected to Parliament. In 1991, there were 36 MPs (the total number of MPs is 200) with no business positions; ten years later the figure was up to 62. If an MP had an elective office in one business, they held such positions in others, too. In 1991, MPs had on average three positions in business companies, and ten years later almost the same amount or 2.8. In other words, these business positions are increasingly concentrated in the hands of an ever smaller group of MPs. The same trend also applies to elective offices in public and party organizations (*Helsingin Sanomat*, Nov. 22, 2001).

The reasons why MPs are less involved with businesses than before have to do both with the MPs themselves (i.e., supply) and with the business sector (i.e., demand). Firstly, although MPs, unlike ministers, have no constitutional obligation to disclose their business affiliations, a voluntary procedure has been created for this purpose in Parliament. For reasons of political pressure and public (via the mass media) interest, MPs' business affiliations no longer remain a personal, private matter. On the other hand, as a result of the mergers in the banking sector and company bankruptcies during the 1990s recession, the number of elective positions decreased, and hence, ever fewer local banks and companies invited politicians to take up elective positions of responsibility in their organizations, making it clear to politicians that these roles are not just arenas for networking, but they may also involve personal financial risks and, by the same token, political risks. Another reason why there is less demand for politicians in such roles is that the transition from a regulated economy to a liberalized market economy has made politicians less valuable to businesses. Key decisions affecting the environment of doing business are now made in a free competitive economy and within the EU, and therefore companies no longer need to have politicians representing their interests vis-à-vis the national authorities.

But this cannot be a full explanation for the declining number of elective positions in business companies, because the trend is the same across all elite groups.

Another reason has to do with the fact that more and more major corporations, and state-owned companies in particular, have closed down their supervisory boards since the early 1990s in order to streamline company management. Furthermore, globalization and economic crises have increased the pressures of competition felt by businesses, and it is no longer thought appropriate for business directors to join the elected bodies of several other companies: the thinking now is that directors should devote most of their time to running their own business rather than some other business. According to Mikael Pentikäinen, former editor-in-chief of Finland's biggest daily, *Helsingin Sanomat* (2013, 156), "in the editor-in-chief role you become involved in many networks, even if you try to avoid getting involved in associations and organizations. I personally learned that an editor-in-chief should not be a member of any outside boards and associations, because that's bound to lead to conflicts and to erode the reader's confidence in the newspaper's independence."

This is not to say there are no significant cross-connections via company boards, for instance, between earnings-related pension institutions and listed companies. In sum, the decline in elite members' elective offices in business companies is explained by both the declining demand and the declining supply.

The proportion of elite members serving in elective positions on central government committees and other similar bodies has fallen from 33 percent in the early 1990s to 20 percent in 2011. This type of position has also served as an arena linking together different sectors of society and decision-makers representing different organizations. Given that formal committee-type bodies representing Finnish consensus and corporatist political culture have been used much more sparingly since the early 1980s (Wiberg 2009, 37), it is hardly surprising that this type of elective office has become rarer among elite members, too. Increasingly, committee-type preparatory bodies have been replaced by the use of single rapporteurs and consultants (see Kuusela and Ylönen 2013).

Having explored the level and extent of the power elite's involvement in society, we can now return to the question of cultural capital and ask to what extent this involvement is a pattern of behavior inherited from childhood and youth. More specifically, in the context of power elite recruitment, do the elite members come from a background where involvement in society was more common than average? Direct comparisons are not in fact possible because no data are available on the involvement of the general population of the same age as the parents of power elite members in public and NGO elective offices.

One way of studying how actively the parents of elite members were involved in society is to examine their memberships and active involvement in various associations. It is difficult to develop an unambiguous measure for the level of involvement (cf. SOU 1990, 44), but the elective positions held by parents serves as a useful proxy indicator.

The power elite come from homes that were quite actively involved in society (table 4.9). In practice, active participation in society is mostly inherited from the father's side, as mothers have held only few elective positions. The positions most commonly

Table 4.9.   Elective Offices Held by Elite Members' Parents (%)

	Father			Mother		
	1991	2001	2011	1991	2001	2011
Member of the government	1	0	0	0	0	0
Member of parliament	1	1	2	0	0	0
Political party: national organization	3	3	2	0	0	2
Political party: regional organization	7	7	8	1	3	2
Political party: local organizations	17	20	15	2	3	3
Municipality or joint municipal authority	22	23	17	3	3	3
Business company	15	13	16	1	0	1
Church	13	9	9	5	6	6
Employee association	7	9	6	2	2	4
Employer or other business association	10	7	7	0	1	0
Agricultural producer association	10	9	9	1	1	1
Sports club	16	15	16	1	1	1
Social and health care association	3	3	3	7	5	7
Rotaries, Lions, Zonta clubs, etc.	13	12	16	2	2	1
Veterans' or reservists' association	17	17	14	1	1	3
Cultural association	7	5	4	5	5	7
Women's association	0	0	0	20	21	20
Religious association	2	2	2	5	3	2
Pensioners' association	2	4	4	5	5	5
Other association	8	9	10	5	7	6
N	698	619	434	698	619	434

held by the fathers of the 2011 elite members were in a local government or joint municipal authority, a business company, a sports club, or Rotary, etc., club. However, the power elite's cultural capital has decreased since the early 1990s in that parents have been involved less often than before in elective offices in public bodies or NGOs. Fathers' positions have slightly increased only in business companies, in regional level political party organizations, in other associations, and especially in Rotary, etc., clubs. In fact the involvement of fathers in this last-mentioned local networking forum has increased the most (+3 percentage points) since the early 1990s. As was discussed earlier, the number of elite members working in such roles has increased accordingly.

Although elite members' mothers have held elective offices less often than fathers, mothers' involvement in these roles has increased somewhat in a larger number of public or other associations than fathers'. Mothers' involvement in society is more often channeled into women's associations, but also into social and health care associations, religious associations, and pensioner associations.

However, the involvement of elite members' parents is on the local level, through local government and political party organizations. In 1991, eight fathers of power elite members had been a cabinet minister, in 2011 three, and in

2011 not one. None of the power elite's mothers had been a cabinet minister in 1991–2011. The corresponding figures for members of Parliament were 10, 6, and 7 (fathers); and one in 2001 and two in 2011 (mothers). In 2011, 2 percent of elite members' fathers held an elective office in a national party organization (3 percent in 1991 and 2011), 17 percent in a local government or joint municipal authority (23 percent, 23 percent), and 16 percent in business and industry (15 percent, 13 percent). In sum, based on an examination of the elective offices held by parents of elite members, it appears that a very small proportion of power elite members come from a power elite background.

This does not, however, mean to say that no inheritance effect is to be seen in elected offices. According to the calculations of Jaakko Numminen, a former permanent secretary of the Ministry of Education and Culture, it is not at all uncommon that a membership of the Finnish Parliament is inherited, or rather handed down in the family. Before the 1999 parliamentary election there had been some 30 married couples and almost 80 siblings in the Finnish Parliament, and more than 60 MPs whose father, mother, grandfather, or grandmother had earlier been elected to Parliament. Among the members of the first unicameral Parliament (1907), one in five handed down a legacy of political involvement either to their children or other close family members. Although it has since then become much harder to "bequeath" votes, 10 candidates who were elected to Parliament in the 1995 elections came from families who had MP experience (*Suomen Kuvalehti,* Sept. 18, 1998). However, these figures cannot be compared with the political elite in this study, as the strict definition applied here excludes three-quarters of all MPs from the political elite.

Memberships of the cabinet have also been handed down in Finland across two, and even three generations. For instance, Kerttu Saalasti and Katri Kaarlonen, daughters of the multiple minister and Prime Minister, President of the Republic Kyösti Kallio, served as MPs for the Agrarian League: Saalasti even became a cabinet minister. Rafael Paasio served as prime minister, his son Pertti Paasio as a minister, and Pertti's daughter Heli was an MP. While the members of the Paasio family all represented the Social Democrats, ministerships may also be handed down in the family across party boundaries. During World War II, Jalo Aura, a Social Democrat, was a minister in four successive cabinets. His son Teuvo, a Liberal, was a multiple cabinet minister and prime minister of a non-partisan caretaker government in the early 1970s. His son Matti, representing the Conservatives, served as minister of transport and communications in the late 1990s.

The inter-generational inheritance of municipal elective positions is far more common than the inheritance of such positions at state level. In the early 2000s, 39 percent of the elective officials of six municipalities in southern Finland had a father, mother, or other close family member who had served in a municipal elective position before their own recruitment (Ruostetsaari and Holttinen 2004, 282). One-fifth or 22 percent of the fathers of the 1990s power elite had held a municipal elective position; in 2001 the figure was 23 percent and in 2011 17 percent.

5

Coherence of the Elite Structure

Chapter 4 above discussed the changes that have taken place in patterns and avenues of recruitment into the Finnish elites. In this, the fifth chapter, we turn our focus to the second dimension of the elite typology (table 2.1), that is, the coherence of the elite structure. To this end, we have to move forward in time on the career trajectory and examine the actions of elites in the positions they have attained. Our main interest centers around the coherence of the elite structure: is it accurate to say that the different elite groups form a tight-knit network, a cohesive power elite?

The chapter is divided into four sections. Section 1 deals with elite members' lifestyles as reflected in their leisure activities, memberships in informal social networks, means of communication and contact, and connections with the mass media. Section 2 investigates elites' national and international networks of interaction.

Section 3 discusses the degree of attitudinal unanimity between elite groups, on the one hand, and between elite groups and the citizenry, on the other. In addition, separate analysis is focused on the interests that elite members share in common and to their views on the principles of public decision-making. Finally, section 4 is concerned with horizontal mobility among elites, that is, elite circulation. It discusses the accumulation of elite positions to certain individuals, the ability of elite members to retain their positions of power, and the mobility of elite members from one elite group to another over time. The elements of elite coherence addressed in this chapter are interwoven with one another, so that mutual communication and interaction promotes greater attitudinal similarity through processes of social comparison, which in turn may promote role transitions and circulation between organizations (Knoke 1990, 11).

FORUMS FOR THE CONSTRUCTION OF SOCIAL CAPITAL

The Power Elite's Lifestyle

This section discusses the nature of the power elite and the way it has changed since the early 1990s by describing elite members' leisure activities and interests as part of their lifestyle. Have the leisure activities in which Finnish elites took part in their youth contributed to building up social capital assets that have later helped them achieve and excel in their leadership positions? And what about elite members' current leisure pursuits: do they enjoy exclusive leisure activities, do these activities reflect their social status, do they maintain that status?

Social capital—personal networks and memberships in various informal and formal clubs and associations—is closely related to other forms of capital, that is, economic and cultural capital. Bourdieu (1989) made it clear that, under certain conditions, social capital can even be exchanged for economic and cultural capital. In Finland, too, it has been found that active involvement in associations and in society is related to a high social status and serves as a resource for individuals. On the other hand, there is evidence that cultural leisure pursuits (e.g., choirs and drama clubs) have a positive impact on the individual's well-being and even health (Purhonen et al. 2014, 350).

The concept of lifestyle refers to regular, meaningful activities and choices that fill people's everyday life: their work, consumption, living, leisure, family life. Lifestyle is often reduced to a single dominant characteristic (family orientation, work, physical exercise, etc.), but it is more accurate to describe a lifestyle as a cluster of characteristics (Roos 1989, 9). Key elements of a lifestyle include everyday life, the way in which everyday life is woven into a single fabric, and the way in which this fabric is interwoven with the structure of society and its overall changes (Allardt 1983, 87). Lifestyle choices materialize within the wider set of choices made by each individual: their lifestyle evolves gradually over the course of their life, through internalized rules of choice-making (Roos 1989, 9).

Erik Allardt (1986) offers a useful analysis of the how lifestyle relates to the system of concepts describing people's functions of everyday life. He describes lifestyle as one vertex of a triangle whose other vertices are rational choice and fashion. Lifestyle is characterized by non-awareness and constancy; fashion by irrationality and variability; and rational choice by awareness and rationality. Lifestyle is about recurrence and repetition, about something that changes slowly. On the other hand, lifestyle is largely controlled by internalized, embodied choices that are beyond our control.

Bourdieu (1989) suggests that people's lifestyles, consumption, and tastes are hierarchically organized and that this hierarchy is structurally compatible, or "homologous" with the hierarchy of individuals' and groups' social status, and ultimately with the social class hierarchy. The definition of what is regarded as valuable, good, and "high culture" is open to contest and inextricably interwoven with the more general struggle for social status and prestige. Bourdieu's main thesis is that the status struggle is waged primarily within the domain of culture, using cultural distinctions.

Social status must be demonstrated by symbolic means, which by definition implies the involvement of culture. Bourdieu developed the concept of cultural capital as an analytic tool for understanding how cultural resources—and more generally differences in lifestyle and taste—are involved in the production and reproduction of inequality in society. The perspective of cultural capital brings social differentiation, struggle, power, and inequality into the focus of culture. Cultural capital is first and foremost an indicator and foundation of class positions—a resource that finds expression in various cultural orientations, or tastes and practices. In its most pared down form, Bourdieu's argument equates cultural capital with education, which together with economic capital (income, property assets) structure the "social space." As theories of mass society are based on the opposition of the elite and the masses, the concept of mass culture usually implies an automatic contrast and distinction between the high culture of elites and the popular culture of the masses (Purhonen et al. 2014, 11–18, 120; see also Peterson 1992, 255).

However, criticisms have been raised against the generalizability of Bourdieu's theorization. In Finland, the sociologist Klaus Mäkelä argued as early as the mid-1980s that this was such a small country and small language area with such a homogeneous culture that it is inconceivable that cultural distinctions and lifestyle differentiation could be a significant source of social inequality. For this reason there are no grounds to describe Finland as a socially organized cultural hierarchy in a Bourdieuan sense (Mäkelä 1985, 254–57; see Purhonen et al. 2014).

Mäkelä's critique was based on the history of Finnish society. Long a predominantly agrarian country, Finland got off to a relatively late start with modernization and industrialization, which only got underway after World War II. In the 1960s and 1970s, Finnish society was developed on the basis of the welfare state idea, with the aim of reducing income and other disparities between social classes and ultimately achieving equality among all citizens. From very early on, the educational system and universities gave all population groups the chance to pursue their social and educational ambitions, which contributed to enhance social mobility. In contrast to France, for instance, farmers in Finland retained their freedom and played an important role in state building. Finland has never had a feudal noble class within which cultural distinctions could have slowly evolved and developed, nor has the Finnish working class (in contrast to its British counterpart) ever become culturally separated from the farmers or middle class. Although the working class showed high political fighting spirit, it was keen to adopt middle class values, especially an appreciation of education. All of these factors together explain why Finland was to be considered a country of minor cultural differences (Mäkelä 1985, 254–57).

Purhonen et al. (2014, 22–25) have since argued that Mäkelä's critique does not stand on its own merits. There are two reasons for this. Firstly, his critique has never been backed up by empirical research. Secondly, Finnish society has changed decisively since the 1980s. Most importantly, we have seen the growth of income inequalities and social inequalities more generally, accelerating urbanization and rural depopulation, post-industrialization, and the rise of ICT technologies and the knowledge economy in the wake of the 1990s recession and globalization, particularly cultural globalization (the unprecedented proliferation of cultural products, influences, and trends). All this, Purhonen and colleagues maintain, undermines the argument of a local and remote, homogeneous culture in Finland.

Purhonen and colleagues fail to recognize, however, that despite ongoing and often rapid changes in society, political culture is very slow to change. It continues to reflect a country's history and traditions. "And there lies the essential importance of political culture: it is the means by which a country's history influences its current politics and through which a form of government perpetuates itself. To dismiss the significance of political culture would be to deny history itself." The building blocks of political culture are the beliefs, opinions, and emotions of individual citizens toward their form of government (Hague and Harrop 2001, 79, 81).

J. P. Roos (1989, 10–11), however, points out that in modern society, lifestyle has become increasingly conscious and variable in nature: we make reasoned choices and change our lifestyles, at least in part, based on our day-to-day preferences. This is exactly what leisure pursuits are about: conscious choices. In some instances leisure pursuits undertaken in youth are also about choices made by parents.

Roos (1989, 12) argues that lifestyle is ultimately a group phenomenon, something that is specific to a generation, class, family, youth group, etc. Groups express themselves to one another via their lifestyles. They use their lifestyles to compete with one another, to create their own territories to which others are denied access. Through their lifestyles, people define the area they consider to be their own. It has been suggested that in the current post-modern situation, a change is going on from organization to cultural meanings and processes that create imagined communities on the basis of lifestyles and value commitments (Kivinen 2002, 142).

Within each social stratum it is possible to find a great diversity of lifestyle combinations, if lifestyle is broken down into various educational, living arrangement, leisure activity, and habitus determinants. For example, all the basic groups mentioned above share in common a physically active lifestyle, but each of them will have their favorite sports and forms of exercise (Roos 1989, 25–27).

Based on his studies of French people's exercise pursuits in the 1970s, Bourdieu (1978) observes that there are social class differences in both the frequency of participation and in the capital requirements of different sports. The upper classes are far more active participants than the working class. They tend to favor individual sports, such as golf, horse riding, skiing, tennis, gymnastics, and hiking, all of which require both economic and cultural capital. Middle-class activities, then, are characterized by rationality, asceticism, and health consciousness. They require less capital: favorite sports include walking, jogging, and various team sports, such as basketball, handball, and soccer. Bourdieu notes that for the working class, walking is connected with the job and its requirements of physical strength. Typical working class sports, he says, include bodybuilding, weightlifting, wrestling, and boxing (Purhonen et al. 2014, 155).

In Finland, Roos maintains that leisure pursuits are closely associated with social strata. He observes that different types of sports or distinctions within a sport have characteristics that are homologous to the characteristics of the social field. In other words, based on where the individual is located within the field of different sports, we can more or less accurately deduce the individual's position within the social field, and vice versa. "In proletarian sports the body is often exposed to great physical exertions, blows, and violence: every ounce of energy is drained out of the body, which is used as a means to victory and results, even at the cost of total exhaustion and incredible risk-tasking. Upper-class sports, in contrast, require extreme self-control, elegance of performance, efficiency, economy." Indeed, the associations with social stratum are more clear and apparent in the physical manifestations of habitus. "It's easy for us to understand that there are clear differences between, say, wrestling and tennis, and we might be bemused about Finnish wrestlers who have an academic degree (which probably has to do with the strong local Ostrobothnian culture), but we can make equally clear distinctions within different sports" (Roos 1989, 25–27).

Different groups' lifestyles are also interconnected: they change according to the increasing or decreasing relative distance to other groups' lifestyles. They are influenced by one another, but this process of influence is not a one-way road, even though it usually flows from above to below: more often than not, it is an elite or new middle class discovery that filters down into the lifestyles of ever larger groups. Examples of such leisure activities that have trickled down are skiing, holidaying in the Mediterranean, winter holidays in the Alps, sailing, eating out in Italian or Chinese restaurants, wines, healthy diets, the avoidance of fats, etc. Examples of leisure pursuits spreading in the opposite direction, in a process of upward diffusion, include the arrival of the sauna in towns in the wake of the rural flight, the growing popularity of cross-country skiing and running, folk music, etc. (Ibid., 12).

The Finnish power elite's lifestyles and the changes in their lifestyles are here analyzed on the basis of their leisure activities. A study of leisure activities obviously taps into just one facet of the concept of lifestyle. Members of elite groups were asked in an open-ended question about the leisure pursuits in which they took part in their youth, and about the leisure pursuit that they continue to enjoy at the moment. Youth leisure pursuits are especially important, for it is in youth that the foundations are laid for networking and for the build-up of social capital that will remain with people for the rest of their lives (Salverda and Abbink 2013, 13).

The main category of sports includes all references to sport in general and to specific sports. The main category of outdoor recreation and exercise includes jogging, fishing, and keep-fit exercise. There is some inevitable overlap between these categories: it was not always clear from the responses whether the leisure pursuits concerned were more about sport or exercise. The main category of cultural pursuits includes various forms of culture and arts, collecting, and travel. Study and research includes learning languages, research of the natural environment, history, and folklore. The main category of home, family, and friends includes chores around the home and

spending time at home, spending time at the summer cottage, forestry and gardening, social interaction, the family and children.

In their youth, elite members were quite active in physical exercise. In 2011, three-
fifths of the power elite said they took part in sports and one-fourth in outdoor
recreation and physical exercise. In response to the question concerning life stages
important to career advancement, one respondent said that sports had taught him
about winning and losing. Three-fifths said they had been active in cultural pursuits.
Over one-quarter had been active in associations, and one in ten mentioned studying and research, politics and social issues in general as well as the home, family,
and friends. Overall there is nothing exceptional about the youth leisure pursuits of
Finnish elite members. In the United States, too, elite members have been actively
engaged in sports and student associations in their youth (Lindsay 2014, 27).

A comparison of Finnish elites from 1991 to 2011 shows that involvement in
youth leisure pursuits has increased somewhat. The only category where activity
has decreased since the early 2000s is study and research. While there has been no
change in involvement in cultural pursuits, the figures for sports, outdoor recreation and exercise, involvement in associations, politics and societal issues as well
as for relaxing at home and spending time with family and friends have all increased. The sharpest relative increase is observed for spending time at home and
with family and friends, and the second sharpest increase for involvement in associations. These changes can be considered to reflect both the privatization of
lifestyles and a movement toward greater sense of community. Involvement in associations and in political and societal arenas has increased since the early 1990s,
suggesting that elite members have been working from an ever younger age to
build up the skills they will need in their roles later in life (table 5.1).

Far and away the most common youth leisure pursuits among elite members in
the early 1990s were reading and literature as well as music. These leisure activities
have continued to gain in popularity in 2011. The third most common leisure activity was scouting: in 1991 one in ten power elite members were involved in scouting
and in 2011 one in seven. According to Jorma Ollila (2013, 188), CEO of Nokia
(1992–2006) and chairman of the Shell board of directors (2006–2015), many of
those who carved out a successful career at Nokia came from an entrepreneur or
otherwise middle-class family, and many of them were active in scouting or other
leisure activities when at school. In the United States, too, many elite members were
scouts in their youth (Lindsay 2014, 27–28).

The next most popular leisure activities were fishing, hunting, and the outdoors.
These were mentioned equally often in the 1990s and 2010s. Hardly any of those
recruited to elite positions played golf in their youth. In the 1991 power elite no one
played golf, in 2011 just 3 percent (5 percent of the mass media elite and 2 percent
of the business elite).

A comparison of the leisure activities pursued by different elite groups in their
youth suggests that life careers have indeed to some extent been influenced by the
youth home environment: people recruited to different elites have had slightly dif-

Table 5.1. Elite Members' Leisure Pursuits in Their Youth (%)

	Political Elite			Administrative Elite			Business Elite			Organizational Elite			Mass Media Elite			Scientific Elite			Cultural Elite			Power Elite Total		
	1991	2001	2011	1991	2001	2011	1991	2001	2011	1991	2001	2011	1991	2001	2011	1991	2001	2011	1991	2001	2011	1991	2001	2011
Sports	61	76	76	61	63	55	71	71	70	74	60	64	53	67	73	63	49	57	57	36	54	60	62	61
Outdoor activities and exercise	25	24	17	28	25	34	22	26	28	22	28	35	28	26	17	25	26	20	22	27	16	25	26	27
Culture	58	51	45	56	60	59	53	40	48	56	56	65	77	88	71	61	71	63	81	85	81	62	62	62
Studying and research	9	1	0	13	14	8	11	11	9	13	8	3	9	0	2	24	16	16	10	19	9	10	10	7
Associational activities	30	29	43	23	25	28	20	23	33	23	31	25	19	19	27	21	24	22	26	19	23	23	25	28
Politics and social issues	19	16	14	7	8	13	7	11	4	7	12	1	7	10	15	4	10	6	3	15	2	8	11	9
Home, family, friends	5	5	10	4	6	11	1	0	0	6	3	9	5	5	2	4	3	12	4	2	7	4	4	8
Other	3	3	0	5	6	2	4	5	0	3	3	3	1	2	0	1	1	2	4	2	9	3	3	1
N	77	80	42	119	162	130	98	84	46	134	108	69	75	58	41	72	70	49	68	59	43	643	582	409

ferent interests. The group that most clearly stands apart from others in this respect is the political elite. People recruited into the political elite have most often been involved in sports and associations, and second most often (after the mass media elite) in politics and societal issues. The political elite have shown less interest than other elite groups in cultural pursuits and study and research. While the share of political elite members engaging in sports has increased, the figure for those enjoying outdoor recreation and exercise has fallen accordingly. In other words, politics either attracts competitively minded young people, or competitiveness is a factor that promotes recruitment into the political elite. Of course, sport can also be an important source of social contacts that may be useful later on in life. The administrative elite has moved closer to the political elite in the sense that increasing numbers in this group have been involved in associations and politics.

People recruited into the business elite do not seem to have been particularly competitively minded in their youth: in 2011 both the political and mass media elite took part in sports more often than the business elite. In their youth, those recruited into the business elite were typically less interested than others in cultural pursuits and in spending time at home and with family and friends. The business elite has moved closer to the political and organizational elites in that increasing numbers since the early 1990s have built up social capital through their involvement in associations.

In the mass media elite, scientific elite, and cultural elite—the "intellectual" elite groups—the most popular youth leisure interest was culture, although the 2011 mass media elite was slightly more interested in sport. It is no surprise that even in their youth, those recruited into the scientific elite took a stronger interest than others in study and research. The 2011 scientific elite also had the largest share of those who in their youth enjoyed spending time at home and with family and friends. Like the political elite, the cultural elite differs quite noticeably from other groups in its youth leisure pursuits. The 2011 cultural elite took part in sports and outdoor recreation less often than any other group, and its involvement in associations and politics was second lowest. It comes as no surprise that members of this elite group have shown the greatest interest in cultural pursuits.

Over time, elite group differences in youth leisure pursuits have grown wider. In the early 1990s, the youth leisure pursuits of the mass media elite and cultural elite in particular differed from other elite groups' pursuits, whereas in the early 2000s the cultural elite and in the early 2010s the political elite had different leisure interests in their youth. The growth of these differences points at a trend of increasing diversification in the habitus of Finnish elites.

Youth leisure pursuits may also play a part in the creation of social contacts and relationships that will continue into adulthood. The respondents were presented with a structured question in which they were asked to what extent they had work-related contact with people they knew from their youth. Rather than leisure pursuits, the examples mentioned in this item were student mates and army buddies (Finland has universal male conscription). Among the power elite in 2011, only 6 percent reported a very large number of such contacts (6 percent in 1991, 10 percent in 2001), and 28 percent reported rather many contacts (27 percent, 31 percent). In other words, one-third of the 1991 power elite had very many or rather many contacts with persons they knew from their youth. This share increased to two-fifths in 2001, but dropped back to one-third in 2011. As this question specifically concerned work-related contacts with acquaintances from youth, these figures can be considered quite high. No more than 5–6 percent of elite members have had no contact at all with acquaintances from their youth. In the early 1990s and 2000s, the largest number of contacts was reported by the political elite, but in the early 2010s by the mass media elite. In 1991, the lowest number of contacts was reported by the cultural elite, in 2001 by the organizational elite, and in 2011 by the business elite.

The elite groups diverged increasingly from one another from 1991 to 2001 not only in terms of their youth leisure pursuits, but also their *current leisure pursuits*. In 2011, however, the differences were smaller than before. In 1991, the elite group that most differed from other elite groups in terms of its current leisure pursuits was the business elite, in 2001 the cultural elite, and in 2011 the political elite. A comparison of elite members' youth leisure pursuits with their current pursuits shows that sports activities have clearly decreased, and at the same time outdoor recreation and exercise has slightly increased.

The most common leisure activity for the 2011 power elite was culture: two-thirds engaged in various cultural pursuits. This is not surprising: results from a survey conducted among the general population in 2008 show that education is associated with an interest in literature. People with an academic education are more interested in literature and read a wider range of books. Likewise, involvement in traditional forms of high culture (classical music concerts, opera, theater, museums, art galleries) correlates closely with high social status. Having said that, the motive for taking part in cultural events is not always or primarily to enjoy artistic pleasures, but often it is a case of being on show and creating contacts (Purhonen et al. 2014, 75, 250, 346). The growing popularity of cultural pursuits and exercise compared with involvement in cultural pursuits in youth is largely explained by ageing, which imposes its own inevitable limitations. While sports and culture were the two most common youth leisure pursuits for elite members, culture has clearly overtaken sports among current leisure interests. However, around one-half of the power elite engage in both sports and exercise. In fact, the numbers who take part in sports have increased since the early 1990s. The popularity of sports is probably explained by efforts to maintain one's fitness for work, work-related networking, and more generally by the cultivation of social relations through informal forums of leisure pursuits (table 5.2).

The biggest change compared with youth leisure pursuits is that much larger numbers say they enjoy spending time at home and with family and friends. In 2011, one-quarter of elite members mentioned home, family, and friends among their leisure pursuits, a higher proportion than in the early 1990s. Spending time at the summer cottage, which also falls under this main category, is not a socially dissociative leisure pursuit in that it is very popular among both elites and the general population. In the total population, though, the popularity of this leisure pursuit increases with a higher level of education and social status (Purhonen et al. 2014, 277). Although social interaction is a subgroup of this category, enjoying time at home and with family and friends is of course precisely about spending time with a small circle of friends and acquaintances. Indeed, it is impossible in Finland to distinguish a less active and home-centered lifestyle from a more active, events-oriented lifestyle (Ibid., 346). By contrast, the proportion saying that they are involved in associations, a "real" social leisure pursuit, has slightly decreased. Involvement in politics and societal issues has not increased since the early 1990s. Indeed, in his analysis of how the Finnish field of associations changed in the 1990s, Martti Siisiäinen (2002, 90) found that the production of symbolic capital increasingly takes place in the context of leisure associations, while in earlier decades it was mainly built up and accumulated in political and professional associations.

Bourdieu (1989) has underscored the differences between different elite groups' tastes: the economic elite is more conservative and "classical" in its art tastes, while the cultural elite favors experimental, modern, even avant-garde art (Purhonen et al. 2014, 110). It is impossible here to describe in detail these group differences in art tastes, but we must content ourselves with a more general examination of how elites differ in their leisure pursuits. It is hardly unexpected that the political elite are more actively involved than other elite groups in associations and politics. Work and leisure, in this instance, clearly shade into each other. Even in the political elite, though, the most common leisure pursuits are culture as well as outdoor recreation and exercise. It is noteworthy that the administrative elite's participation in cultural pursuits has decreased since the early 1990s, and been replaced by exercise and involvement in associations and politics. The business elite, then, takes part in outdoor recreation and exercise more often than other elites, and it has the second lowest proportion of members who engage in cultural pursuits. However, the business elite's lifestyle has changed significantly over the career trajectory: in their youth, none of the business elite mentioned spending time at home and with family and friends, but in 2011 this elite group had the highest proportion of those who mentioned home, family, and friends. This can be explained by the search for a counterbalance to the intense competition and performance pressures at work, which is provided not only by sports and exercise, but also by enjoying the company of family and friends. The finding that the mass media elite engage in sports more often than other elite groups may be an indication of their searching for a counterbalance to work pressures stemming from dwindling circulation numbers and advertising revenue.

The scientific elite seek a counterbalance to work in a different direction altogether. This elite group participates in sports and exercise less than others, but it is more interested in cultural pursuits and study and research. Research may indeed be a leisure pursuit for the scientific elite as many of its members work in administrative roles as rectors and heads of research institutes, which means they have to do much of their research outside office hours. The culture elite (together with the scientific elite) spend the least time at home and with family and friends and participate the

Table 5.2. Elite Members' Current Leisure Pursuits (%)

	Political Elite			Administrative Elite			Business Elite			Organizational Elite			Mass Media Elite			Scientific Elite			Cultural Elite			Power Elite Total		
	1991	2001	2011	1991	2001	2011	1991	2001	2011	1991	2001	2011	1991	2001	2011	1991	2001	2011	1991	2001	2011	1991	2001	2011
Sports	28	38	45	33	38	50	41	51	50	39	29	49	41	46	63	26	37	43	33	28	46	35	39	49
Outdoor activities and exercise	47	55	52	54	54	54	63	65	59	46	64	55	44	44	49	40	46	43	45	29	43	49	53	52
Culture	66	56	57	71	70	64	50	55	59	62	61	70	83	83	66	64	69	76	80	79	71	67	66	66
Studying and research	5	5	7	10	14	11	4	7	7	13	10	4	12	5	7	21	16	14	13	19	9	11	11	9
Associational activities	14	18	14	7	11	10	10	5	11	14	15	10	7	2	7	7	9	10	12	3	0	10	10	9
Politics and social issues	26	30	31	7	8	14	10	9	7	13	7	3	7	5	12	8	6	2	7	14	7	11	11	11
Home, family, friends	34	23	24	24	33	30	16	24	35	22	23	22	17	31	22	23	17	31	16	19	16	22	25	27
Other	5	3	10	5	5	4	9	1	2	7	4	3	8	5	5	3	3	2	6	5	7	4	4	4
N	76	80	42	121	162	132	100	86	46	135	71	69	75	59	41	73	70	49	69	58	44	649	586	412

least in outdoor recreation and exercise. The proportion reporting cultural pursuits is second highest in this group. In the cultural elite, too, it is hard to draw a clear distinction between work and leisure pursuits.

Some sports have something of an elitist aura about them: examples include golf, sailing, and (in earlier years) tennis. A survey conducted among the general population in 2008 found that 8 percent enjoyed skiing, 4 percent played golf, 3 percent played tennis, and 2 percent did horse riding. The relatively low figures reported for these leisure pursuits can be explained, at least in part, by the fact that they require not only economic capital, but also some degree of special skills and special facilities. Among tertiary degree graduates, playing golf is more than 10 times as common as among those with a lower secondary education. In the latter category, just 1 percent played golf as compared with 9 percent among tertiary degree graduates (Purhonen et al. 2014, 158).

The elite members do not participate in these "elitist" sports very often, either. In 1991, just 5 percent of elite members played golf, and in 2011 the figure was only slightly higher at 8 percent. In the early 1990s, the keenest golfers were the business elite (10 percent), in 2011 the mass media elite (17 percent) followed by the business elite (15 percent). These are quite minor shifts when compared with the rise in popularity of golf in the general population. In 1994, the number of golfers in the population aged 19–65 was 35,000, which almost tripled by 2009–2010 (OSF 2011, 540). The number of sailing and boating enthusiasts in the power elite has fallen from 7 percent in 1991 to 6 percent in 2011. At the same time, the numbers playing tennis have dropped from 6 percent to 4 percent both in the power elite and in the whole population aged 19–65. The number of skiers in the power elite has remained unchanged at 2 percent since the early 1990s.

The number of elite members who take an interest in fishing as a leisure pursuit has dropped from 11 percent in 1991 to 7 percent in 2011, whereas in the general population the figure in 2002 was 43 percent. At the same time, the proportion of hunting enthusiasts in elite groups doubled from 5 percent to 10 percent. Hunting in the total population (8 percent in 2002) has been more or less as popular as in the power elite. However, it is noteworthy that hunting has continued to gain in popularity in elite groups, but in the total population its popularity has waned somewhat.

Hunting and, to a lesser extent, fishing have also had a role to play in elites' social networking. In 1991, both fishing (15 percent) and hunting (16 percent) were more common leisure pursuits in the business elite than in other elite groups. In 2011, the keenest anglers were the administrative elite (11 percent), while the business elite were the most active hunters (22 percent). Hunting has always been a traditional leisure pursuit among others for forest industry executives in Finland. For instance, hunting and fishing played a very prominent part in President of the Republic Urho Kekkonen's (1956–1981) conduct of foreign relations with the Soviet Union.

Pietiläinen et al. (2013, 225–26, 327) describe how, for a long time, the nobility in central Europe used hunts for purposes of showing off their wealth and power, for impressing both visitors and subjects. Even today, hunting remains a leisure amusement above all for wealthy and influential men, but rather than an embodiment of ostentation it is now seen as an opportunity for extending contacts and networking. Business executives will get together on invitational hunts in order to exchange information. In Finland, Björn Wahlroos, chairman of the boards of Sampo Bank, Nordea Bank, and the forest giant UPM, "worked long and hard at building up his network, and took a very pragmatic approach to the task. He wanted to know everyone of any importance, and he would invite people to his hunts and dinner parties based on their positions and titles. He rarely made friends in these circles." Iiro Viinanen, who was minister of finance (1991–1996) during the great recession, describes in his diaries how, despite his heavy workload, he always managed to find the time to go hunting, almost on a weekly basis. In fact, these hunts are the only aspect of his private life that Viinanen mentions in his diaries (Viinanen and Heiskanen 2014).

Social distinction, in its Bourdieuan (1989) sense, refers to a process where in their quest for upward mobility, the lower classes start imitating the lifestyles and leisure pursuits of the upper class, while the upper class moves on to adopt new ways of social distinction. However, it seems that Finnish elites have found no new leisure pursuits to replace those appropriated by the common folk. In 2011, no more than 2 percent of elite members said they liked opera, very much an elitist leisure interest, and 4 percent mentioned food or cooking. Only two elite members say they were interested in wines.

The level of elite interest in opera is quite low if considered against the 2008 results which show that 5 percent of the total population go to the opera at least a few times a year. Furthermore, going to the opera is four to five times more common in the highest than in the lowest educated groups. Likewise, the higher the level of education, the more common it is for people to drink wine with meals. The power elite probably underreport their interest in opera and wines, both of which have gained an "elitist" reputation, although even the general population is known to underreport its cultural leisure pursuits. Bourdieu (1989) maintains that there can be no surer way to deduce an individual's social class than on the basis of music taste. In Finland, too, listening to classical music is clearly segregated by social status, above all by level of education (Purhonen et al. 2014, 38, 66, 188, 254–57).

The French sociologist Bernard Lahire (2003) has critized Bourdieu's assumptions of a coherent and uniform habitus and a consistent class taste and lifestyle based on that habitus. Lahire insists that Bourdieu's research approach, which emphasizes the internal coherence of classes and groups and their relative mutual differences, is in many ways misleading. Bourdieu fails to sufficiently recognize that much of culture unites different groups. In the end there are many elite members who do not enjoy high culture or go to the opera, for instance (Purhonen et al. 2014, 314). Studies of Finland (Mäkelä 1985, 257; Purhonen et al. 2014, 122) and France (Lahire 2003) have shown that the spread of television has brought together and created greater unity within social groups and between their lifestyles.

The American cultural sociologist, Richard A. Peterson (1992, 2) has likewise maintained that music preferences among people in high social positions have changed. He discovered that high status groups were no longer exclusive in their tastes, but on the contrary inclusive, incorporating many different elements: "While those in the upper occupational groups are more apt to like symphonic music and to engage in elite arts activities, they are also more apt to like a number of kinds of music and engage in a wide range of non-elite activities." In fact, the taste of high status groups has shifted from high culture snobbery to cultural omnivorousness. The thesis of a tendency toward omnivorousness in the cultural taste of high status groups—effectively highly educated groups—has gained support from studies all around the world. In North America, for instance, attendances and visitor numbers at many traditional high culture institutions, such as museums, concerts, and dance shows, have been dwindling, and this tendency has been most noticeable among higher educated audiences (DiMaggio and Mukhtar 2004, 189). In Finland, too, it has been found that in the general population omnivorousness—measured in terms of enjoying various cultural objects and the number of leisure pursuits—is associated with high social status (measured by education, income, or occupational category), female gender, living in an urban environment, and middle age (Purhonen et al. 2014, 310–11, 321). In the United States, though, it has been reported that, contrary to expectations, the number of omnivorous people in highbrow groups with wide-ranging tastes is no longer necessarily increasing (DiMaggio and Mukhtar 2004, 189).

The thesis of cultural omnivorousness stands in a critical relationship both to Bourdieu's model of the homology of taste and social status and, particularly, to theories of mass society. At least implicitly, the latter have suggested that the highbrow taste of elites and the popular taste of the masses are mutually exclusive. The current basic distinction between culture consumption and taste would no longer run between the elite and the mass, but rather between the omnivore and the univore (Purhonen et al. 2014, 310–311, 321). Whereas omnivorousness is thought to be typical of the highly educated cultural elite, Bernard Lahire (2003) stresses in his study on France that there is interindividual variation in all social classes. Although it is possible to detect some social conformity in tastes, they are nonetheless highly individual and rarely predictable on the basis of, say, level or type of education (Purhonen et al. 2014, 289–90).

The main difference between the Finnish power elite's and the general population's leisure pursuits is that the elites prefer far less often those recreations that are popular among the masses. Examples include films, handicraft, travel, visual arts, photography, and mushroom and berry-picking. The one exception to this rule is exercise: statistics for 2002 show that 45 percent (summer) and 32 percent (winter) of the general population exercised at least once a week, but the corresponding proportion for the power elite in 2001 was 53 percent (see OSF 2011, 538–40). According to a survey conducted among the population in 2008, 79 percent of Finnish people reported taking part in sports or physical exercise (Purhonen et al. 2014, 156). The above supports the observation by Roos (1989, 31) that exercise is a common cultural characteristic among Finnish people. In fact, it seems that there has even been some convergence in the leisure pursuits of the elites and the citizenry. According to an international comparison by the European Commission, people in Finland as well as in other Nordic countries take active part in physical exercise. In France, exercise is very clearly a leisure pursuit of the cultural middle class. In Finland, too, there is evidence that high social status and high education are associated with active participation in exercise. People with less education, in working-class occupations, older people, and men are overrepresented in the group that does not engage in exercise at all (Purhonen et al. 2014, 153–56).

Based on the findings of Purhonen et al. (Ibid., 414–18), there is no disputing the role of highbrow taste in upholding the boundaries of the upper middle class and especially the elite, in building these groups' self-understanding and solidarity, or as an instrument of networking. As cultural taste varies systematically by social status, questions of taste—regardless of content—are necessarily and inevitably also questions of power and inequality, for taste automatically becomes a way of symbolically representing differences between capitals. In Finland, a highbrow cultural orientation may provide concrete benefits in other areas of life in that cultural capital can be exchanged for other capitals and resources. Purhonen et al. maintain that Finland has become culturally more hierarchical in recent years, at least if compared with the picture drawn by Mäkelä (1985) of 1980s Finland as a unified culture with few differences and inequalities. In the 2000s, Finnish tastes and lifestyles are in fact even more hierarchically organized that the British. However, even today, a certain degree of social uniformity and an egalitarian educational system mean that Finland remains a country of universal cultural classifications, even though cultural diversity is certainly increasing.

The findings of the present study are consistent with those of French political scientist Jean-Pascal Daloz in his studies of the behavior of Nordic elites. He says that in Nordic political culture, (political) elites are expected to display "conspicuous modesty" in their lifestyles. It is not acceptable to show off one's wealth and success, as citizens expect the elites to have dedicated their lives to serving their country. In many other cultures, such as in France and Africa, elites do show off, indeed they are expected to show off their power in their lifestyle choices. Elites enjoy valuables that not only make their life pleasant and comfortable, but also serve as symbolic representations of their status. Dominant groups often seek to define themselves—and to judge and value others—based on material symbols. Elegant clothes, large houses, luxury cars, and even fine food serve as indicators of social status, reflecting the superiority of elites vis-à-vis lower social groups (Daloz 2007, 181; 2010, 61; 2013).

Matti Alahuhta, CEO of Kone Corporation in 2005–2014, has been described as Finland's most respected business leader on grounds that he "represents almost everything that Finnish people value. He comes across as an ordinary, even modest guy." (Väisänen 2013, 49) The modesty of elites is not an unknown phenomenon in the United States, either. As Lindsay (2014, 99) observes, "many leaders I encountered made token gestures such as refusing bonuses or traveling by the subway instead of by limousine in order to communicate economy to their constituents. Depending on the individual leader, these self-denials may come out of a genuine respect for their employees, or they may simply be a manipulation of public perception. Especially in a climate of recession and layoffs, leaders recognize that conspicuous modesty reflects well in the eyes of the public."

Daloz's Finnish examples are President of the Republic, Mrs. Tarja Halonen (2000 –2012), who enjoyed shopping in a department store, and Prime Minister, Mr. Matti Vanhanen (2003–2010), who during his premiership was renovating himself his own house. In Finland the popularity of DIY renovation, agriculture and forestry, as well as gardening and spending time at the summer cottage has increased among elites since the early 1990s. Daloz (2007, 189) writes: "It is always fascinating for a political scientist specialized in elite studies to be at the parliament cafeteria—whether in Oslo, Stockholm, or Helsinki—watching top political figures queuing like others before getting their food. From a foreign perspective, this may look quite strange and, for instance, a Russian senior official once asked 'but where is the VIP room' when invited for lunch at the Storting [Norway's Parliament]." Daloz (2007) believes this Scandinavian and Finnish ideal of modesty is explained by several factors, including Lutheranism, with its moral code of austerity, the absence of feudalism, the major role of civic movements driven by underprivileged strata, and the ideal of general egalitarianism, which frowns upon making any kinds of distinctions between people.

In Finland, lifestyle modesty has most rigorously been followed by the political elite, who depend directly on the support of the electorate. However, the avoidance of ostentation is such an integral part of Finnish culture that the same fundamental thinking cuts across all elite groups. But the winds of change are picking up. The Finnish icons of the 1990s ICT boom were the brothers Rytsölä—the overnight millionaires who later lost their fortune—and their Lamborghini sports cars. In the 2000s, Björn Wahlroos, son of a member of the administrative elite and famous for rebuilding and restoring a manor of historic importance and throwing lavish parties (with guest lists including the King of Sweden), was hailed as a symbol of the booming economy, setting the standard for how to make a fortune on business acquisitions and sales and option programs. Are these examples just exceptions that prove the rule about the modesty of Finnish elites, or do they reflect a changing climate of opinion and real changes in elite lifestyles? Since the early 1990s, business elite earnings have skyrocketed far beyond the reach of other elites, never mind ordinary citizens, and this is now inevitably being reflected in their lifestyle. Capital gains and bonus systems have brought so much wealth to the business elite that there is more than enough for the next generations to inherit, which might lead to the emergence of a new upper class.

Informal Contacts

Interaction between elite groups may be created and maintained not only through leisure pursuits and job roles, but also in the context of discussion groups, which are a long-standing tradition in Finland. It's a well-known adage that "Finland is not a country, it's a club" (e.g., Sipponen 2000, 171); and that "in Finland, everyone who counts knows everyone else who counts."

However, it is impossible to gain a proper understanding of elites just by studying the connections they have through elective positions in public administration or business companies. Many scholars who have concentrated on these highly visible, formal networks, have failed to appreciate the importance of informal networks at elite level. C. Wright Mills, who was preoccupied in his work with formal networks, was by no means unaware of informal networks. On the contrary, he took the view that in order to understand elite cohesion, it is necessary also to explore various forums of face-to-face contacts (Salverda and Abbink 2013, 12).

Finnish decision-making culture has traditionally included various kinds of informal discussion groups working both within and between organizations. Among the best known of these was the O-group of economists, which was active from the mid-1950s to the early 1990s. The group consisted of individuals who were to hold key leadership roles in society, such as Mauno Koivisto (president of the republic 1982–1994) and Jaakko Lassila (CEO of the country's largest commercial bank 1983–1991) (see Suvanto and Vesikansa 2002). Other, more recent discussion groups include the Kairamo–Väyrynen group, which was formed in the mid-1970s around Nokia CEO Kari Kairamo and Centre Party MP and cabinet minister Paavo Väyrynen. This group wound down in 1990 (Kiander and Vartia 1998, 170). Even earlier, in the 1960s, a group of financial directors from companies under the umbrella of the Union Bank of Finland set up a formal and exclusive "billion club" in order to enhance mutual contact and exchange. In the 1970s, it was realized that effective interest representation required that members from the other major banking group as well as state-owned companies also be involved. Hulkko and Pöysä (1998, 129–131) point out that by virtue of its expertise and position, this club came to have a major influence on the legislation concerning accounting and joint stock companies.

During his tenure as minister of finance in 1991–1996, Iiro Viinanen had two support groups with whom he discussed economic policy issues and that served as a sounding board for his ideas. Both these groups took a critical view of devaluation and were in favor of a stable national currency. The first, "economist" group consisted of representatives of business corporations, business and industry associations, the Research Institute for Business Economics, and the Bank of Finland. The second, "big boy" support group was created in 1991 at an informal sauna evening at Nokia Research Centre. During Viinanen's tenure, this group met on more than 30 occasions, usually for discussions at business companies' entertainment and hospitality facilities. This group was put together by director of the "blue-and-white bank" Kansallis-Osake-Pankki Matti Korhonen, who served as political state secretary in the cabinet under Harri Holkeri (1987–1991). The composition of this CEO-level group varied depending on the situation, but it always attracted CEOs from Finland's biggest corporations. The group played a vital part in Viinanen's plans to rekindle relationships between the business community and the government, which had soured during Holkeri's premiership. Sauli Niinistö continued with this practice when he was appointed minister of finance (1996–2003, president of the republic 2012–). Nokia CEO Jorma Ollila joined the support group during Niinistö's tenure (Uimonen 2010, 111–14).

In the Finnish elite surveys, the respondents were presented with a statement which said that "informal personal relations have a major influence on the wielding of political power in society." In 1991, 40 percent of the elite members fully agreed with this statement, but in 2011 the figure dropped to 28 percent. However, when both "fully agree" and "agree to some extent" responses were included, the proportion who believed informal personal relations have a major influence on the wielding of power was 94 percent in 1991 and 87 percent in 2011. Not a single elite member fully disagreed with this statement at either time point, although the share of don't know responses increased from 4 percent to 10 percent.

As informal personal contacts are thought to play an important part in the wielding of power in society, to what extent and on what kinds of forums are these social contacts created and maintained? In the early 1990s, three-fifths of the power elite said they belonged to an informal contact group. This figure increased significantly to three-quarters in the early 2000s, but in the early 2010s dropped back to three-fifths again. Membership in informal contact groups has been most common in the political elite.

A separate open-ended question was included in the surveys to query about elite members' involvement in any such informal contact groups. It is not straightforward to classify these informal groups because they are a diverse and eclectic mix with inevitable overlap.

Political groups refer here to various kinds of political discussion groups (e.g., ideological discussion group, Wednesday club, discussion group composed of researchers and public officials with similar aims of societal and political reform) and political background groups (e.g., group of influential figures analyzing political issues, past and present influential political figures meeting once a month, background lobby group). Furthermore, political groups include various intra-party groups, such as a political discussion group of same-minded people, various professional groups, a group of like-minded people with the same bourgeois vision of society, a green discussion group, a party background group for the Ministry of Social Affairs and Health, and women MPs from the same parliamentary group). Examples of cross-party groups include a group of influential members of local council groups, which meets ahead of council sessions to hammer out agreements, a group of youth policy activists, a friendship group promoting collaboration among MPs, a contact network among people interested in human rights issues, and women's groups that cut across party boundaries.

Another major category consists of *spiritual discussion groups and single-issue groups*. The latter refer to informal groups focusing on one relatively closely defined issue (e.g., groups addressing environmental or equality issues, national defense questions, or children's schooling). In addition to these groups with a specific content focus, it is possible to identify the more general category of *discussion groups*, which includes groups formed around various subject areas (e.g., societal issues, culture, international questions) and involving people representing different fields of expertise.

A *cooperation group*, then, refers to groups devoted to cooperation and interaction generally (e.g., inter-organizational preparation teams, fishing and foreign travel group sponsored by private companies, old boy networks), and groups promoting cooperation with some field of education, regional collaboration (e.g., local think tank), and cooperation between different sectors of public policy (e.g., annual meeting with trade and industry representatives for information exchange, former cabinet ministers' contact group with business and industry, contact group between businessmen and state civil servants). *Professional groups* refer to collaboration among people working in the same branch (e.g., informal contact group for insurance professionals, ICT experts groups, companies involved in Russian trade, women engineers, a group discussing science policy issues, international contact group for theater professionals, gray eminence group for the culture sector).

Exercise groups refer to various leisure groups engaging in some form of exercise but also having discussions about societal issues (e.g., "sports club" of acquaintances from student days, cross-country skiing group who also meet in the summer, cross-country skiing group of same-minded influential figures, a group of business and industry leaders meeting for ball games, an elk hunting group, a sports club which engages in discussions to "heal the world").

The criterion that sets *clubs and societies* apart is not the content of their activity, but rather its form, the experience of exclusivity afforded by club membership. Some of the groups in this category are clearly informal, but others are formally organized (Round Table, Rotaries, Lions, Freemasons). The most common type of club is the "lunch club," which brings together decision-makers active either in the same or different branches (e.g., the lunch club of past and present professors). The category also includes groups that are described as clubs and that meet more or less regularly (e.g., administrative clubs, Tuesday clubs), as well as sauna clubs.

Earlier, in connection with the examination of recruitment into elites, reference was made to the importance of old school ties at later career stages. The category of *course reunions* includes classmate or alumni reunion groups, national defense course meetings, management training course reunions, etc. *Friendship circles* include various leisure groups, such as choirs and language courses, army buddies, family societies, and a group of people who grew up in the same region.

In 2011, the most common type of informal group among the Finnish power elite was the discussion group: one-third of elite members who said they had been involved in some type of informal group were members of a discussion group. The next most common types of group were professional groups (one-quarter), clubs and societies (one-fifth), and course reunions (less than one-fifth). Elite participation in exercise groups, clubs and societies, course reunions, discussion groups, and friendship circles has increased since the early 1990s. For instance, in 2011 one-sixth of elite members attended national defense course meetings. All elite groups except the scientific elite took part in these meetings. Organized by the Defence Forces, the national defense course is a highly respected invitation-only series of lectures attended by key influential figures from various sectors of society. Elite involvement in political groups, cooperation groups, single-issue groups, and spiritual groups, on the other hand, has shown a tendency to decline. Participation in professional groups increased noticeably after the early 1990s, but in 2011 was at a lower level than in 1991. In other words, membership in informal groups has since 1991 moved away from work-related interaction and become increasingly oriented to social interaction.

Not surprisingly, the political elite have been more actively involved than other elite groups in various political groups, but also in cooperation groups and single-issue groups. Until the early 2000s the administrative elite took more active part than other elite members in course reunions. Since then, administrative elite members have participated more actively than others in exercise groups. In 1991, the business elite were still the most active participant in exercise groups, but in 2011 business elite members were more actively involved than other elite groups in clubs and societies and in course reunions. In 1991, the organizational elite were involved more actively than others in cooperation groups and professional groups. However, the involvement of organizational elite members in discussion groups has all the time increased. Mass media elites have been involved in various informal groups more than average. In 1991 they participated more actively than other elites in exercise groups, in 2001 in clubs and societies, and in 2011 not only in discussion groups but also in friendship circles. The scientific elite, then, have been more actively involved than other elites in professional groups, while the cultural elite have had no distinctive features in their affiliation with informal groups.

Forms of Contact

Leisure pursuits and informal discussion groups are just some of the arenas in which elites can network with other elites as well as non-elites. Forms of elite interaction were inquired with identical structured questions in 1991, 2001, and 2011: "What forms of communication and contact do you consider most important in advancing the goals of your organization or field of work?" The question was intended to shed light on ways in which elites seek to exercise influence on society *both* through their job roles *and* through informal social interaction. Elite members were presented with a list of 12 ways of exercising influence and asked to identify which for them were the three most important. In 2011, two new forms of communication and contact were added to the list, that is, e-mail and social media (e.g., personal blog, Facebook).

In 1991, personal informal meetings were by far the most important form of communication and contact: 87 percent of the respondents included them in their top-three list. The key role of informal contacts has been stressed among other by politicians, journalists, and researchers. According to Hannele Pokka (1995, 19–20), minister of justice in the Aho Cabinet (1991–1995), "Finland's political table manners still mean that issues are very rarely addressed directly in the same places where the formal decisions are made. . . More often than not I learned about what was going on from a colleague in my parliamentary group, who in turn would have heard about it in an informal sauna meeting or through some insider's contact in the field." Indeed, it has been suggested that the higher up one moves in the hierarchy of society, the greater the importance of orally transmitted information and the shorter the memoranda and background papers (Kulha 2000, 76). Personal contacts are considered vital, for instance, in collective bargaining, in which vast amounts of diverse interests must be reconciled. It would be difficult to keep such negotiations on track without informal networks where the parties involved can freely exchange views and test one another's tolerance (Uimonen 1995, 153–54).

Despite the growth of electronic communications and social media, personal contacts still remain the most important form of influence in the 2010s (81 percent). In the early 1990s the next most important forms of influence after personal meetings were phone calls (58 percent), mass media (e.g., written content contributed, interviews given), contacts in associations and organizations (27 percent) and at seminars (25 percent), official letters from one's own organization (20 percent), governmental committees and working groups (17 percent), and personal letters (14 percent). Only very few elite members mentioned statement procedures of central government (4 percent), expert consultations in parliamentary committees (4 percent), and paid PR services or expertise from an advertising agency, for instance (1 percent). Despite the growing number of communications agencies and former aides of MPs and ministers recruited on their payroll, it seems that professional interest representation, for the time being at least, has little more than a marginal role in elite communications and contacts. On the contrary, it is the elites who are being subjected to influence by non-elite groups and individuals who are hiring communications agencies that are familiar with national and EU-level political decision-making processes and key individuals.

In 2011, the power elite consider almost all these forms of influence less important than two decades earlier. This is largely explained by the increasing use of e-mail as a channel of influence: e-mail is the second most important (54 percent) form of influence after personal contact. Social media, by contrast, are still to make their breakthrough as a means of influence: only 4 percent of elite members consider social media an important means of communications and contact. E-mail has increasingly replaced both formal and personal letters as a means of contact. Somewhat surprisingly, the weight of two very traditional forms of influence and networking has increased since 1991: in the early 2010s contacts created at seminars are considered much more important (41 percent) than earlier, and likewise a slightly larger proportion (21 percent) than earlier think that governmental committees and working groups are useful channels of influence, even though these preparatory bodies have a less prominent role in state administration than they used to. It is quite possible that this in itself is the explanation: that since these bodies have fewer assignments than before, it is thought that the lesser amount of work they are doing carries greater weight.

In 2011, the political elite (together with the business elite) considered seminars to be an important forum of contact less often than other elite groups. Similarly, official letters and e-mail appear to be less important to the political elite than to other groups, but personal letters are more important. The political elite attach more importance to social media as a channel of influence than other groups, although one only in ten ranks social media among the top three forms of contact. For the administrative elite, the most important channels of influence are the bureaucratic instruments of official letters and governmental committees.

The business elite have attached more importance than other elites to informal personal contacts ever since the early 1990s: it appears on the top three list of more than nine in ten business elite members. In 2011, the business elite also considered phone calls more important than other elite groups, but they attached less importance to seminars and especially to governmental statement procedures and the social media. The organizational elite attached less importance to phone calls than other elite groups, but more than average importance to the role of mass media. It is not surprising that the media elite consider the mass media a more important channel of influence than other elite groups. The media elite also attach more importance than other elites to e-mail, but place the least importance on the role of governmental committees.

The scientific elite consider seminars, the traditional forum of information exchange in academia, a more important form of contact than other elite groups. No one in the scientific elite considers the social media an important channel of influence. The cultural elite continue to believe in the effectiveness of meetings in the 2010s: they rated associations, governmental statement procedures, and parliamentary committee hearings as important channels of influence more often than other elite groups. The cultural elite accordingly attach less importance to personal contacts.

The key role of informal personal contacts in elite interaction is largely explained by the consensual nature of Finnish society. This consensus-mindedness is attributable not only to some important shared historical experiences (the "winter war spirit"), but also and importantly to the multiparty system under which political parties have been forced to seek collaboration across the left-right divide. Until the early 1990s, the constitutional qualified majority provisions still favored a collaborative orientation, as it was not possible to wield political power through a minority government.

Even today, the situation is completely different in Sweden, for instance, where the government cooperation across the left-right divide is in practice not an option, and therefore the country has had minority governments. According to Christoffer Taxell, former CEO of Partek Corporation and former chairman of the board of the Finnish employers' confederation, "we have good dialogue between the different sectors of society and we're capable of reaching decisions together. . . . My theory is that distances in Finland are shorter than anywhere else in the world. This has been a strength of our society that we must continue to draw on in the future. After all we've negotiated collective agreements together for tens of years" (*Helsingin Sanomat*, Jan. 13, 2002). Taxell says that in Sweden, decision-makers in business and politics are far more removed from one another than in Finland, and he is convinced that Finland and Nokia Corporation have benefited from people working in different positions being able to have informal discussions (*Talouselämä*, Oct. 18, 2013).

Ralf Sund (2002, 170), former Left Alliance party secretary (1995–2001) and trade union secretary, describes how at "a trade union meeting I once told my Nordic colleagues about our relationship with the employers. About how our union officials had been on a skiing trip to Lapland with employer counterparts, about how we might sometimes go out for a beer together without any formal reason, about how we can even be family friends at some level. Swedish colleagues experienced this more or less as class traitorship. In their labor market climate, this would have been unprecedented. In the end, however, it was never clear to me which of the two parties was the bigger traitor. In southern Europe a trade union leader would immediately be fired for the kind of shoulder rubbing that was commonplace in Finland."

Taking Advantage of the Mass Media

The mass media had a very important role among the methods of contact used by elites to further their interests. In 2011, the only forms of contact more important than the media were informal personal meetings, e-mail, and seminars.

The following discusses the role of the mass media in elite interaction strategies. Elites can use the media as a tool for exercising influence and try to put onto the political agenda issues that they believe are important, or to shoot down viewpoints and arguments put forward by the opposite camp. It is widely felt that the attention generated by the media can contribute to increasing one's potential power: anyone who is taken seriously by the major mass media will gain increased bargaining power in the networks of power (Kunelius et al. 2009, 459–60). The frequency and forums of elite appearances in the media were inquired with a structured item in all three years of the study. The response options were "once or twice a month," "a few times a year," and "less often or not at all."

The power elite's most common media strategy in the 2010s is giving an interview to a newspaper. Four in five elite members do this at least a few times a year. The next most common types of media appearance are giving an interview to some other media than a newspaper (seven in ten), writing an article, column, etc. (two in three), giving an interview or making an appearance on a talk show on national radio (three in five), making a local television or radio appearance (less than three in five), an appearance on national television (over half), and appearing as an anonymous expert or news source (over two-fifths). One-quarter said they have a blog on the Internet.

However, as far as exercising real influence is concerned, it is clear that making media appearances "at least a few times a year" is such a rare occurrence that it can hardly count as a core strategy in the attempts of elites to further their interests. It's obviously necessary to consider their more frequent media appearances. In the case of media appearances made "at least once or twice a month," giving an interview to a newspaper is still the most common way in which elites make public appearances. One-third of the power elite give newspaper interviews at least once or twice a month. The next most common forms of media appearance are writing an article, column, etc. (one-fifth), appearing as an anonymous expert or news source in the media (less than one-fifth), writing a blog on the Internet (one-sixth), giving an interview to some other media than a newspaper (one-seventh), and appearing on national radio (one-tenth), local television or radio (one-tenth), and national television (less than one-tenth). Compared to 1991, elite members today appear somewhat more frequently on national television and give slightly more interviews, whereas they less often appear as anonymous experts or information sources, write articles or columns, or appear on local television or local radio. All these shares are so low that it is certainly unwarranted to talk about the mediatization of the power elite's channels of influence.

The political elite's media strategy, however, differs clearly from that of other elite groups, suggesting a stronger tendency of mediatization within this particular group. The political elite use virtually all forms of media exposure more actively than other elite groups. They are particularly active bloggers: while just one-sixth of the whole power elite say they write their own blog at least once or twice a month, the proportion in the political elite is one-half. Up to one-fifth of the political elite write in their blog once a week or more often. At their best, blogs provide a way for the political elite to put issues onto the political agenda, or at least to bring them into public debate and to make clear their own views without journalistic filtering (e.g., Herkman 2011). Despite their blogging enthusiasm, the political elite still tried in 2011 to maintain contact with their electorate first and foremost by traditional means, even more so than in 1991, that is, by giving interviews to newspapers and by making appearances on local television or local radio. The mass media elite, not surprisingly, write articles and columns more often than other elites. The administrative and organizational elites give interviews to other media than newspapers more frequently than any other groups.

NETWORKS OF POWER

Research Approach

The following analyzes the structure of elite groups' interaction network and looks at how its density has changed since the early 1990s. Elite interlinkages with various institutions can be examined via the social networks they form. To this end it is useful to apply a research approach known as network analysis.

In the social sciences the concept of network has long been used in a general, metaphorical sense as a model or image of reality. In the 1990s, the concept of network and networking became something of a universal panacea that was applied even to old existing structures, and new networks were found within and between just about every organization. One particularly noteworthy promotor of the Finnish network-ing boom was Manuel Castells's work *The Rise of the Network Society* (1996), which shot to worldwide fame. The Finnish debate and discussion on networking has in part been normative in the sense that networks have been characterized axiomatically as democratic structures, and networking has been considered to lead inevitably to the decentralization of power. In reality, the nature of any network depends on its structure, which can be located anywhere along the centralized-decentralized axis, meaning that the network can be more or less democratic (Ruostetsaari and Holt-tinen 2001, 100; see van Waarden 1992; Kenis and Schneider 1991).

In fact, governance through networks can create a completely new topography of power: the actor's position on the center-periphery dimension will be replaced by the actor's position within the network, or exclusion from the networks. In municipali-ties, for instance, the composition of governance networks based on the interaction and collaboration between public authorities and actors of civil society is not neces-sarily democratic by any means, but within networks may arise new kinds of elites (Peltonen 2002, 172).

Networks have a significant role to play even in public decision-making, because individuals' preferences, views, and decisions are shaped and influenced at least in part by their interaction with other individuals. In other words, networks shape both individuals' stable characteristics, such as values and identities, and more variable characteristics, such as opinions and preferences (Passy 2009, 23).

In the context of the public debate, then, the concept of network has largely lost its original link with sociometric network analysis, which developed specific concepts, variables, and analytical tools for studying networks. There has also been growing interest in quantitative network analysis (see Mattila 2000), in part at least as a result of the development of software. The growing popularity of network analysis can be explained by the flexibility of the network concept, which has enabled researchers to deal with such changes in society that are difficult to include within the boundaries of formal bureaucracies or nation states or at the other pole, individual actors. Refer-ence to networks thus provides clues for defining specific actors' social positions and for identifying general structural models from a relational perspective (Diani 2009, 4).

However, social network analysis can be qualified neither as a scientific theory nor as a research method. Rather, it is best described as a broad approach to studying social relationships. Network analysis is concerned not so much with organizations as with interorganizational interaction. The basic idea is that actors are interconnected and these connections create a network of social relationships whose characteristics cannot be reduced to the characteristics of the single actors making up the network, even though it is their actions that create the network. In order to understand the nature of a social network, we need to look not only at the direct contacts between individual actors, but also consider the characteristics and structure of the whole network (Scott and Griff 1984, 9; Knoke 1990, 235–36; Marsh 1998).

Studies based on network analysis have two basic premises in common. Firstly, they are usually focused on organizations (or institutions) and the positions or roles within them, not on the individuals engaged in these roles (see, e.g., Laumann and Knoke 1989, 22–23). Roles can be seen as rights, duties, obligations, and expectations that guide the characteristic conduct of the persons in such positions. Furthermore, a role indicates how its holder is expected to interact with other social actors in certain situations. For instance, political party or business leaders are subjected to different expectations in their environments that will also influence their actions. Role holders come and go, but the configurations of interaction among positions and roles remain fairly stable. The basic idea of a social structure is a stable, recurring order or pattern of social relationships among positions occupied by actors (Knoke 1990, 7).

Secondly, the actor's structural position in the network is to a lesser or greater degree associated with the actor's influence. Galaskiewicz (1989, 82–83) argues that the influence of an organization is a function not simply of its own resources or control over significant events, but also of its potential to access the resources of other organizations. Knoke's (1983) explanation for the connection between the actor's structural position and its perceived influence is slightly different. For him, power—whether actual or potential—is directly associated with the actor's autonomy.

All interaction involves power (Giddens 1979) because it is about the production and reproduction of structure, which creates rules and resources (Clegg 1989, 141). Indeed, the resource dependency theory posits that power is grounded in interorganizational relationships: organizations attempt to avoid becoming dependent on others and at the same time seek to make others dependent on themselves. In order to avoid dependence and limitations, organizations seek to manipulate the information flow about themselves and their actions. The more an organization interacts with several organizations, the less dependent it is on one organization. The existence of alternative sources of strategic resources will strengthen the actor's power position. Conversely, the more power an actor possesses, the more dependent other actors are on the scarce resources controlled by that actor (see, e.g., Aldrich 1979, 119; Pfeffer and Salancik 1978, 261).

In the network approach, a resource can be defined as anything that 1) is controlled by an actor, 2) is desired by another actor, and 3) can be transferred or exchanged in some meaningful sense. Resources, therefore, can be very diverse and include such things as legal authority, mass power, economic resources, information, expertise, and control of the public realm (Compston 2009, 19–26). Policy networks that cut across the public, private, and third sector boundaries are created out of the mutual resource dependence among actors. For example, the political elite can influence the business elite by enacting laws on corporate taxation, but the political elite is in turn dependent on the companies controlled by the business elite as a source of employment and government tax revenue. The political elite, then, is dependent on the expertise of the administrative elite in the drafting and implementation of legislation, while the administrative elite depends on the political support and authority of the political elite. Changes in the distribution of resources among actors may also lead to changes in governmental decision-making (Ibid., 36–39; van Waarden 1992, 31).

It is thought that social networks are held together by a mutual sense of trust among their members and by related normative rules and reciprocal expectations. The social network and its relations of trust provide its members with a source of capital or, in Bourdieu's terms, a resource that members can alone or together draw upon when necessary. However, social capital is not like economic capital in that it cannot be detached from its holders or their relationships (Ilmonen 2002, 20–21).

Being part of a network can be seen as an integral element of modern leadership. In fact, an elite network is necessary for leaders to get anything done, and aspiring leaders have to recognize this fact. A strong network serves to tighten the bonds of a leader's own ranks and selectively escorts others into the upper echelon. To gain access, rising leaders seek out opportunities to interact with respected leaders (Lindsay 2014, 3).

Predictable problems can often be solved by formal networks, but when unexpected problems arise it may be necessary to make use of informal networks. Successful leaders spend much time networking with people whose services they may need in the future to resolve problems. However, networks must exist before they are needed. A leader may have profound expertise on some subject matter, but without trust this leader may be excluded from informal networks and therefore find it difficult to do his or her job (Pentikäinen 2014, 190–92). Another person may be trusted simply on the basis that he or she is a member of the network, even if this person is not known personally (Ilmonen 2002, 25). At elite level, networks may thus create cultural bonds of trust that reinforce the mutual solidarity and shared interests among elites (Salverda and Abbink 2013, 11).

Relationships of interaction have both form and content. The former refers to the properties of the relationship regardless of its substantive meaning. The form and content of the relationships between social positions have important implications for the formation of political attitudes and behavior (cf. Knoke 1990, 235–36).

Various indicators have been developed to assess the significance of different network positions. Firstly, the indicator of *centrality* does not differentiate sending from receiving relations, but simply treats all connections as symmetric. The most central actors in a network are those involving many reciprocated ties to other actors. Actors in the center of the network are influential because other actors are dependent on them in transmitting information or material resources. This kind of centrality is a useful indicator for analyzing positional power in a symmetric exchange network, such as communication networks (Knoke 1990, 10).

In reality, all organizations do not have equal value as channels of interaction. A part of an actor's contacts focuses on other actors occupying a central position in the network, while other contacts are with actors in a more peripheral position. Interaction with central actors—who have contacts with several organizations—contributes more to strengthening the actor's centrality than contacts with isolated organizations.

Contacts with central organizations provide access to significant communications fora, which adds to the actor's influence in the network (Bonacich 1972, 17).

When an actor's network position is assessed based on the concept of *prestige*, interaction is interpreted as asymmetric so that an actor is considered influential if that actor receives many contacts but sends few. In other words, the sheer volume of contacts is not what counts, but their quality: an actor's prominence is determined in part by the prominence of that actor's contacts. Indeed, the centrality of an actor in a communication network has been regarded as synonymous with its influence. This kind of centrality is particularly useful in analyzing the influence related to roles or positions in networks where commands or material resources are not reciprocally exchanged (Knoke 1990, 10–13). As the current study is focused on elites who by definition are influential, it is reasonable to assume that the interaction between elites and societal organizations is asymmetric.

We begin our examination of the structure of elite interaction network from the targets of interaction, and then proceed to the content and direction of interaction. However, the challenge with applying the network approach in this connection is that it is not possible to directly analyze the mutual contacts among elite members. There are two reasons for this. Firstly, for reasons of space alone it was impossible to list in the questionnaire the names of more than one thousand elite members and to ask the respondents about their contacts with each of them. The second, even more important reason was that listing these names would have breached the respondents' anonymity they were guaranteed. It follows that the contacts between elite members cannot be directly analyzed, but it is possible to explore their contacts with organizations included in the elite structure.

The direction of Finnish elites' contacts was inquired in the 1991–2011 surveys by listing institutions and organizations with which elite members might have had contact through their work, elective offices, leisure pursuits, etc. In each case the respondents were asked to assess the frequency of contact and its nature. The question was designed to capture both formal and informal contacts, which together structure the societal power structure. In practice there is no justification for distinguishing the work-related contacts of people in leading positions from their other contacts, as they can just as well attend to work in their own office or outside the office, while performing the duties of an elective office or in connection with leisure pursuits.

C. Wright Mills placed greater emphasis on the constitutive role of informal rather than formal factors as a basis of the power elite's self-consciousness. Economic and political interests take shape through informal interaction in small groups and through networks of social relations. Through their similar upbringing and constant informal interaction, members of the power elite are capable of creating cohesion and social exclusion and thus of maintaining consensus amongst themselves (Scott 1991, 123). At elite level, dense networks of contacts created in company boards, foundations, clubs, and various policy planning organizations are considered crucial to preventing dissension and disintegration within the power elite (Higley and Moore 1981, 584). Personal level contacts are resources of information and influence that can be mobilized directly or indirectly to promote career advancement. Social capital—in the form of information and helpful contacts—can serve as a mediating factor among educational achievement and professional status and income level. It has even been argued that the higher the individual's level of network contacts, the greater that individual's prospects of career advancement (Knoke 1990, 102–3).

Based on his personal experience as Left Alliance party secretary and trade union secretary, Ralf Sund (2002, 170) has stressed the pivotal role of personal contacts in networking: "Good personal relations between different sectors of society are one manifestation of consensus. As we furthermore have a large number of organizations involved in facilitating personal contacts, it is clear you will have a dense network. Finland is such a small country that you can find a school, army, university or childhood friends around every corner. Everyone speaks the same language, which makes information exchange easy." Nina Kopola, however, Finland's only female CEO of a listed company, Suominen Corporation, decouples the link between the small size of the country and networking: "Finland is such a small country that they'll find you if you're really good. There's no need for any networks." (*Talouselämä*, Apr. 4, 2014)

The key research question of this section is this: How do Finnish elites network with different organizations and institutions in society, and have their contact networks moved toward greater concentration or fragmentation since the early 1990s?

Density of Elite Network

In each of the three years of study, Finnish elites were presented with an identical structured question: "The following lists some instances and institutions with which you might have had contact in connection with your job, elected positions, leisure pursuits, etc. For each of these instances, please indicate the 'frequency of your contacts' and then the 'nature of your contacts.'" The response options for frequency were "at least once or twice a month," "a couple of times a year," and "less often or not at all." The three categories were enough to distinguish between regular and random contact.

The following discusses the position of different institutions and organizations and changes in those positions in elites' interaction networks using an index based on the responses to the question about the frequency of contacts. The higher the index value, the closer the elite members' contacts with institutions or organizations. This is a sum variable that takes into account both the number of contacts and their intensity. In order to calculate the intensity of interaction, coefficients are assigned to the frequency of contacts. The coefficient assigned to the response option "at least once or twice a month" is 100; for a "couple of times a year," 50; and for "less often or not at all," 0. The weight of recurring, at least monthly contacts in the intensity of interaction is thus twice as high as the weight of contacts that happen a couple of times a year. The last response option indicates such a low frequency of interaction that it carries no weight at all in the intensity index. The *intensity* of interaction between the elite members and organization/institution A is obtained by multiplying by 100 the percentage of those who have had contact with A at least once or twice a month and by adding to this figure the percentage, multiplied by 50, of those who have had contact with A a couple of times a month and by dividing this sum by the total number of contacts, that is, the percentages of both those with one or two monthly contacts and those with a couple of contacts a year. The maximum intensity value is 100, which is obtained if all members of the power elite have had interaction with A at least once or twice a month. The index describing the *density* of interaction is obtained by multiplying the total number of contacts by intensity divided by 100. Therefore the maximum value for the density index is also 100; the higher the score, the more frequent the interaction of the elite members with institution A (cf. Petersson 1989, 36–37). For example, the intensity of interaction between the elite members and the mass media in 1991 is obtained from the equation (63 x 100 + 24 x 50): 87 = 86. This yields a density value of (87 x 86): 100 = 75.

In the early 1990s, the most central institution in the power elite's contact network was the mass media (including journalists), whose position is characterized by a density index of 75. The mass media retained this position in 2001 and 2011. However, when the centrality of organizations in the power elites' contact network is described using the circles-of-power model, the mass media were relegated to the second circle by 2001 (index value 68 in 2001 and 67 in 2011). In the early 1990s, there were three institutions on the third circle of the interaction network (index value 50–59): the government, private companies, and banks. The government was relegated to the fourth circle (index values 40–49) by 2001, but was then revived to the third circle in 2011 (53). Private companies retained their position in 2001, but were relegated to the fourth circle one decade later. Banks in particular became less important targets of elite members' interaction: in 1991 they still belonged to the third circle, in 2001 they were relegated to the fourth circle, and in 2011 to the fifth circle (index value 30–29). In the early 1990s there were two institutions on the fourth circle, that is, universities/polytecnics and central government agencies. Universities/polytechnics were then revived to the fifth circle, whereas central government agencies were relegated to the third circle.

In all, four-fifths of Finnish institutions saw their role decline in the power elite's interaction network after 1991 (table 5.3). The few exceptions whose density increased in these networks were the Ministry of Justice (+3), the judiciary (+3), state regional administration (+3 since 2001), employer associations (+3), municipalities or joint municipal authorities (+2), the Ministry of Social Affairs and Health (+2), regional councils (+2), the Ministry of Agriculture and Forestry (+2), and the president of the republic (+2), and universities /polytechnics (+2). Institutions whose density in the elite network of interaction increased slightly less (+1) than those listed above were political parties' parliamentary groups, parliamentary committees, the Ministry of Employment and the Economy/the Ministry of Trade and Industry, the Prime Minister's Office, the Ministry of Transport and Communications, and other associations or organizations. The sharpest decline was recorded for power elite contacts with banks (–21), state-owned companies and public utilities (–10), the

Table 5.3. Density of Interaction between Elite Members and Various Institutions (Index Value)

Institution	1991	2001	2011
Mass media	75	68	67
The government	52	48	53
University/polytechnic	48	52	50
Private business	50	51	41
Municipality or joint municipal authority	34	38	36
Other research institute	36	37	34
Central government agency	42	39	33
Business association	36	33	33
Political party: national organization	33	30	32
Employer association	34	37	31
Ministry of Education and Culture	34	32	31
Other association	30	36	31
Bank	51	49	30
Ministry of Finance	34	28	30
Parliamentary group	29	29	30
Employee association	36	33	29
Ministry of Employment and the Economy	28	26	29
State regional administration	*	26	29
Cultural association	34	30	27
Parliamentary committee	26	25	27
State-owned company or public utility	35	30	25
Prime Minister's Office	22	23	23
Ministry of Social Affairs and Health	20	21	22
Political party: regional organization	23	21	22
Regional council	20	25	22
Ministry of Transport and Communications	20	23	21
Political party: local organization	25	23	21
Defence Forces	23	23	20
Ministry for Foreign Affairs	29	25	20
Cooperative	23	19	19
Ministry of Agriculture and Forestry	16	18	18
Ministry of the Interior	22	23	18
Agricultural producer association	20	20	17
Church	19	17	17
Ministry of Defence	19	16	16
Ministry of Justice	13	16	16
Ministry of the Environment	24	18	16
Judiciary (courts, police)	12	13	15
Environmental protection association	16	13	13
The president of the republic	10	15	12
Women's association	11	11	11
Consumer association	9	10	8
N	696	609	431

Ministry for Foreign Affairs (–9), central government agencies (–9), private companies (–9), the Ministry of the Environment (–8), the mass media (–8), wage earner
associations (–7), and cultural associations (–7).

Overall the interaction network of the Finnish elites has been eroded since the
early 1990s. In other words, there are fewer institutions than before with which
the power elite has very close contact. The interaction network therefore does not
tie elites to institutions in society as closely as before. The number of institutions
within the core of the power elite's interaction network also decreased and to some
extent changed after the early 1990s. There are only a few exceptions to this general
trend. Each elite group has the closest contact with the institutions in their respective
sector: the political elite has the closest contact with political parties, parliamentary
groups, and the government; and the business elite has the closest contact with private companies, banks, and employer associations.

The elite group whose contacts with the institutions concerned have declined
most of all is the business elite. This is true even of its density of interaction with
institutions in its own sector, that is, state-owned companies, banks, private companies, entrepreneurial or other business associations, and the Ministry of Employment
and the Economy, and the Ministry of Finance.

The contacts of the mass media elite and to a lesser extent the contacts of the
scientific elite with different institutions increased more than those of other elite
groups. The mass media elite differs from other elite groups in the sense that its contacts have increased with two-thirds of all institutions, but decreased with no more
than one-quarter in 1991–2011. This suggests that the mass media have a prominent
and even strengthening role as a hub of the power elite interaction network.

The media elite recognize that the journalists' close contacts with various elite
groups are useful, even indispensable for them but they should be too intimate.
Mikael Pentikäinen (2014, 271), former editor-in-chief of Finland's biggest daily,
Helsingin Sanomat, describes the advice he was given by the newspaper's CEO Jaakko
Rauramo when he was appointed editor-in-chief of a smaller regional newspaper:
"Remember. You're to be friends with no one. I remember this advice well because
it was all I got. It was how I tried to perform in my role as editor-in-chief and how
I've instructed my staff writers. Journalists need to know those who are in power,
the people they're writing about, and to keep in touch. But you must keep enough
distance so that if needs be, you can write about every one of them without the pain
of close friendship."

Pekka Seppänen, former editor-in-chief of business magazine *Talouselämä*, says
the mate syndrome is the biggest problem for Finnish media: "In journalistic work,
you can't go looking for anything else: no friendship, no adulation, no back-slapping.
. . . The elite and those in power will keep feeding their liturgies and absolute truths
that journalists all too easily take as given, without bothering to find out for themselves. Desk staff keep complaining of a shortage of time. We might in fact be suf-
fering from a shortage of attitude." (*Helsingin Sanomat*, Sept. 14, 2010).

However, Martti Ahtisaari, 2008 Nobel peace laureate who from his administrative elite background became the president of the republic (1994–2000), also came to experience the power of the media: "All along [during the presidency] it was clear from the attitude of the media that I wasn't part of the political elite, which was very close with the media elite. I wasn't part of them but an annoying outsider, a stranger. It's easier to criticize someone like that." (Merikallio and Ruokanen 2011, 383–84)

Direction of Elite Contacts

As well as considering the density of elite interaction networks, it is important to look at the form of these networks, that is, the direction of communications between elites and different institutions. In 1991–2011, elites had three response options to a question concerning the nature of their interaction: "you usually provide information for decision-making by the other side"; "you usually receive information for decision-making from the other side"; and "more general information exchange or social interaction." Non-response to the question concerning the nature of interaction with an institution is open to different interpretations. For instance, it is possible that the respondents were reluctant to give this information, or that they had no interaction with the institution in question. The latter seems a more plausible interpretation: as they had nothing against answering questions about their socioeconomic status, for instance, it is unlikely that the respondents would have considered the question about their interaction too sensitive to answer.

The wording of this question has the added benefit that it allows us to examine the direction of elite interactions—although we cannot of course conduct a genuinely bidirectional analysis of the network, with descriptions provided by both sides. The important thing, however, is that the question allows us to make a distinction between sending and receiving information. Secondly, it separates the sending and receiving of information relevant to decision-making from more general information exchange and social interaction, although the latter type of information may of course also be relevant in the wielding of power.

In 1991, the power elite sent more often information than they received in the case of 24 institutions. In 2001, the number of such institutions was 17; and in 2011, 23. Conversely, the power elite received more often information than they sent information in the case of 16 institutions (1991), 22 institutions (2001), and 15 institutions (2011). Overall, the power elite's contacts became more general in nature: "more general information exchange or social interaction" was the most common form of interaction with 20 institutions in 1991, with 29 institutions in 2001, and with 33 institutions in 2011 (table 5.4).

Since 1991, sending information has been the most common form of elite interaction with parliamentary groups, parliamentary committees, the government, national political party organizations, the Ministry of Finance, the Ministry of Education and Culture, the Ministry of Employment and the Economy, and the mass

Table 5.4.   Direction of Information Flow between Elite Members and Various Institutions in 2011 (%) and Changes in 1991–2011 (Percentage Points), N=431

Institution	Direction of Information Flow							
	Mainly from Self to Other		Mainly from Other to Self		General Information Exchange		No Answer	
Mass media	59	−4	6	1	20	1	16	1
The government	47	−2	11	3	21	4	21	−5
University/polytechnic	27	3	20	−3	31	2	22	−2
Private business	20	−2	19	−3	26	4	35	1
Municipality or joint municipal authority	26	4	12	−1	25	7	38	−10
Other research institute	16	−1	22	−3	26	6	37	−1
Central government agency	23	−10	15	2	24	4	38	3
Business association	17	0	18	−2	30	5	36	−3
Political party: national organization	29	−2	9	3	23	3	39	−4
Employer association	17	0	18	−3	27	6	39	−2
Ministry of Education and Culture	23	−8	19	7	23	4	35	−3
Other association	17	5	13	−2	31	7	40	−8
Bank	13	−8	22	−2	24	3	42	7
Ministry of Finance	24	−7	18	4	18	3	41	1
Parliamentary group	32	−1	9	3	22	6	37	−8
Employee association	15	−2	16	−4	29	5	41	2
Ministry of Employment and the Economy	25	0	15	2	19	2	41	−4
Cultural association	11	−2	13	−5	35	7	41	0
Parliamentary committee	44	1	7	2	13	4	36	−7
State-owned company or public utility	13	−4	16	−4	26	6	45	2
Prime Minister's Office	19	−2	13	1	23	7	45	−7
Ministry of Social Affairs and Health	18	1	13	1	24	7	46	−8
Political party: regional organization	18	2	6	−1	26	7	50	−8
Regional council	17	4	13	1	25	6	46	−10
Ministry of Transport and Communications	18	−1	13	0	25	5	48	−5
Political party: local organization	18	0	7	2	24	4	52	−5
Defence Forces	10	0	15	−2	30	3	46	0
Ministry for Foreign Affairs	14	−7	14	−3	26	7	45	1
Cooperative	9	−1	12	−2	27	4	52	−1

Institution	Direction of Information Flow							
	Mainly from Self to Other		Mainly from Other to Self		General Information Exchange		No Answer	
Ministry of Agriculture and Forestry	14	0	11	1	25	5	51	−6
Ministry of the Interior	14	−4	16	3	20	4	50	−3
Agricultural producer association	9	0	12	−3	26	2	53	1
Church	10	3	10	−2	30	0	50	−2
Ministry of Defence	11	−3	14	3	25	3	50	−3
Ministry of Justice	13	0	13	3	24	6	50	−9
Ministry of the Environment	16	−4	12	0	21	3	51	1
Judiciary (courts, police)	12	3	11	0	27	6	50	−9
Environmental protection association	6	1	12	−5	28	7	54	−4
The president of the republic	13	3	3	−2	41	10	43	−11
Women's association	5	0	9	−1	30	8	56	−8
Consumer association	5	1	8	−5	29	9	58	−6

media. In 1991, sending information was also the most common form of interaction with the Ministry for Foreign Affairs, the Ministry of the Interior, the Ministry of Transport and Communications, and the Ministry of the Environment. In the case of central government agencies and the Prime Minister's Office, sending information was the most common form of information exchange in 1991 and 2001, and in the case of municipalities and joint municipal authorities in 1991 and 2011.

Sending information is clearly associated with influence at elite level. The institutions to which elites send information most often, rank among the most influential institutions in Finland. According to the power elite's assessment in 2011, the most influential institutions of the 24 listed were (in this order) the government, Parliament, television and radio, the print press, political parties, and major corporations (see table 5.11). Although Knoke (1990, 10–13) suggests that the most influential actors are those who receive several relations, it is evident that at elite level the situation is reversed: elites actively send out information to persuade the recipients to comply with their goals. Even so, sending information as a form of elite interaction has increased in the case of just 12 institutions, while it has decreased in the case of 20 institutions since the early 1990s.

Receiving information, then, was not the most common form of interaction with any institution during the whole research period 1991–2011. It was, however, the most common form of elite interaction in 1991 and 2001 with employer associations, other research institutes, banks, and private companies. All forms of contact were equally common in elite interaction with private companies. Further, in the early 1990s receiving information and general information exchange were equally common forms of elite communication. Sending information as a form of elite contact has increased with 17 institutions, but decreased with 21 institutions since the early 1990s. The role of more general information exchange or social interaction, then, has increased as a form of interaction between elites and all institutions. The conclusion that can be drawn from these changes is that the elite interaction network has become increasingly fragmented and dispersed over the past two decades not only in terms of the density of interaction, but also the form of interaction.

An examination at the aggregate power elite level hides from view some significant group differences in forms of interaction. Only the political elite and the mass media elite mainly receive information from most institutions, whereas other elite groups are predominantly senders.

For the political elite, receiving information has been the most common form of contact with the Ministry of Finance, the Ministry of Education and Culture, employee associations, employer associations, entrepreneurial or other business associations, producer or other agriculture and forestry associations, other research institutes, and state-owned companies and public utilities. Many of these institutions perform an interest representation role, seeking to lobby political decision-makers with a view to furthering their own goals. For the political elite, sending information has been the most common form of contact vis-à-vis political institutions since 1991, that is, parliamentary committees, parliamentary groups (with the exception of 2011), the government, political party organizations, and the mass media, but also vis-à-vis municipalities and joint municipal authorities in 2011. Sending information to the government and all levels of political party organizations has even increased as a form of communication for the political elite. This trend illustrates the growing tendency of the political elite to try to influence both institutions within its own sector and the public realm through the mass media. Not only the political elite but also the mass media elite are predominantly receivers of information. This is explained by the fact that a key part of the job description of journalists, including those in leading positions, is to collect information from various institutions as material for journalistic reporting.

One characteristic that virtually all elite groups share in common is that general information exchange or social interaction has gained in importance as a form of interaction since the early 1990s. Its role has declined only among the mass media. Sending information as a form of interaction with various institutions has gained in importance in the political, administrative, and organizational elites, while it has lost importance in the business, mass media, scientific, and cultural elites. On the reverse side of the coin, the role of receiving information as a form of communication has strengthened in the business, mass media, and cultural elites, but declined in the political, administrative, and organizational elites since the early 1990s. In the scientific elite, receiving information was as common in 2011 as it was two decades earlier.

One distinctive feature of the cultural elite is that a much larger proportion of this than other elite groups did not answer the question concerning the form of interaction. The most plausible explanation is that the cultural elite has probably had quite limited contact with institutions outside the cultural sector: if you have no contacts, then obviously it is hard to describe their form. In contrast to other elite groups, the role of neither sender nor receiver of information was clearly predominant in this group of elite members, and social interaction was an even more common form of interaction than in other elite groups.

Elites' International Contacts

Finnish elites' contact networks are not confined to Finland, of course. Finland's membership in the European Union in 1995 and globalization have greatly expanded elites' playing field. Internationalization is likely eroding the traditional Finnish model of interaction that is based on personal contacts, as is reflected in the declining role of informal meetings as a way for elites to further their own interests. As distances grow longer and linguistic and cultural divides grow wider, personal meetings no longer work as well as they used to in the Finnish and Swedish-language environment. However, the picture that emerges of the internationalization of elites is somewhat contradictory.

In terms of *studying abroad*, the internationalization of the power elite has hardly advanced at all since the early 1990s. Until the early 2000s, over one-fifth of the power elite had not studied abroad at all, but in 2011 this share increased to one-quarter. The proportion of those studying longer periods abroad (one year or more) has not increased from the one-fifth share recorded in 1991. The only indicator of advancing internationalization is the statistic that the share of those who have studied abroad for more than three years has increased from 3 percent to 6 percent in 2001, but since then this figure has no longer risen.

The group showing the strongest trend of internationalization is the scientific elite: since 1991, two-fifths of them have studied abroad for at least one year. The sharpest increase, however, is recorded for the cultural elite, rising from one-fifth in 1991 to over one-third in 2011. It is noteworthy how studying abroad has declined in the business elite: the proportion with no experience of studying abroad has increased from one-seventh to one-quarter, while the proportion of those with more than three years of foreign study has dropped from one-fifth to just 2 percent in 2011. The political elite has the largest proportion, over one-third, of those with no foreign studies, which is a higher proportion than in the early 1990s. Having said that, the share of political elite members who have studied longer periods abroad has increased from one-eighth to one-fifth in 2011.

As regards *working* abroad, the power elite has made more progress in its internationalization than in studying, and it has furthermore clearly increased. Whereas in 1991 two-thirds of the elite members had never worked abroad, in 2011 the corresponding proportion was one-half. At the same time, the proportion of those who had worked abroad for at least a year increased from one-fifth to one-third. The proportion of those who had worked abroad for long periods, that is, over five years, rose from 5 percent to 16 percent.

In 2011, the political elite were less internationalized that other elite groups in the sense that seven out of ten had never worked abroad, and the proportion with at least one year's international work experience was clearly lowest (one-seventh). The scientific elite, for their part, had the lowest proportion (one-quarter) of those who had no international work experience. Accordingly, the proportion of those who had worked abroad for more than a year was highest in this elite group (over one-half). The second highest figure was recorded for the cultural elite (two-fifths), followed by the administrative elite (over one-third) and the business elite (over one-third).

The biggest increase since 1991 in the proportion of elite members with more than one year's foreign work experience was recorded for the administrative elite. This is explained in part by rotation related to EU membership: a number of Finnish central government civil servants are posted for temporary assignments at Finland's EU mission and EU institutions in Brussels, only to return to Finland on completion of their assignment. This alone is not enough to explain the internationalization of the administrative elite; however, as the sharpest increase in the administrative elite is seen for the proportion of those who have worked abroad for more than five years. In other words, the administrative elite are making headway toward greater internationalization more generally.

It is noteworthy, though, that longer than 12-month foreign work placements increased significantly from 1991 to 2001 in the two most naturally internationalized elite groups, the business elite and the scientific elite, but since then there has been no noticeable increase. In the business elite in particular, internationalization has clearly slowed down. Furthermore, the proportion of those with no international work experience has no longer fallen since 2001. However, the share of those with more than five years of international work experience has increased from 5 percent in 1991 to 17 percent in 2011. This change has been driven by rapid restructuring in business and industry, including the loss of Finnish companies to foreign countries and takeovers of foreign businesses by Finnish firms, but one might have expected to see larger shifts in international work experience in the business elite. In the scientific elite, internationalization is reflected both in a sharp decline in the proportion of those with no international work experience and in the rise in the share of those with more than five years of international experience from 6 percent to 16 percent. In academia, researchers' interest in gaining international work experience is effectively dampened by the uncertainty of employment prospects on return.

While elite internationalization and changes in internationalization are more or less in line with expectations as far as working abroad is concerned, the results for *personal contacts* are even more surprising than those for studying abroad. That is, Finnish elites' contacts with foreign citizens have actually decreased since the early 1990s. This change cannot be explained away by the fact that the question concerning the orientation of international contacts was worded in a slightly different way in each year. In 1991, the question only concerned the frequency of elite members' personal contacts with people in other Nordic countries, European countries, and non-European countries, whereas in 2001 and 2011 the question was expanded to concern not only contacts with people, but also with foreign institutions.

In 1991, over half of the power elite reported contacts with other Nordic citizens at least once or twice a month. In 2011, this proportion was down to one-third. In the early 2010s, Nordic personal contacts were reported most frequently by the scientific elite (one-half), followed by the organizational elite (almost two-fifths) and the business and administrative elites (over one-third), and least often by the political elite (less than one-third).

In the wake of Finland's membership in the European Union and the country's main international reference group shifting from the Nordic countries to Europe, one would have expected to see Nordic personal contacts be replaced by European contacts. This has not taken place, however. The power elite have less frequent personal contacts in Europe, too. In 1991, almost half of the elite members were in contact with citizens from other European countries at least once or twice a month, but by 2011 this share dropped to one-third. In 2011, the group with the most frequent European contacts was the scientific elite (almost three-fifths), followed by the business elite and the cultural elite (almost two-fifths), while the political elite had the least frequent contacts (over one-quarter).

The power elites' personal contacts with citizens from non-European countries have decreased as well, from one-quarter in the early 1990s to one-fifth in the early 2010s. In 2011, the most frequent contacts were again reported by the scientific elite (two-fifths), the cultural elite (over one-fifth), and the business elite and political elite (one-fifth). Although the business elite have more contacts than most other elite groups in the Nordic, European, and non-European countries, this group has seen the sharpest fall in the number of contacts since 1991. The turning point came after the 2000s, because figures for 2001 show that the business elite had the closest contacts with persons from all these country groups.

The elite members' contacts with *foreign institutions* are clearly less frequent than their contacts with citizens from the above countries. These contacts, too, have become less frequent from 2001 to 2011. However, an examination at the overall power elite level gives an incomplete picture since contacts in different elite groups are heavily clustered in their respective sectors. When the analysis considers contacts occurring at least once or twice a month, the group reporting the most frequent contacts in 2011 is the scientific elite with universities and research institutes (three-fifths), the business elites with foreign companies (one-half), the organizational elite with foreign associations (two-fifths), the cultural elite with cultural institutions (less than two-fifths), the mass media elite with mass media (one-third), the administrative elite with national authorities (one-third) and EU institutions (less than one-third), and the political elite with foreign governments (less than one-third), and foreign political parties and MPs (one-quarter). With the exception of organizational elite contacts with foreign associations and organizations, the contacts of all elite groups with their "own" foreign counterparts have become less frequent since the early 2000s.

The picture of increasingly infrequent international contacts changes very little if instead of looking at contacts occurring once or twice a month, we turn our attention to very frequent, weekly contacts. With the exception of contacts with political parties/MPs and associations, interaction has decreased with both foreign institutions and citizens. The situation in different elite groups shows slightly more diversity. For instance, the contacts of the political elite with associations and Nordic citizens have increased somewhat, as have the administrative elite's contacts with EU institutions, the organizational elite's contacts with the public authorities, business firms, associations, and Nordic citizens, and the administrative elite's contacts with universities and research institutes.

Overall, then, the internationalization of the power elite since the early 1990s has increased with respect to working abroad; become polarized with respect to studying abroad (both the proportions of those with no foreign studies and those studying abroad for extended periods have grown); and decreased with respect to personal contacts. These patterns are hard to explain. One might be inclined to think that elite members' less frequent personal contacts abroad are explained by the relatively limited effects of European integration on elites. However, this does not seem to be the case. In the early 2000s, 15 percent of the Finnish elite members took the view that Finland's EU membership had had a major effect on decision-making in their respective branch, 56 percent said they thought membership had had some effect, 16 percent thought this effect was minor, and 13 percent thought EU membership had had no influence at all. By and large, the power elite thought the effects of Finland's EU membership had been positive. One-eighth thought it had made no difference, one-third that the effect was a positive one, almost one-quarter that it was negative, and the remaining one-third described the effect more vaguely. The most positive assessment was given by the business elite (43 percent) and the most negative assessment by the political elite (29 percent).

Another tempting explanation is to suggest that the declining frequency of elites' international personal contacts is due to the waning hype of internationalization after Finland's accession to the European Union and monetary union. However, this does not seem credible as the process of European integration is bound to have increased Finnish elites' foreign contacts, especially in the administrative elite. The question this raises is this: Are Finnish elites now turning in on themselves, within the confines of their own country?

ATTITUDINAL UNANIMITY

Attitudinal Unanimity between Elite Groups

The following discusses the degree of attitudinal unanimity among the power elite and changes in the degree of unanimity since the early 1990s based on the elite

Table 5.5. Elite Members Perceiving Various Dimensions of Social Conflict as Very or Fairly Intense (%)

Conflict Dimension	1991	2001	2011
Growth centers vs peripheral regions*	52	90	75
Rich vs poor	49	62	73
Native population vs immigrants**	61	73	68
Politicians vs the people	73	62	73
Employed vs unemployed	58	62	50
Industrial companies vs nature conservation***	86	40	51
Employers vs employees	64	30	56
Socialists vs bourgeoisie	18	11	24
Men vs women	21	12	11
Finnish-speakers vs Swedish-speakers	14	12	19
N	689	619	434

* in 1991: people living in developing areas vs southern conurbation
** in 1991: Finns vs foreigners living in Finland
*** in 1991: business and industry decision-makers vs nature conservationists

members' views of the intensity of societal conflicts, attitudes, interests, and normative principles of decision-making.

Table 5.5 illustrates the attitudes of elites to 10 dimensions of societal conflict that have been frequently discussed in the public debate in Finland. The response options were very intense, fairly intense, fairly weak, has not occurred, and don't know. An overall examination of the conflict dimensions shows that the proportion of respondents who saw them as very or fairly intense declined from 1991 to 2001, but then increased so that by 2011, they were regarded as slightly more intense than in the early 1990s. However, a linear change in attitudes is only seen on the dimensions of rich/poor and men/women: the former is seen as an intense conflict dimension by an increasing proportion of elites and the latter by a decreasing proportion. In each year of study, the group that has stood most clearly apart from other elite groups is the cultural elite and the second most clearly the business elite: the former elite group has regarded societal conflicts as more intense than others, while the latter has felt they are less intense.

To gain more insight into the coherence of the elite structure, table 5.6 shows the mean standard deviations for 10 conflict dimensions. The mean standard deviation of power elites' assessments of different conflict dimensions fell from 0.732 in 1991 to 0.626 in 2001; in other words, there was greater attitudinal unanimity among elites. After 2001, however, the mean standard deviation climbed to 0.647, indicating a reduced level of attitudinal unanimity, although it was still higher than in 1991. With the exception of the organizational elite, the same trend can be seen in all elite groups, that is, their internal coherence increased up to 2001, but then fell back slightly to a level that was still higher than in the early 1990s. Elite group internal coherence has increased linearly since the early 1990s in just one group, that is, the organizational elite.

Table 5.6.   Elite Members' Attitudes to Various Dimensions of Social Conflict: Means of Standard Deviations

Elite Group	1991	2001	2011
Political	0.750	0.635	0.676
Administrative	0.736	0.587	0.599
Business	0.692	0.579	0.609
Organizational	0.695	0.662	0.623
Mass media	0.651	0.606	0.625
Scientific	0.756	0.633	0.685
Cultural	0.717	0.648	0.741
Power elite	0.723	0.626	0.647

As well as looking at power elites' attitudes to conflict dimensions, it is useful to analyze their responses to different *attitudinal statements*. Table 5.7 illustrates the attitudes of the elite members to eight attitudinal statements that are commonly used in surveys to tests citizens' perceptions of society. In all three years the response options for both the elite members and citizens were "fully agree," "agree to some extent," "don't know," "disagree to some extent," and "fully disagree."

Elite satisfaction with how democracy is working and with ordinary citizens' chances to participate in society has increased, at the same time as their concerns about the increasing influence of experts have grown linearly since the early 1990s.

Table 5.7.   Elite Members Agreeing Fully or to Some Extent with Attitudinal Statements (%).

	1991	2001	2011
In the future, science and technology will be able to solve most present-day problems	48	43	49
Democracy is working so well in Finland that talk about citizens' lacking influence is groundless	28	49	55
The increased number of foreign workers would increase exposure in our country to beneficial international influences	80	85	89
I am prepared to compromise my standard of living in order to reduce pollution and other environmental problems	80	69	71
There is a worrying trend for ownership to become more concentrated in our country	53	49	55
Socio-economic status differences are acceptable because they serve as a measure of how well individuals have seized their opportunities	41	33	30
There is no foundation to the claims that experts have gained increasing power in recent decades at the expense of representative decision-making bodies	26	32	39
A large part of our public services should be privatized in order to increase the efficiency of service provision	52	26	20
N	694	602	434

Table 5.8. Elite Members' Responses to Attitudinal Statements: Means of Standard Deviations in Different Elite Groups

	1991	*2001*	*2011*
Political elite	1.134	1.112	1.014
Administrative elite	1.037	1.005	0.964
Business elite	1.046	1.020	0.996
Organizational elite	1.110	1.090	1.033
Mass media elite	1.029	0.964	0.987
Scientific elite	1.035	1.048	0.964
Cultural elite	1.058	1.031	1.034
Power elite total	1.090	1.073	1.016

However, optimism in technology has in 2011 returned to the same level as in the early 1990s, having dipped slightly in 2001. Environmental concerns have clearly subsided since the early 1990s. On the other hand, elites are increasingly concerned about the concentration of ownership, and there is progressively less support for the privatization of public services. Acceptance of socioeconomic status differences has decreased linearly since the early 1990s.

The mean standard deviations for the eight statements above (table 5.8) have declined linearly since 1991. This means that there is greater attitudinal unanimity among Finnish elites. However, the changes have not been entirely consistent across the different groups. The mass media elite's internal coherence declined from 2001 to 2011, while the scientific elite's coherence decreased in 1991–2001 and the cultural elite's in 2001–2011.

Apart from the requirement of coherence, another criterion for the existence of an elite, in most elite theories, is that the elite members are aware of their position and that they are prepared and willing to take joint action. In other words, the elite shall function together as a group that shares certain purposes in common (Parry 1969, 31–32). However, it is extremely difficult to measure elite members' awareness of their position at the apex of power, especially in the context of empirical postal surveys. Indeed, this question has received very little attention even in qualitative elite research (but see Daloz 2010). In this connection we can only examine the identification of elites for 2011, when the elite respondents were presented with the following structured question: "To what extent do you feel you share interests in common with decision-makers in different sectors of society?" The response options were "to a great extent," "to some extent," "rather little," "not at all," and "don't know" (table 5.9).

It is no surprise that elite members felt they had the most interests in common with decision-makers in their "own" sector: the proportion of those reporting that they had shared interests "to a great extent" or "to some extent" varied in different elite groups from 86 percent to 100 percent. Four out of seven elite groups (political, administrative, organizational, and business elites) reported the fewest interests in common with decision-makers in the cultural sector. The mass media elite felt they

Table 5.9. Elite Members Perceiving They Share Many or Rather Many Interests in Common with Decision-makers in Different Sectors of Society in 2011 (%)

				Sectors				
Elite Group	Politics	Public Administration	Business	Organizations	Mass Media	Science	Culture	N
Political elite	100	98	76	87	71	49	45	45
Administrative elite	78	96	70	63	75	54	37	134
Business elite	59	54	91	57	43	74	22	46
Organizational elite	88	82	67	92	76	45	25	72
Mass media elite	72	57	70	63	94	46	57	46
Scientific elite	47	55	57	45	39	86	59	51
Cultural elite	50	50	41	61	52	41	89	46

had the fewest interests in common with the science sector and the second fewest interests in common with the cultural sector. Accordingly, the scientific elite identified the least common interests with mass media decision-makers, but the second most with cultural decision-makers. The cultural elite found the least interests in common with decision-makers in business and industry and in academia.

Sharing interests is not always a reciprocal experience. Identification is weakest between business and culture: 24 percent of the business elite did not feel they had any interests in common with decision-makers in culture, while 17 percent of the cultural elite thought they had no reason to identify with business decision-makers. Whereas the business elite felt they had quite strong interests in common (74 percent) with decision-makers in academia, the scientific elite reported much fewer (57 percent) common interests with business decision-makers. Overall, with the exception of the cultural elite, Finnish elites are quite closely integrated with decision-makers in different sectors of society, reflecting a sense of cohesiveness, an awareness that they are an integral part of the "core of power."

Another way to test the attitudinal coherence of the power elite is to study their views on the principles of political decision-making within their respective fields. In 2011, the elite survey included for the first time an item about the perceived importance of certain normative principles in political decision-making within the elites' respective fields (see Ruostetsaari 2010). The responses provide insight into the elites' notions of an ideal democracy, that is, about how transparent decision-making should be, what factors should be considered in decision-making, and who should be involved in making decisions or who actually make the decisions. The response options for the importance of different principles were "very important," "rather important," "not very important," "not at all important," and "don't know." Table 5.10 shows the results for the very and rather important categories.

Fourth-fifths of the power elite thought it was important that citizens have a say in political decisions, whereas two-fifths considered it important that business companies and NGOs were involved in decision-making. There is surprisingly little support for consensual decision-making among elites: only 5 percent consider it a very important and 41 percent a rather important principle. Support for consensus is lowest in the administrative elite (two-fifths) and highest in the mass media elite (more than nine in ten).

According to Jacob Söderman, former MP, cabinet minister, and European Ombudsman, the 1960s experience was that reforms were to be pushed through in the government by lobbying, which meant that preparation was power. "Ninety per cent of power is preparation. Whoever drafts a proposal will usually come out on top." (Saari 2014, 168) There is surprisingly strong support for the power of experts among elites, as over half of them consider it important that decisions are made by experts (very important 17 percent, rather important 36 percent). Differences between elite groups are quite noticeable. Support for the power of experts is strongest among the culture elite, 76 percent of who consider it important that political decision-making rests with experts. The figure is lowest in the political elite at 37

Table 5.10. Elite Members Perceiving Certain Principles as Very or Rather Important in Political Decision-making Concerning Their Own Sector (%)

	Elite Group							
Principle	Political Elite	Administrative Elite	Business Elite	Organizational Elite	Mass Media Elite	Scientific Elite	Cultural Elite	Power Elite Total
Decisions are prepared in a transparent manner	94	84	83	93	91	90	93	89
Decisions are prepared by experts	96	100	98	99	100	98	100	99
The media foster discussion and debate around the issue from the earliest stages of preparation	81	67	64	81	96	65	71	73
Communication about decisions made is as transparent as possible	100	98	96	99	100	98	98	98
Decisions made take broad account of their impacts on the national economy	98	90	96	95	98	96	82	93
Decisions made take broad account of their impacts on society	100	99	98	99	96	96	89	97
Decision-making is based on sound research knowledge	93	96	96	90	100	98	89	95
Decisions are reached unanimously in a process of negotiation	64	39	38	53	96	50	47	46
Decision-making rests with experts	37	48	55	51	60	63	76	54
Representatives of business and industry take part in decision-making	72	29	76	45	59	39	37	41
Representatives of NGOs take part in decision-making	43	84	26	53	50	42	42	39
Decision-making rests with those who have political responsibility to the electorate	96	88	64	88	89	63	43	79
Citizens have influence over decision-making	94	79	62	89	83	71	56	77
N	47	133	47	72	46	49	42	436

percent. In the scientific elite 63 percent consider this principle important, in the mass media elite 60 percent, in the business elite 55 percent, in the organizational elite 51 percent, and in the administrative elite 48 percent.

These figures for the support of expert power are also quite high when compared with the results of earlier studies on attitudes to the principles of energy policy decision-making, a 2007 postal survey among citizens, and a 2008–2009 interview study with elites in the energy sector. The biggest difference between elites and citizens concerned the role of politicians and experts in the decision-making of energy policy. While the elite stressed the role of institutions of parliamentary democracy, the views of citizens reflected a feeling of distrust in political decision-makers. Among the energy elite, 92 percent as compared with only 54 percent of the citizenry considered it (very or rather) important that decision-making rests with those who have political responsibility to the electorate. As many as 90 percent of citizens, but only 38 percent of the energy elite considered it important that experts make the decisions (Ruostetsaari 2010).

In contrast to the energy elite, citizens' attitudes to energy policy decision-making were indicative of their support for stealth democracy. Supporters of this form of democracy do not routinely want to be involved in political decision-making, or to constantly monitor and assess the doings of politicians. Rather, they want to see efficient and objective decision-making without too much discord. Ultimately, stealth democracy supporters want to see representative democracy work more efficiently, to have altruistic and knowledgeable politicians make all the decisions. For instance, they are firmly in favor of using more experts and business professionals in political decision-making, at the expense of politicians. Stealth democracy includes features that are reminiscent of Joseph Schumpeter's 1940s model of democracy, which is based on elite competition and where the influence of citizens is limited to voting in elections (Bengtsson and Mattila 2009, 307–9; see also Hibbing and Theiss-Morse 2002).

However, a study of the 2007 parliamentary election found that most people in Finland do not unreservedly support public debate and direct civic participation. In other words, people in Finland are very much in favor of strengthening both direct democracy and expert authority (Bengtsson and Mattila 2009, 316). While a clear majority of Finnish people had long felt their views were not sufficiently taken into account in energy policy decision-making, it was evident that the support for expert authority in this area was due to their lack of trust in political decision-makers rather than their reluctance to take part in the decision-making process themselves (Ruostetsaari 2010).

Although the Finnish power elite are quite strongly in favor of expert power, they still believe in the principles of democracy in that four in five consider it important that decisions within their own field are made by those who are answerable to the electorate, that is, politicians. This principle, not surprisingly, enjoys the strongest support in the political elite, while it is weakest in the cultural elite (43 percent). In other words, a larger proportion of the cultural elite would like to see experts rather than politicians make key decisions concerning cultural policy. In the scientific elite, the same number are in favor of experts and politicians making science policy decisions. Other elite groups show a stronger preference for decision-making by politicians rather than by experts.

The cultural elite attach more importance than other elite groups to the role of experts not only in decision-making, but also in the drafting of decisions. However, this expertise does not mean that decision-making should be evidence-based, as the cultural elite consider research less important than any other elite group. The same goes for their views on taking account of the economic and societal effects of decisions as well as their views on the opportunities of citizens to influence decision-making. In other words, support for stealth democracy is strongest in the cultural elite.

Since many of the above mentioned principles are related to the role of publicity in political decision-making, it is no surprise that the mass media elite differ most clearly from the power elite as a whole. The mass media elite attach more importance than other elite groups to the role of the media in inspiring public debate ahead of the actual decision-making process, to the transparency of information about decision-making, to evidence-based decision-making, to the role of experts in the drafting of decisions, and to the formation of decisions based on a consensual bargaining process.

As many of the decision-making principles discussed are related to the political elite's "own" field, it is also no surprise that the political elite differ the second most clearly from the whole power elite. The political elite attach more importance than any other elite group to the transparency of the drafting of decisions, the openness of information about decisions made (together with the mass media elite), the role of those responsible to the electorate in decision-making, citizens' influence on decision-making, and taking account of decisions' socioeconomic effects. Another indication of the political elite's reluctance to accept expert knowledge is that a smaller proportion of the political elite (38 percent) consider it very important that decisions are based on research evidence. By contrast, the political elite are prepared to afford the business elite a significant role in political decision-making: only the business express more support for the involvement of business representatives in decision-making.

The administrative elite express stronger support than other elite groups for having experts take control of the drafting of decisions (together with the cultural elite)—in other words, for both the administrative elite themselves—and NGOs participating in political decision-making. By contrast, the administrative elite attach less importance than other elite groups to consensual decision-making and business firms' involvement in decision-making. The business elite, on the other hand, place more emphasis than other groups on the involvement of companies, but less on the involvement of NGOs in decision-making. Furthermore, the business elite are less concerned than other elite groups about the need for open information about decision-making concerning business and industry, or about the need for public debate inspired by the media before the actual decisions are made.

Attitudinal Unanimity between Elites and Citizenry

It is often claimed in the public debate that divisions in our society are getting deeper and that elites and the citizenry are separated by a widening gulf, to the extent that they no longer live in the same world. For populist political parties that in recent years have enjoyed increasing support both in Finland and around Europe, this argument of a growing rift between the elite and the people effectively constitutes their *raison d'être*. Although populism has different expressions in different countries and political parties, there are two universal elements: praise of the people and criticism of elites. This is ultimately what populism is all about in modern democratic societies: appealing to the people and a critique of the established power structure and the dominant ideas and values of society (Canovan 1981, 294; 1999, 3). Paradoxically, the populist notion of power falls closely in line with the views of classical elite theory, which can be reduced to Gaetano Mosca's (1939, 50) thesis: there are in all societies two classes of people—a class that rules and a class that is ruled.

The focus of studies on the relationship between elites and the citizenry, both in European (e.g., Engelstad and Gulbrandsen 2007; Best and Cotta 2010) and Nordic (e.g., Munk Christiansen et al. 2001; Gulbrandsen et al. 2002; Lindvall and Rothstein 2006; Togeby et al. 2003; Østerud et al. 2004) elite research, has been on recruitment into elites from below (openness vs. closure of elites) and interaction between elite groups rather than on the confluence of attitudes between elites and citizens. In Finland, too, comparative research on the views and opinions of elites and citizens has been quite scarce (Julkunen 2001, 82). Yet it is important to explore and try to understand the relationships between elites and non-elites, because elites do not exist and operate in a vacuum. On the contrary, elites and other groups in society are mutually dependent on one another, and those groups can challenge the power of the elite. In order to understand the relationship between elite members and citizens, we need to explore the way they construct the reality around them, how they understand the world, and what relationship they have with the world as self-conscious actors (Salverda and Abbink 2013, 16).

Opinion polls in Finland suggest that elites' opinions differ consistently from those of the majority population both in ideologically charged issues and in issues that symbolize something greater, either in good or bad. Examples of such themes include the size of the public sector, the provision of municipal services, equality of income distribution, care for the underprivileged (Julkunen 2001), immigration (EVA 1991), European integration (Wiberg 1998), NATO membership (Ekholm 2006), and nuclear power (Ruostetsaari 2010).

The following discusses the gulf separating elites and the citizenry in two different ways: first, based on their responses to attitudinal statements, and second, based on their views on the distribution of power. The focus here is on indicators that in the public debate have not had quite the same symbolic significance as, say, Finland's membership in NATO or the decision on whether or not to build new nuclear power plants. For instance, nuclear energy is for some a symbol of wealth and the welfare state, while for others it is a signal of old-fashioned technology and unnecessary risk (Berg 2009, 107).

We start with a sum variable composed of four attitudinal statements discussed earlier (table 5.7): "In the future, science and technology will be able to solve most present-day problems," "Democracy is working so well in Finland that talk about citizens lacking influence is groundless," "There is a worrying trend for ownership to become more concentrated in our country," (reversed scale) and "A large part of our public services should be privatized in order to increase the efficiency of service provision." Since these attitudinal statements measure, firstly, trust in the regime and its ability to resolve problems in society, and secondly, the growing tendency since the 1990s to liberalize the economy, to reduce the role of the state in the economy via the privatization of state-owned enterprises and service provision, and the deregulation of capital markets (see, e.g., Boas and Gans-Morse 2009), this sum variable can be characterized as neoliberal support for the regime (table 5.11). The component statements of this sum variable correlate quite well with one another, that is, they measure the same phenomenon (Cronbach alpha 0.51 in 1991, 0.67 in 2001, and 0.59 in 2011). Therefore, the removal of any one variable would impair the sum variable. The higher value of the sum variable, the higher the support for neoliberalism.

Measured on the basis of mean values, neoliberal support for the regime decreased both in the power elite and among citizens from 1991 to 2001, but then started to increase again, although in 2011 it had not yet recovered to the 1991 level. In each year of study the elites have shown stronger support for neoliberalism than citizens. However, there are marked differences between elite groups. While

Table 5.11.   Neo-liberal Endorsement of the Regime among Elites and the Citizenry: Means (M) and Standard Deviations (SD)

	1991			2001			2011		
	M	SD	N	M	SD	N	M	SD	N
Political elite	2.58	0.78	86	2.68	0.80	87	2.66	0.75	47
Administrative elite	3.03	0.65	128	2.82	0.74	168	2.85	0.63	135
Business elite	3.33	0.63	109	3.43	0.69	93	3.28	0.66	47
Organizational elite	2.84	0.78	142	2.87	0.81	112	2.83	0.76	73
Mass media elite	2.75	0.66	80	2.51	0.70	59	3.03	0.78	46
Scientific elite	3.03	0.68	81	2.88	0.83	77	2.99	0.62	51
Cultural elite	2.67	0.72	72	2.40	0.74	60	2.54	0.79	46
Power elite (A)	2.91	0.74	698	2.83	0.81	616	2.86	0.72	434
Citizenry (B)	2.75	0.67	2420	2.56	0.69	2240	2.72	0.58	1327
Difference (B-A)	−0.16	−0.07		−0.27	−0.12		−0.14	−0.14	

the business elite have shown much greater support than any other groups for neoliberalism throughout the research period, support was lowest in 1991 in the political elite and in 2001 and 2011 in the cultural elite, when it was even lower than in the citizenry. Measured in terms of standard deviations, the internal coherence of both the power elite and the citizenry decreased from the early 1990s to the early 2000s, but then started to increase so that in 2011, they were both internally more homogeneous than in the early 1990s.

Hence, the different indicators of the attitudinal distance between the power elite and the citizenry gave somewhat different results. When measured on the basis of standard deviations, their attitudinal distance increased linearly from 1991 to 2011, but when measured in terms of means, it increased from 1991 to 2001, but then declined, to a level even lower than in 1991.

Secondly, the attitudinal distance between elites and the citizenry is assessed based on opinions about the distribution of power and influence in society. In each of the three years of study, identical questions were presented to elite members and citizens about how much influence they thought the listed organizations or institutions had over decisions that affected the lives of citizens or groups of citizens. The response scale was designed to reflect traditional Finnish school grades from 4 to 10 (4=no influence, 10=very much influence). Table 5.12 converts the influence grades given into rankings, firstly because this makes the table easier to read and secondly, and more importantly, because influence is in any case a relative concept: the best way to assess the influence of an institution is to compare it with the influence of other institutions.

The biggest changes in assessments of the distribution of influence in society have concerned political institutions and market forces. The power elite have ranked the government as the most influential institution since the early 1990s, but the citizenry only since the early 2000s. The influence of both Parliament and political parties has increased significantly according to both the power elite and the citizenry since 1991. At the same time, the position of the president of the republic has weakened significantly in the view of both groups. Both the elites and the citizenry take the view that the judiciary (police, courts), local civil servants, and local elected officials have gained increasing influence.

The greatest loss of influence, according to both elites and the citizenry, has been suffered by banks, major corporations, and insurance companies. Banks were also rated by residents as having lost the most influence in decision-making in their home municipality from 1992 to 2011 (Foundation for Municipal Development 2012, 53).

Wage earner associations, agricultural producer associations, and, surprisingly, the mass media were also among the institutions that both elites and citizens thought had lost some of their influence. Opinions between the two groups of respondents differed most in the case of banks and the judiciary, with citizens believing they had much greater influence than the power elite.

Table 5.13 shows the *mean deviations* of the grades given by elites to different institutions and their sums (the distance between elites). Only the political elite's

Table 5.12. Views of the Citizenry and the Power Elite on the Influence of Various Societal Institutions (Rank Ordered)

	Citizenry			Power elite		
	1991	2001	2011	1991	2001	2011
Banks	1	8	8	6	14	14
Major corporations	2	3	4	7	4	6
TV, radio	3	4	6	2	2	3
Press	4	5	7	4	3	4
Employer associations	5	12	10	11	11	11
The government	6	1	1	1	1	1
Employee associations	7	10	12	5	7	10
Judiciary	8	7	5	14	13	12
President of the Republic	9	9	14	3	9	15
Political parties	10	11	9	9	12	5
Insurance companies	11	15	16	16	18	19
State civil servants	11	13	11	8	8	8
Parliament	13	6	2	12	5	2
Agricultural producer associations	14	19	21	13	19	17
Municipal civil servants	15	14	13	10	10	9
Defence Forces	16	16	18	17	16	18
Municipal elected officials	17	17	15	15	15	13
NGOs	18	18	17	18	17	16
Universities (researchers)	19	20	19	19	20	20
Representatives of culture (art and literature)	20	23	23	20	23	22
Church	21	21	22	21	22	23
Individuals citizens	22	24	24	22	24	24
European Union	*	2	3	*	6	7
Regions	*	22	19	*	21	21
N	728	738	1340	698	560	434

*not inquired

and the business elite's attitudinal distance from the means for the power elite increased linearly from the early 1990s onward. The administrative, mass media, and scientific elites moved closer to the power elite from 1991 to 2001, but after 2001 their attitudinal distance from all elites grew again. The attitudinal distance of the organizational and cultural elites increased from 1991 to 2001, but then decreased. However, when all elite groups are considered, there was less consistency and agreement about the distribution of influence from 1991 to 2011 (distance between elite groups). In other words, the attitudinal coherence of Finnish elites declined. The *standard deviations* of their assessments point in the same direction: in 1991 the standard deviation of the power elite's assessments of the distribution of influence was 0.60, rising to 0.61 in 1991 and further to 0.63 in 2011. By contrast, the attitudinal distance between the power elite and citizens, as measured

Table 5.13. Views on the Distribution of Influence in Society: Differences between Elite Groups and between the Power Elite and the Citizenry (Sum of Mean Deviations)

	1991	*2001*	*2011*
Political elite	0.099	0.171	0.204
Administrative elite	0.122	0.063	0.100
Business elite	0.102	0.127	0.200
Organizational elite	0.102	0.140	0.129
Mass media elite	0.171	0.146	0.159
Scientific elite	0.139	0.134	0.157
Cultural elite	0.182	0.189	0.185
Difference between elite groups	0.917	0.970	1.134
Difference between power elite and citizenry	0.373	0.249	0.326

by mean deviations, decreased from 1991 to 2001 and then began to increase, but did not recover to the same level as in 1991.

The power elite and the citizenry view power relations from different vantage points: the former take the point of view of those in power, the latter the point of view of subjects of power. However, their largely uniform assessments especially concerning the increasing influence of political institutions but decreasing influence of market forces are unforeseen in the light of public debate; these evaluations could have been expected to be reversed. The section below looks in closer detail at how far the assessments of elites and citizens about the influence of societal institutions are supported by the research literature on Finland's political system.

CHANGING POWER RELATIONS IN THE FINNISH POLITICAL SYSTEM SINCE THE EARLY 1990s

Governmental and Political Institutions

The argument that the power and role of parliaments is declining has received much attention in the research literature. Governments and public administration, it is suggested, have gained increasing power at the expense of parliaments. This argument is based on three main factors: party discipline and the concentration of power in the hands of political party leaders, who also serve as government ministers; the increasing number and complexity of issues on the political agenda; and the growing significance of external restraints, such as the European Union, various international obligations, and the judiciary (Raunio and Wiberg 2014, 8). However, the evidence from Finland does not lend unambiguous support to this argument.

Studies on how European integration has affected everyday life in member states suggest that the European Union has had a greater impact on the content of politics than on the structures of political systems in member states. The influence of Europeanization has been greatest in areas where member states have delegated exclusive authority to the European Union, such as monetary policy and trade policy.

However, the effects of integration do also extend to questions that remain within member states' jurisdiction. The Economic and Monetary Union, for instance, which Finland joined in the first wave in 1999, has effectively curtailed the scope of economic policy autonomy (Raunio 2007, 133–34).

In a comparison of the ability of national parliaments to control their cabinets in EU matters, the Finnish Parliament ranks a strong second after the Danish Parliament. European matters are addressed not only by the Grand Committee which is charged with the oversight of these matters, but a major strength of the Finnish system is that other special committees are actively involved as well. In the parliaments of other EU countries, special committees tend to have a much less prominent role (Raunio 2006, 59–60).

Another strength of the Finnish model of addressing EU matters is that the role of Parliament is anchored in the Constitution. This was endorsed in the 2000 reform of the Constitution, which defined Parliament's role in the national preparation of EU matters and its right to be informed. Furthermore, EU legislative proposals are brought to Parliament very soon after their publication; special committees are systematically involved in the consideration of EU matters; Parliament has unlimited access to information; European Council meetings are systematically taken up in an advance reading; decisions taken at these meetings are reported post hoc; and the principle of transparency is universally applied. Ministers are consulted in the Grand Committee before and after the meetings of the EU's Council of Ministers. Regular hearings have improved or at least intensified dialogue between the government and Parliament, which in turn is reflected in the supervision of domestic legislative drafting (Ibid., 60).

It is noteworthy that in the wake of Finland's EU membership and the new Constitution, Parliament and especially its Foreign Affairs Committee have also gained a stronger position in foreign and security policy. Foreign and security policy used to be conducted primarily by the president of the republic and the Ministry for Foreign Affairs under the foreign minister, but when Finland joined the European Union it was reassigned to the domain of domestic policy because the EU's common foreign and security policy belongs to the competence of the government, which is responsible to Parliament.

Even though Parliament has taken steps to increase its efficiency in drafting EU matters, this cannot fully offset its loss of legislative powers (Raunio 2006, 64). The most extreme estimates are that up to 80 percent of new national legislation in Finland and other member states originates from the European Union (see, e.g., Vogt 2007, 90). However, just 12 percent of all acts passed by the Finnish Parliament in 1995–2009 made reference to the European Union, which is quite closely in line with figures in other member states. The main reason why the European Union has such limited influence on Finnish legislation is that national legislation is mainly concerned with policy sectors over which the EU has no authority. Only some 2 percent of all acts coming under the administrative branch of the Ministry of Education and Culture made reference to an EU regulation, whereas in the case of acts under the Ministry for Foreign Affairs the corresponding proportion was the highest at over one-third. However, the number of EU matters as a proportion of all matters handled by Parliament is much greater than the share of EU-related national legislation. In 2005, Parliament itself estimated that EU matters accounted for almost half of all matters it has under consideration. The number of matters brought to parliamentary committees has doubled as a result of Finland's EU membership (Raunio and Wiberg 2008; Raunio 2013; Wiberg 2004).

Kaarlo Tuori suggests that the Finnish legislator has actually relinquished a greater portion of its legislative powers than would have been necessary under EU conventions and related secondary legislation. He argues that far too often, EU directives are nationally implemented by simply copying the wordings of EU directives, without any effort to align them with national regulatory frameworks or legal terminology. Some EU directives are implemented in Finland *carte blanche*, incorporating them into the national judicial system by reference provision (Tuori 2013, 7–9).

In the past few years, democracy problems related to the EU, particularly in the eurozone countries, have had to do not so much with legislative powers as with financial and budgetary powers. When Finland joined the EMU in 1999, responsibility for national monetary policy was transferred from the Bank of Finland to the European central banking system. The emergency measures introduced in spring 2010 to fight the eurozone debt crisis have impacted the sovereignty of both aid recipients and aid providers. The financial sovereignty of eurozone members states has been curtailed. National sovereignty and budget authority are under threat not only from the huge financial bailout obligations, but also from the gradual tightening of fiscal policy controls, which have now been extended to national budgetary procedures (Tuori 2013, 10–11).

The European Fiscal Compact came into force in 2013, giving the European Commission the powers to scrutinize member states' budget proposals in advance. The main purpose of the compact is to create guarantees that member states will respect the requirements of budgetary balance or surplus. If the Commission feels that a member state is in serious non-compliance with the EU's Stability and Growth Pact, it can issue a negative assessment and ask the member state to revise its draft budget. Although the EU Commission does not have the powers to compel member states to change their budget plan, it can impose sanctions for failure to respect budget discipline. German Minister of Finance Wolfgang Schäuble has proposed that the Commission should have the power to veto member states' national budgets. From a democracy point of view the problem with EU monitoring here is that the budget is central to national autonomy and to determination of the direction of national policy, not only in terms of revenues and expenditures, but also more generally. However, the European Central Bank, to which the eurozone countries have relinquished their monetary decision-making, have no way to influence what services are made available to citizens, whereas the Commission can, through its budgetary control, directly influence the position of different population groups and income distribution between generations (Tuori 2013, 11–13; Henriksson and Kajaste 2014;

Korkman 2014). Furthermore, EU regulation is being stepped up with the gradual introduction of a banking union, which will bring the biggest banks under a supranational monitoring mechanism.

During the eurozone debt crisis, EU citizens have felt the impacts of European policy decisions immediately, without the dampening and legitimizing effects of national democratic processes. In the crisis states, national decision-makers have put in place belt-tightening programs jointly prepared and imposed by the "troika" of the European Commission, the European Central Bank, and the International Monetary Fund. On the street there has been a strong sense that political decision-makers at home have been reduced to marionettes whose role it is to implement decisions made elsewhere. In Finland and other aid-providing countries, too, there is a feeling that decisions affecting citizens' everyday life are increasingly made by eurocrats, and that the national Parliament has only limited freedom to maneuver. Both the European Parliament and national parliaments are thought to have little more than a bystander role, both in the fiscal stability mechanisms and in Europe's new economic governance system. There is a growing need for democratic legitimation of European decision-making in both the aid-providing and aid-receiving countries, yet at the same time it is increasingly difficult to satisfy that need through national democratic procedures (Tuori 2013, 12; see also Sailas 2013).

Finland's EU membership has strengthened the government's and the prime minister's position vis-à-vis Parliament and the president of the republic (see Myllymäki 2010). The prime minister has become the country's key political leader. The government and the prime minister in particular have a pivotal role in shaping Finland's EU policy. Although the European Parliament has gradually gained increasing legislative powers, the EU's most important legislative body is still the Council of Ministers. The prime minister's role is underscored by the fact that the PM regularly attends European Council meetings, which is the main forum for strategic decision-making on EU development. As Finnish foreign policy is increasingly tied to the EU's common foreign and security policy, the prime minister also has a prominent leadership role in foreign policy (Raunio 2006, 58, 64).

The prime minister's position has also strengthened for other than EU reasons. The government's power vis-à-vis the opposition has increased after the qualified minority rules were abandoned in the early 1990s, meaning that, with the exception of the Constitution, Parliament can now pass an act on a simple majority vote. Since the late 1970s, Finland has had a string of broad-based majority governments that have served out their full four-year terms, with the exceptions of the short-lived cabinets of Jäätteenmäki (2003), Kiviniemi (2010–2011), and Stubb (2014–2015). Relying on rigorous party discipline, strong majority governments are in the position to absolutely control Parliament's legislative work, which undermines Parliament's position. Declining party membership numbers and the erosion of local party organizations, in respect to which Finland is a typical rather than a deviant case in a west European comparison (Karvonen 2014, 56), have strengthened the position of national party organizations and party leaders in particular. Party leaders have furthermore been increasingly in the spotlight with the personification of politics in the media, their high visibility roles in election campaigns, the strengthening of the prime minister's and the government's position, their increasing influence over the appointment of government ministers from the party's ranks, and their increased involvement in international cooperation.

The curtailing of the president of the republic's powers coupled with the stronger position of Parliament and the government have moved political parties out of the president's shadow into the center stage of politics. It is the political parties that form the government and run the country with the support of their parliamentary groups. Indeed, it is the role of parliamentary groups that has strengthened the most vis-à-vis national party organizations outside Parliament. This is explained by the erosion of party organizations, the increasing resources and personnel available to parliamentary groups and individual MPs, and an increasingly specific and detailed political agenda. Political party organizations outside Parliament very rarely directly address legislative issues (Forsberg and Raunio 2014, 14–16, 30; Ruostetsaari 2005).

In Finland the president of the republic has had exceptionally strong powers when compared with other countries; only the presidents of the United States and France have exercised stronger powers. In fact, Heikki Paloheimo (2001, 100) has argued that in the heyday of Urho Kekkonen's presidency (1956–1981), his powers were far greater than the US president's. Finland has been characterized as a semi-presidential government which combines a president directly elected by the people and per-forming a political task with a prime minister who heads a cabinet accountable to Parliament. The prime minister, who is appointed by the president, is responsible for day-to-day domestic government (including relations with the Parliament), but the president retains an oversight role, responsibility for foreign affairs, and can usually take emergency powers (Hague and Harrop 2001, 245; Gallager et al. 1995, 20).

Gradual constitutional reforms were put in place in the mid-1990s to curtail the president's powers and to parliamentarize the distribution of governmental power at the highest level. These reforms paved the way to a wider overhaul, the need for which became increasingly apparent when Finland joined the European Economic Area (EEA) in 1994 and the European Union in 1995. The new Constitution came into force in March 2000, establishing the role of Parliament as the most important branch of government and the division of powers between the president, the govern-ment, and Parliament (Wiberg 2006, 122).

The Constitution of 2000 changed above all the position of the president. The president no longer "determines Finland's relations with foreign states," as was the wording of the 1919 Constitution. The new Constitution says that "the foreign policy of Finland is directed by the president of the republic in co-operation with the government." The Constitution assigns responsibility for the national prepara-tion of EU matters to the government, which shall decide on concomitant Finnish measures, unless the decision requires the approval of Parliament. This provision brought EU matters under the realm of domestic policy and very much curtailed the president's role in these matters. However, the president could still attend European

Council meetings alongside the prime minister and minister for foreign affairs (and possibly the minister of finance), especially when these meetings discuss questions of foreign and security policy. Although the formal decision over the president's participation in European Council meetings was now to be made by the government, in practice presidents have continued to make this decision themselves—and, if approved by the government and prime minister, attended these meetings.

The question of who was to represent Finland at European Council meetings was finally resolved with a constitutional amendment that came into force on 1 March 2013. The Finnish Constitution now states unequivocally that the prime minister represents Finland on the European Council. Furthermore, unless otherwise decided by the government, the prime minister shall represent Finland in other EU activities that require the participation of the highest governmental leadership. The new Constitution curtailed the powers of the president in other ways, too. Bills are no longer submitted to Parliament by the president, but by the government. In certain categories of matters the president's discretion in decision-making was tied to the government's motion, implementation of Finland's international obligations was charged primarily to the government, and the government gained expanded rights to make appointments to offices. Although provisions on Parliament's involvement in the national preparation of EU matters and its right to information were already included in the Constitution of 2000, it was only the 2013 amendment that made explicit mention of Finland's membership in the European Union. The president's role in forming the government is limited to the formal appointment of the prime minister, who is elected by Parliament, and the other members of government. In foreign and security policy, the president's powers are now effectively limited to Finland's relations with non-EU states, although even these are largely managed under the umbrella of the EU's common foreign and security policy, which is the government's responsibility. In domestic policy-making, the president's role is largely restricted to opinion leadership. In short then, the parliamentarization of the Finnish Constitution has greatly increased the power of Parliament (Raunio and Wiberg 2014, 13).

All in all, the constitutional reforms of 2000 and 2013 transformed the Finnish political system from a semi-presidential regime—sometimes bordering on pure presidentialism—into a basically parliamentary form of government (Karvonen 2014, 85–86). The epithet of "semi-presidential government" no longer applies to Finland.

Although parliamentarization has given political parties a stronger role in governmental decision-making, their significance as civic associations has declined. In particular, dwindling memberships have meant that political parties carry less weight and importance as popular movements. Parties' links with civil society, through local party organizations, are ever weaker, further underlining their increasing integration with government. Indeed, political parties have increasingly turned into mere electoral machines (Wiberg 2014, 182).

The research literature provides support then for the views of both the power elite and the citizenry of the increased influence of Parliament and political parties. But the picture is not entirely straightforward: there is also research evidence that points the other way and suggests that the influence of Parliament and political parties is waning. This latter argument is supported by evidence which shows that government officials now enjoy a stronger role and position than before. The power elite thought governmental officials had greater influence than the citizenry did, but neither group felt that that influence had increased since the early 1990s.

Public Administration

Although political parties remain irreplaceable political actors, other centers of power have increasingly taken on roles that used to be performed by parties in the traditional division of labor in society. Political parties do not in fact exercise their power potential to the full. Government officials, on the other hand, exercise both their formal powers of preparation and execution, but also powers of a distinctly political nature. It has been suggested that the everyday political agenda is formed in the offices of civil servants and lobbying organizations rather than in ideological discussions at party meetings (Wiberg 2014, 181).

Although Parliament has adopted an active role in European Union policy, the advance of Europeanization has also contributed to the strengthening the role of civil servants. Civil servants play a key role in drafting the country's official positions and in presenting these positions to the EU Commission and Council working groups. In general it has been suggested that with the internationalization and particularization of politics, civil servants have inevitably gained a stronger role (Forsberg and Raunio 2014, 37). Cabinet ministers, senior civil servants, and MPs have so much work with domestic issues that they rarely have the time or the resources to familiarize themselves with EU matters in any detail. The increasing involvement of civil servants in politics is not just a Finnish phenomenon, but comparative studies suggest that European integration has had the same effect in virtually all member states. The Parliament in Finland has attempted to curb this trend—and has had some success in doing so—by conducting regular hearings on EU issues with cabinet ministers and officials responsible for the matter. However, it has been suggested that civil servants in Finland occupy a less prominent role in political decision-making than their colleagues in other members states (Raunio 2006, 65).

Regardless of EU membership, the reason why the balance of power between cabinet ministers and civil servants is tilted in favor of the latter is that the ministers have charge of their respective ministries for no more than one electoral term at a time, whereas civil servants are hired staff and therefore represent continuity. A long-standing career in the civil service will inevitably strengthen civil servants' expertise and make them specialists in their respective administrative branches. Ministers, by contrast, are generalists in charge of running the ministry, professional politicians who have neither training nor experience in that particular administrative branch—nor is such training or experience expected or required (Nousiainen 1992).

An important doctrine of reforms in the public sector is that of New Public Management (NPM), which has incorporated business principles into public administration: accountability, professional management, privatization, decentralization, deregulation. Competitiveness and competition-mindedness have become the order of the day with the introduction of new accounting systems, budget discipline, benchmarking, monitoring, and evaluation. In Finland, NPM reforms were launched above all after the 1990s recession, and by the end of the decade privatization of the public sector in Finland had advanced further than in any other OECD country. Indeed, complaints have been heard from the field about the difficulty of performing even basic administrative functions as the number of civil servants has been cut and as significant resources have to be deployed for running various projects and commissioning outside reports. At the same time, experts and consultants from outside public administration—professors, management consultants, development experts, business gurus—have gained a prominent role in steering the state. This has been described as shadow governance or consultancy democracy: experts of all manner are penetrating the field of political power by redefining political issues as administrative and managerial problems (Heiskala and Kantola 2010, 143–44, 136; Kuusela and Ylönen 2013).

On the other hand, there are some counterarguments to be made to the growing influence of the civil service. Firstly, there have been no caretaker governments composed of senior civil servants in Finland since the mid-1970s, but every government since the late 1970s has been a majority government and, with just a few exceptions, they have served out their four-year term. Through political appointments, each cabinet has been able to recruit individuals of the appropriate political color into senior posts in ministries and government agencies and so to strengthen their political steering.

A system of political permanent secretaries was introduced in Finland in 2005 with a view to strengthening the political staff of cabinet ministers. Prior to this, each minister had at least one special assistant. As virtually all ministers are chosen from the ranks of serving MPs, they have also been able to call upon the services of their personal representative's assistant. This reform was intended to strengthen political steering at the stage when matters are under preparation at ministries. Finland's membership in the European Union in particular has increased government ministers' workload and job demands. However, with the single exception of the prime minister's permanent secretary, political permanent secretaries do not have general management and coordination functions, but their role is to assist the minister in preparing matters under the minister's authority. In other words, they do not serve as heads of the civil service in their ministry, nor do they have the authority to suspend the preparation of matters by the ministry's civil servants. Political permanent secretaries are not deputy ministers in the sense that in the absence of the minister, they cannot vote at the EU Council of Ministers' legislative meetings, although they can represent the minister at other meetings (Tiihonen 2006, 106–13). The number of government ministers' political aides—political permanent secretaries and special assistants—has doubled from 24 in the Holkeri Cabinet (1987–1991) to 48 in the Katainen Cabinet (2011–2014). When the personal assistants of ministers serving as MPs as well as other aides, advisers, and secretaries are included, the total number of aides in the Cabinet of Jyrki Katainen was 149 (*Helsingin Sanomat,* 20 July 2013).

It is a common finding in studies of the municipal power structures that power tends to be concentrated in the hands of a relatively small number of (leading) civil servants (e.g., Karila 1998; Möttönen 1997; Lehväsvirta 1999; Heuru 2001; Ruostetsaari and Holttinen 2001). The single most influential actor in the municipal organization is the mayor, who in contrast to most other countries is not an elected political leader, but a civil servant. In practice, however, the mayor does exercise power of a political nature and is often appointed on political grounds. The second most influential institution after the mayor is the municipal board, which is composed of elected officials. The municipal council, officially the highest municipal decision-making body, ranks only as the third most influential body (Ruostetsaari and Holttinen 2001, 23).

Since the late 1980s, the same NPM principles applied to the development of central government have also been put to work in developing management in local government. Decision-making powers have been decentralized from elected officials to civil servants. The mayor's role has changed from that of a traditional leading civil servant to a position that resembles the role of a business company's managing director (Haveri and Anttiroiko 2009, 200).

The municipal council, which according to the Local Government Act should represent the highest level of democratic decision-making, has been losing its power and in practice is unable to assume overall responsibility for running the municipality. This tendency has been reinforced above all by the adoption of strategic management practices, under which the council concentrates on setting the broad parameters for development, while decisions as to how the targets set shall be achieved have been delegated to civil servants. In practice, the council is restricted in its decision-making to the set of alternatives prepared and presented by civil servants and the municipal board (Heuru 2001, 355–57).

This separation of administration from politics can be described as the govermentalization of politics. There is some tension in the relationships between elected officials and civil servants in local government, which can be assumed to reflect the fact that the power of civil servants is not yet entirely exempt from democratic control, even though they have gained increasing influence (Möttönen 1997, 386–87). In the 2000s, a couple of municipalities have moved to strengthen political steering over municipal administration by introducing a system where the duties of the mayor and the chair of the municipal board (who is elected by the council) are all given to the mayor, or where the chair of the municipal board is hired to serve in this role as a full-time politician.

The surveys conducted for this research found that both elites and citizens thought the influence of local government elected officials and civil servants had increased since the early 1990s. To suggest that both poles of power have strengthened is an impossible equation in the context of an individual municipality. Based on the research literature it is evident that municipal influence has mainly shifted from elected officials to civil servants. On the other hand, the research evidence is that, in contrast to the power elite's and citizens' assessments, the influence of civil servants in central government has increased since the early 1990s, which has eroded the power of both the government and Parliament.

Judiciary

The Finnish constitutional culture and the judiciary have seen significant changes since the early 1990s. It is fair to say that the Finnish Constitution has become increasingly Europeanized (Salminen 2010, 64–67) and that we have witnessed a growing trend of constitutionalization (Lavapuro 2010, 16). Finland's EU membership has constrained country's legislative elbow room, and the role of national and international legal norms protecting individuals' fundamental and human rights has increased significantly, which has implied a shift in influence from Parliament, representing legislative power, toward the system of courts (Husa 2004, 147).

Processes of judicialization can occur at various levels, both in politics, in citizens' everyday life, and in society at large. As far as the political system is concerned, judicialization can take the form of the judicialization of politics or the politicization of justice. The judicialization of politics can be seen as referring to the limitations imposed by constitutional considerations and fundamental rights on the legislator's free political discretion. In other words, the judicialization of politics limits the options available in democratic law-making. The politicization of justice, or governance by judges, then, refers to the transfer of the locus of political discretionary and decision-making authority to courts of law that in a democratic rule of law framework should belong to Parliament and the government (Wiberg 2006, 156; Tuori 2007, 273–74). Politicization is not necessarily about courts of laws attempting to gain more power, but it may be the result of the legislators' passiveness and their wish to pass on difficult problems, in the form of loosely written legislation, to courts of law (Husa 2004, 154; Sipponen 2000, 126).

The new Constitution of 2000 introduced significant changes to the supervision of the constitutionality of legislation by expanding the powers of courts of law to assess the constitutionality of laws. If in a case being processed by a court of law the application of an act of Parliament would be in evident conflict with the Constitution, the court of law must give precedence to the provision in the Constitution. In other words, the court has the discretion not to apply the provision of an act if it clearly conflicts with the Constitution (Lavapuro 2010, 12).

Several reasons contributed to the formulation of this precedence rule. Firstly, there was a felt need to promote the effective implementation of the Constitution and its fundamental rights provisions in courts of law. At national level, the constitutional reform took effect as early as 1995. Another contributing factor was Finland's decision to sign up to the international human rights convention in 1989 and to join the European Union. As a member of the European Union, Finland's courts of law are obliged to give precedence to Community law over national legislation. This also knocked the bottom out of the 1919 provisions of constitutional control, according to which courts of law were denied the right of post hoc supervision of the constitutionality of an act of Parliament (Nieminen 2004, 126–27). Until the constitutional reform of 2000, the constitutionality of legislation was controlled and verified exclusively beforehand by the Parliament's Committee of Constitution in connection with the enactment of a law.

In connection with Finland's EU membership, two sets of reasons contributed to the increasing powers of courts of law. Firstly, this was the inevitable result of the influx of new norms that followed in the immediate wake of integration, which together with the goal-oriented but loosely worded EU legal regulations has given a more prominent role to bodies applying the law: the content of law is no longer determined exclusively on the basis of the acts and statutes passed by legislative bodies, but also and increasingly via the active steps taken by courts of law to develop the jurisdiction. This means that the court system is having to continue and complete the work done by the legislator, applying loosely worded legislation to individual cases and giving it a more concrete shape. Finland has ranked as one of the most conscientious EU member states in the national implementation of EU legislation on market harmonization (Hix and Høyland 2011, 195). Courts of law ultimately have a major effect on the final content of the goal-oriented and loosely drafted EU rules and regulations (Ojanen 2000, 175).

EU legislation takes precedence over all national legal norms. The duties of Finnish courts of law include interpreting the compatibility of national law with EU law and examining the compatibility of Finnish legal acts with EU law. In practice, the binding effect of decisions made by European Union courts has placed EU law in a position of superiority over Finnish courts of law. Since EU courts of law have an exceptionally strong role in elaborating and developing EU law, and since an act or an omission by Finnish governmental bodies in violation of EU law may be subjected to infringement procedures, the authority of EU courts of law vis-à-vis other Finnish governmental bodies has likewise become increasingly pronounced (Ibid., 177).

A society can be said to be moving toward governance by judges when a growing proportion of matters and cases are subjected to scrutiny by courts of law. The locus of political power has gradually shifted toward courts of law, even though political power should, in a democratic rule of law framework, belong to legislators, Parliament, and the government (Wiberg 2006, 156–57). In Finland, too, the resolution of conflicts is increasingly entrusted to official control and regulatory mechanisms based on legislation, despite the parallel presence of informal means of regulation. The problem with this trend is that, on the one hand, formal regulation easily goes beyond what is reasonably necessary and, on the other hand, formal regulation limits the scope for independent and voluntary intervention by civil society and drives the parties to conflicts further apart from each other and from the event that caused the problems in the first place (Laitinen 2005, 71–72).

But although it would be premature to describe Finland as a state of judges, there are certainly signs of increasing Americanization in our jurisdiction. The reforms of the Finnish litigation system toward the Central European model built around trial lawyers has complicated trial proceedings and driven up costs to the extent that only the wealthiest citizens and indigent persons entitled to legal aid can afford to defend their rights in a court of law. Despite the public debate around this matter, trial costs remain unreasonably high. Paradoxically, the high costs of taking cases to court has slowed the judicialization of society (Ruostetsaari 2003a, 101).

On the other hand, courts of law are in many ways dependent on other governmental bodies. Firstly, courts of law must comply with the laws drafted by the government and passed by Parliament. Secondly, courts of law are fully dependent on the resources made available by the representative political system, such as wages, education, and infrastructure. Furthermore, the appointments of judges are ultimately dependent on politicians: tenured judges are appointed by the president of the republic that is preceded by the selection boards' recommendation and the government's proposal (Wiberg 2006, 157–58). Even so the research literature lends support to the views of the power elite and the citizenry that the judiciary has gained increasing influence since the early 1990s.

Market Forces

Finland has seen deep changes since the 1990s, including a profound globalization of the economy and society; an increasing role of market mechanisms at the expense of governmental intervention; and the breakthrough of ICTs. Foreign investments in Finland have multiplied, integrating Finland more closely with the globalizing world economy (Väyrynen 2000, 5). The first steps to curtail governmental regulation of the economy were taken as early as the mid-1980s. The financial markets were deregulated from 1986 onwards, when business firms and later private households gained the right to take out foreign currency loans. The influx of cheap borrowed money led to the overheating economy, or to what became known as the casino economy and conspicuous consumption. Banks were handing out money to businesses and individuals, who invested it into stocks and shares and real estate speculation. The increased supply and circulation of money drove up not only wages, but also the prices of commodities and housing as well as export prices. This created a real estate and stock exchange bubble. Businesses and households accumulated a heavy debt burden. Banks and bankers were hailed as the flagships of success, alongside and even ahead of forest industry businesses, the traditional cornerstones of the Finnish economy (Kiander 2001).

The casino bubble was burst by a domino effect. The current account deficit was swelling, foreign debt was growing, real interest rates skyrocketing. At the same time, domestic demand was dwindling, and economic policy lost its credibility. Finland was plunged into a banking crisis, which spread to the real economy. The number of bankruptcies multiplied, and even major companies that were considered financially solid and secure went under. Finland sunk into the deepest recession in its history. The effects exceeded even those of the 1930s depression (Kiander 2001).

The great recession was in part caused by external factors, such as the downturn in the international economy and above all by the breakdown of the Soviet Union, which effectively put an end to Finland's bilateral trade in 1991. In the late 1980s, Soviet exports and imports still accounted for one-quarter of Finnish foreign trade. Many companies that were oriented to the Soviet market were not competitive enough in the western marketplace. But home-grown factors were even more important to the unfolding of recession. The Bank of Finland and the Finnish government liberalized the financial markets in an uncontrolled manner and doggedly insisted on maintaining a fixed currency policy, that is, a strong national currency, which pushed up interest rates and eventually under market pressures led to the devaluation of the Finnish markka. As the value of their foreign currency loans suddenly jumped as a result of the devaluation, companies and households found themselves struggling to meet repayments to banks (Ibid.).

The view shared by both the power elite and the citizenry that the balance of power between political institutions and market forces has shifted in favor of the former could thus be explained by financial market liberalization and by the reduced dependence of businesses on banks from the 1980s onward; by the national banking crisis in the 1990s; and by the international financial crisis and eurozone debt crisis in the 2000s. In each case, political institutions have had to address and resolve the ensuing problems caused for private business and the national economy. In other words, political institutions and decision-makers in Finland have had to take a very public role in patching up the anomalies in the markets. One indication that citizens have felt the government is more to blame for the consequences of the financial crisis and the eurozone debt crisis than the banks is that in 2007–2012, Finnish people's trust in economic institutions fell lower than their trust in the government (OECD 2014, 139). As the sense is that the international financial crisis and the eurozone debt crisis were caused by the overheating of financial markets and outright speculation, regulation of the banking and insurance sector has been stepped up with more rigorous solvency requirements. Another sign that banks have been losing some of their weight in society is that since the early 1990s, elite interaction has decreased most of all with banking institutions.

On the other hand, there are also strong arguments to suggest that the influence of major corporations and banks has increased. Although the banking crisis brought down one banking group, which the government split among its four rivals in 1991 and two largest commercial banking groups in the country were engulfed in the merger in 1995, the main concern of governmental authorities was to prevent the financing system from collapsing by handing out governmental subsidies to banks. It was similarly thought that the country could not afford to let major corporations go under, but small and medium-sized enterprises and private individuals were allowed to go bankrupt. Later on the lobbying power of financial institutions has been clear to see in the management of the eurozone debt crisis. For instance, while talks on restructuring the Greek sovereign debt were being stalled, banks and private investors largely got away scot-free as governments and taxpayers were left to pick up the bill (Korkman 2013).

After the recession in the early 1990s, efforts were stepped up to turn Finland into a "competitiveness state" (Heiskala and Luhtakallio 2006). The role of this state was to create the conditions under which industry viewed Finland as an attractive business location where it could run competitive operations and so create jobs and wealth and at the same time generate the tax revenue needed for public welfare services and redistributive payments. It was thought that the only way to succeed in the global economy was to ensure that every aspect of society was permeated by the ethos of competition (Kunelius et al. 2009, 40).

There are plenty of examples of the weight and influence of private business in politics: the lowering of corporate taxes, increased governmental funding for research and development and financial support for enterprises, and the passing of new legislation in 2009 that gave business management the right to monitor employees' electronic communications (Heiskala and Kantola 2010, 131). As the problems of the Finnish economy have been due to the drying up of exports and poor competitiveness, major export companies in particular have gained increased leverage over political decision-makers. This was seen, for instance, in the government's decision in spring 2013 to lower the corporate tax rate from 24.5 percent to 20 percent and to reduce taxes on dividends.

Helsingin Sanomat estimated that in 2012, the total amount of governmental support to enterprises came to 4.8 billion euros. Most of this, 3.7 billion euros, was in the form of tax subsidy, while direct governmental incentives amounted to almost one billion. If the government had suspended the payment of all business grants, the corporate tax rate could have been lowered to around one percent. Even though there have been criticisms that business grants are ineffective and both politicians and business executives have called for them to be discontinued, the amount of direct subsidies paid out over the past decade has increased by more than 50 percent, according the Ministry of Employment and the Economy (*Helsingin Sanomat*, Dec. 17, 2013).

Insurance companies, and especially pension companies that provide compulsory earnings-related pensions, are still significant financiers and shareholders in major corporations, whose representatives wield power together with labor market leaders on the boards of many corporations. Major corporations, for their part, have representatives on the boards of earnings-related pension companies. These companies can in fact be counted among the biggest concentrations of power in Finland. The biggest company of all, Varma, has investment assets worth 36 billion euros, which has been collected from employers and since 1993 from employees in the form of earnings-related pension contributions (*Helsingin Sanomat*, Aug. 10, 2013).

The research literature does not lend clear support to the power elite's and the citizenry's assessment that banks, major corporations, and insurance companies have been losing their power and influence since the early 1990s. Although business firms are less dependent than earlier on banks following the liberalization of foreign borrowing and increased banking regulation, bank lending is still crucial for households and SMEs. Major corporations' power position has been further bolstered by the meta-ideology of economic growth and competitiveness, which enjoys universal acceptance among all political parties and in all sectors of society (see Saukkonen 2012, 40), and on the other hand by major corporations' *de facto* role as export drivers under conditions of economic recession. Insurance companies and employment pension companies in particular remain closely interwoven with major corporations. Perhaps the best indication of the growing influence of market forces is that since the great recession of the early 1990s, Finnish governments have been keen to retain the confidence of international credit rating institutions and have closely followed the comments made by these institutions about Finland's economic policy plans. This same attentiveness has continued in recent years as Finnish governments have attempted to hold on to the country's triple-A rating, which ensures lower interest rates on government debt. However, in October 2014, one of the rating institutions, Standard and Poor's, lowered recession-hit Finland's credit rating from AAA to AA+.

Labor Market Organizations

Labor market organizations, representing employees and employers, gained increasing influence in the late 1960s as Finland moved into an era of centralized incomes policy. This marked the beginning of an incomes policy regime in which the government and peak labor market organizations meet to discuss and agree on various economic, labor market, and social policy issues. The tripartite system of dialogue among the social partners *de facto* curtailed the power of Parliament, which in order to ensure peace and stability in the labor market often had to rubberstamp the proposed agreements put before it, even though the enforcement of these agreements required legislative measures. The power structures of Finnish labor markets became more centralized than in most other advanced democracies.

Increasing membership numbers further strengthened wage earner organizations' bargaining power. In the early 1960s, employee organizations had a combined membership of close to 300,000. By the mid-1970s, the figure soared to over one million, in the 1990s to 1.7 million, and in the early 2000s to 2 million (Sundberg 2008, 77; Suomalaiset osallistujina 2009, 117). It is estimated that in the early 1990s, Finland ranked among the most corporatist countries in the world together with Austria, Denmark, Switzerland, Germany, Belgium, and Ireland (Hague and Harrop 2001, 162).

The influence of labor market organizations in Finland can also be explained by their relationships with political parties. Norwegian political scientist Stein Rokkan has explained the relations between parties and their stakeholders on the basis of a triangular model whose vertices are labor, capital, and agrarian population. This same model also explains the conflicts and contrasts within the Finnish party system and that system's links with the organizational field. Dominant parties at the vertex representing labor have been the Social Democratic Party and the Left Alliance. On the labor market front, the main force is the Central Organization of Finnish Trade Unions (SAK). At the vertex representing owners of the means of production, business and industry, and the affluent middle classes, the leading political party has been the conservative National Coalition Party, and the leading organization in the labor markets the Confederation of Finnish Industries (EK), representing the employer side. The dominant party at the agrarian vertex has been the Centre Party and the main labor market organization the Central Union of Agricultural Producers and Forest Owners (MTK). Other political parties have been less clearly placed at the vertices of the triangle (Sundberg 2008, 75–77).

Since around 2000, however, the Finnish tripartite model has been eroding. The employer side has largely given up seeking centralized agreements between labor market confederations, and consequently bargaining has moved down to a lower union level. The message coming from employers is that comprehensive incomes policy agreements have been made redundant by economic globalization, as it is impossible for businesses to commit themselves to more expensive wage settlements than those adopted in other countries. At the same time, redundancies and business closure or relocations to third countries have undermined the bargaining positions of employee organizations (Heiskala and Kantola 2010, 131).

Another factor that has weakened the bargaining power of employee organizations is the sharp decline in membership rates, which have dropped by more than ten percentage points in less than a decade. At least part of the reason for the exceptionally high levels of membership in Finland and the other Nordic countries has been the earnings-related unemployment benefit system, as entitlement to such benefits has been based on union membership. It was only in the 2000s that an independent unemployment insurance system began to evolve and gain popularity in Finland, severing the link between earnings-related unemployment benefits and trade union membership (Siisiäinen and Kankainen 2009, 117).

The erosion of the power triangle made up of political parties and labor market organizations is seen in the fact that most wage earners are members of one trade union or another, and therefore the distribution of party preferences among union members no longer differs very much from the corresponding distribution for the country's adult population as a whole. Ever fewer MPs have held elective positions in labor market organizations before setting out on their careers in Parliament (Sundberg 2008, 78–79).

Labor market organizations have seen similar patterns of declining influence in all the Nordic countries, and consequently the degree of corporatism has also fallen. However, it is estimated that Finnish labor market organizations play a more prominent role in political decision-making than their counterparts in Sweden (Ruostetsaari 2013a). In Finland, labor market organizations continue to have significant influence in many social reforms that concern not only their membership, but the whole population, and the ultimate decisions on which are made by Parliament. It is extremely difficult for Parliament to change the tripartite agreements reached between the labor market organizations and the government. Sometimes it is not even a tripartite, but a bipartite arrangement: it is not uncommon that labor market organizations decide amongst themselves how they want to resolve tax and social policy issues, for instance (Wiberg 2014, 181). A good example is the recent decision to raise the retirement age: Katainen's Cabinet (2011–2014) delegated and outsourced *de facto* decision-making authority on this matter to the labor market organizations. Through earnings-related pension companies, labor market organizations also exercise influence in the private business sector. Under the conditions of economic recession, the labor market agenda has been dominated by initiatives from the employer's side, which takes a cautious view, to say the least, of persisting with the system of centralized incomes policy agreements, while efforts on the employee side have been concentrated on defending their acquired rights.

The labor market organizations that were affected most by Finland's accession to the European Union were agricultural producer organizations, which before membership had an independent role in the bargaining process between the government and labor market confederations. The agreements hammered out in this process would also dictate the prices that agricultural producers received for their produce, that is, their income level. When Finland joined the EU, national agricultural policy was integrated with EU agricultural policy, and therefore producer prices for Finnish agricultural produce are now decided in that context. National bargaining on agricultural incomes ended with EU membership.

The research literature clearly supports the power elite's and the citizenry's assessment that agricultural producer associations have been losing influence since the 1990s. The picture is less straightforward for changes in the influence of employee associations: under conditions of economic recession, employee associations have found themselves defending their acquired rights, and the initiative in labor market issues has swung over to employer organizations. However, corporatism is still alive and well, as important social issues are decided upon in tripartite settings between employee and employer organizations and the government—and sometimes in bipartite settings between labor market organizations.

Mass Media

The views presented in the research literature on the influence of the mass media have ranged between two extremes. On the one hand, the media has been portrayed as an important locus of power which rewards or condemns people and substance issues following is own "media logic," displacing the power of other institutions such as politicians and civil servants. According to another interpretation, the media has hardly any independent power at all, but it simply reiterates the views of economic and political centers of power. The conceptual framework for the conduct of public discussion and debate is determined by various elites (Kunelius et al. 2009, 11).

In the realm of *politics*, Strömbäck (2008) has identified four phases of mediatization. In the first phase of mediatization, the mass media emerge as the most important channel of communication between the citizenry and political institutions. In the second phase, the media become partly independent of political institutions and can more autonomously decide on the content and newsworthiness of communications, which political actors must take into account. In the third phase of mediatization, media coverage is no longer determined by the political agenda, but that is increasingly determined by the commercial media logic. In the fourth and final phase, political institutions internalize the commercial media logic and standards of newsworthiness and begin to act accordingly. It has been suggested that, historically, Finnish politics has quite closely followed these phases of mediatization (Herkman 2011, 25).

Applied to Finland, an example of the first phase is provided by the decline in political party memberships and the erosion of their local organizations. In this situation, the media has emerged as the principal channel via which parties and politicians address the electorate. The second phase of mediatization in Finland is represented by the declining number of party-affiliated newspapers, a trend that started after World War II and that has continued to accelerate ever since as, under mounting pressures of commercialism, they have had to declare themselves politically non-aligned. Alongside the state-owned public service broadcaster, a commercially funded television channel was launched in 1957. Since the early 1990s, there have been several commercial radio and television channels as well as Internet websites (Kunelius et al. 2009, 64).

Third-phase changes are represented by the reassessment of the newsworthiness threshold: whether or not a given issue moves onto the public agenda no longer depends so much on its societal weight and relevance, but increasingly on its emotiveness and salesworthiness. Increasingly, political news is reported via individuals and their mutual relationships (personification of politics). The fourth phase, then, comes down to the very core of media power: do politicians adapt their public messages according to the media logic, or does the media logic actually begin to determine the political decision-making agenda (Ibid.). It is an instance of the former when politicians convey their message in short and simple sound bites and when they release the message just in time for the evening news. It is an instance of the latter when the media not only react to what politicians are doing, but when they are able to push an issue onto the political agenda in such a way that politicians have to respond and that the issue moves into the decision-making process.

The mediatization of politics needs to be seen as a two-way process so that when politics adapts to the media logic, it not only adopts the media's operating logic, but also seeks to pursue its own logic through the media. The personification of politics, therefore, is not just about the media exercising an influence on politics, but also about politicians taking advantage of the media in an attempt to score political points and to increase their influence, for instance by opening their private life to the media in order to project a softer public profile and to craft an image of an ordinary person. Taking advantage of the media has always been part and parcel of the political logic, rather than a case of the media "colonizing" politics in a one-way process (Kunelius et al. 2009, 73). The media and politics have long enjoyed a symbiotic relationship: politicians need the media in order to reach the electorate, and the media need politicians in order to get good stories (Asp 1986).

In Finland, one indication of the growing influence of the media was the shift in political journalism in the late 1970s and early 1980s which saw the mass media adopt a more critical stance to politics and politicians. In the United States, this same change happened much earlier in connection with the Vietnam war and the Watergate scandal (Aula 1991). More recently, in the 2000s, the focus of independent investigative journalism has turned to individual decision-makers' suspected or actual financial abuses and moral indiscretions. The increasing number of political scandals receiving media attention serves to indicate, firstly, the increasing transparency of the political system; and secondly, the media's commitment to perform, to some extent at least, a political watchdog role (Herkman 2011, 57–58).

The media impact other institutions of the political system in many ways. Firstly, many actors believe that the exposure provided by the media has strengthened their power potential: any serious coverage provided by major news broadcasters and other national media is bound to strengthen their bargaining position in the networks of power. Secondly, the significance of mediatization and journalism is made visible through its rejection. The tendency of decision-makers to keep a proper distance to the media speaks volumes of the influence of the media. Actors constantly have access to publicity and can make use of that publicity to attempt to momentarily increase their influence, although leaking confidential information to the media may also detract from their influence. Thirdly, the influence of the media is seen in the tendency of decision-makers to assess one another's freedom of movement and bargaining position in relation to the public commitments they have made (Kunelius et al. 2009, 459–60).

However, the daily media agenda seems to have little impact on strategic, long-term policy issues and decision-making in society. In these issues the initiative usually comes from the interested parties themselves, who will also negotiate and work together to find a solution. The media covers these issues as well, and can deepen the contrasts between the parties concerned, but the influence of the media is not so much on initiatives and solutions as on the scoring of political points. In other words, it is fair to say that the media is to some extent involved in setting the public political agenda, but its ability to influence the actual decision-making process is much more limited (Ibid., 450, 456). For the most part, then, it is still media publicity that follows politics rather than the other way round (Herkman 2011, 56).

The research evidence is very much at variance with the strongest arguments regarding the mediatization of politics (Ibid., 27). Despite all the noise that is being made, mediatization is not making very much headway, and certainly not penetrating the core of elite power. The elites' bargaining and decision-making processes remain largely unaffected. The influence of the media has been attenuated by the coherence of the Finnish power elite and its traditionally close networks of preparation and decision-making. In its core, the power of networks and elites has been fairly resistant to the media and its influences. However, as commercialization and an increasingly critical journalism have combined to create mounting media pressure, both decision-makers, the officials preparing decisions, and interests groups have sought to protect themselves from this pressure by means of networking. Within their networks, they have been able to work out how to best move forward given the existing facts and circumstances, defending their common interests in a long-term view. One of the most important locuses of networked decision-making at the moment is the non-public negotiations that are conducted after parliamentary elections among major political parties to forge out a government program for the electoral term ahead. Once the major policy directions have been laid out in the government program, all that remains for politicians to do in the glare of media publicity is to try and score some extra political points and moral bonuses in the eyes of the electorate (Kunelius et al. 2009, 448–49, 459–60). However, it is possible that the erosion of elite coherence since the early 1990s has contributed to strengthen the power of the media: elite interaction networks have become more fragmented and less unanimous in their attitudes (Ruostetsaari 2006).

As yet there are no conclusive results on the impacts of the Internet on politics, although this may change in the 2010s with the growing influence of social media. Already, the growth of the Internet and electronic communications has had the effect of reducing newspaper circulation. Internet discussion forums serve as digital "letters to the editor" sections that are closely followed up by journalists in traditional media scouring for news stories. So significant has been the rise in popularity of social media that the gatekeeper role of traditional media between politics and the citizenry has already been dwindling: politicians can now post their own articles in social media and so address the electorate directly, without any editorial interference (e.g., Herkman 2011). Timo Soini (2014, 23), chairman of the True Finns, has described how his party has benefited from social media platforms: ". . . certain opinions would never have found their way into mainstream media such as *Helsingin Sanomat* or the Finnish Broadcasting Company's channels. But as soon as you made a comment on the web that was considered a bit out of order, the media started their onslaught—and that brought you publicity and readers."

In short then, the nature of media power has been changing with the ongoing evolution of the media landscape, in which social media have increasingly wrested power from traditional media and hired journalists. As the staff resources available to traditional media have continued to dwindle with the declining number of paying customers, these media have turned to faster-paced online journalism in search of new readers and viewers, which has eroded the credibility of the whole media field. Journalists have ever less time to be in direct contact with their sources (Pentikäinen 2014, 280–84).

Research supports the view that at its best, the Internet is an important source of political information and increases citizens' knowledge and understanding of politics. This, of course, is particularly important for young people who it is thought are more likely to take an interest in politics through the Internet than through traditional media. According to the most critical views, the Internet and social media may even widen the gulf between the political elite and the citizenry and, on the other hand, between rich people and poor people, as search engines, community website administrators, operators, and the technically most adept individuals have increasing influence in the online environment (Herkman 2011, 157).

The research literature lends support to the power elite's and the citizenry's assessment that the influence of the mass media—television, radio, and the print press—is waning. The media has limited power to set the political agenda, and politicians are not at the mercy of the media, despite its increasing importance as a forum of communication. The influence of traditional media has been undermined by the growing number of mass media, declining circulations, and above all the phenomenal rise of social media and the Internet from the 2000s onwards.

ELITE CIRCULATION

Elite of Elites: Accumulation of Positions

One major area of interest for elite research has been the concentration of power. For the most part, the concern has been to establish to what extent power is concentrated in the hands of elites. Although the mass, which in classical elite theories is constructed as the opposite of elites, is usually described as lacking power, several elite theorists have distinguished between various levels or strata of power within the elite in order to highlight the differences in elite members' amount and type of power (Parry 1969, 33). As citizens today can participate and exert influence in society in a completely different way from citizens in the late nineteenth and early twentieth century when elite theorists made their observations, it is clearly important to avoid a black and white view of power structures and to suggest that some people have power and others don't. Earlier in chapter 2, in connection with a description of the theoretical framework of this study, we suggested that the power structure in society can be visualized as a dartboard in which the core of power—the bulls-eye—is surrounded by progressively weaker rings of influence. It is equally important not to view the elite as homogeneous, to assume that all elites have equal amounts of power.

The following looks more closely at the inner core of power, the elite of elites, to explore the accumulation of elite positions to the same people. This may take place, firstly, within the same elite group. For example, a person who belongs to the political elite has two elite positions if this person is chair of a parliamentary committee and chair of a political party. Secondly, a person may hold influential positions in more than one elite groups, when for instance a person belonging to the political elite serves as chair of a major NGO. The analyses presented below are not based on data from the postal surveys, but they include all people counted as elites (table 3.1.).

Table 5.14 illustrates the accumulation of elite positions over the whole research period from 1991 to 2011. In these past two decades there has not been extensive accumulation, as just 187 persons have held three elite positions or more. The accumulation of elite positions is far and away most common in the business elite, which is explained by the fact that CEOs of major corporations often are chairing the boards of other companies and business and industry associations. The second highest rate of accumulation is found for the political elite: members of this elite group may occupy multiple elite positions if they are serving simultaneously as cabinet minister, party chair, and chair of an NGO. The accumulation of elite positions is marginal and lowest of all in the mass media and cultural elites. Even though the number of elite positions has increased since the early 1990s, their accumulation to the same individuals has decreased. Compared with 1991 when 8.1 percent of elite members held 3–7 elite positions, this figure fell to 7.4 percent in 2001 and further to 7.0 percent in 2011.

The largest number of elite positions held by one individual in 1991–2011 was seven. This record was shared by three persons: Ilkka Kanerva, Jaakko Lassila, and Jorma Ollila. Rising to the elite ranks in the early 1990s, Kanerva is a long-standing member of Parliament for the conservative National Coalition Party (since 1975) and a long-serving cabinet minister (1990–1995 and 2007–2008). Jaakko Lassila, who died in 2003, was CEO of a major commercial bank (Kansallis-Osake-Pankki) in 1983–1991. Jorma Ollila rose to the elite in 2001 when he was appointed to the board of Nokia and was in charge of the company's mobile phone operations. Later, he served as Nokia CEO (1992–1999), president and CEO (1999–2006), and chairman of the board of directors (1999–2012), and as chairman of the Shell board of directors (2006–2015). Jaakko Lassila, however, stands a head taller than other elites of elites, and no one since has come even close to holding as many different positions of power in different sectors of society. Lassila's seven elite positions were in the same year (1991), whereas Ollila's positions span one decade (2001–2011) and Kanerva's two (1991–2011).

Four persons held six elite positions in 1991–2011: Georg Ehrnrooth, Heikki Haavisto, Antti Tanskanen, and Björn Wahlroos. When they rose to the ranks of the elite in 1991, Ehrnrooth was CEO of the engineering company Metra, Haavisto chaired the Central Union of Agricultural Producers and Forest Owners, and Tanskanen was president of the Academy of Finland, later on CEO of the OP banking group and chairman of the board at the University of Helsinki. Wahlroos rose to the elite in 2001 when he served as CEO of the Sampo Bank. These occupants of 6–7 elite positions belong without doubt to the power elite, since they have all held positions in more than one elite group. According to Janne Virkkunen (2013, 125–26), former senior editor-in-chief of *Helsingin Sanomat*, "the

Table 5.14. Accumulation of Elite Positions by Original Position in 1991–2011

Number of Elite Positions	Political Elite	Administrative Elite	Business Elite	Organizational Elite	Mass Media Elite	Scientific Elite	Cultural Elite	Power Elite Total
3	25	24	33	11	4	23	6	126
4	13	4	16	3	0	3	0	39
5	5	1	6	1	0	2	0	15
6	0	0	2	1	0	1	0	4
7	1	0	2	0	0	0	0	3
Total	44	29	59	16	4	29	6	187

role of senior editor-in-chief includes meeting important people and to hear out their views about what's happening in the world. . . . This was how I approached the job when I set about distancing the newspaper from corporations. . . . Two thinkers from the business world stood out from the crowd, Björn Wahlroos and Jorma Ollila. They were internationally well networked and were well informed about what was going on around the world and in Finland. I was in Björn's lunch circle and we met regularly a couple of times a year."

Among women, the largest number of elite positions in 1991–2011 was occupied by two female MPs, Maria-Kaisa Aula (Centre Party) and Tarja Filatov (Social Democrats), both of them holding five elite positions. Filatov, though, rose to the ranks of the power elite in 1991 in her capacity as chair of the Social Democratic Youths. Three women have held four elite positions: MPs Tarja Halonen (Social Democrats, minister of justice 1990–1991, minister of foreign affairs 1995–1999, and president of the republic 2000–2012) and Hannele Pokka (Centre Party, MP 1979–1994, minister of justice 1991–1994, permanent secretary of the Ministry of the Environment 2008–), as well as lawyer Pauliina Haijanen. Haijanen rose to the elite in 2001 as member of the EU's Council of Regions and as chair of the supervisory board of insurance company Lähivakuutus.

Retention of Elite Positions

Retaining and losing elite positions has been a central concern for many classical elite theorists, including Mosca and Pareto. Their theories have often been remarked upon, but rarely empirically tested. For example, Pareto's theory of elite circulation, which laid the foundation for his reputation as a social scientist, has been widely misunderstood, Suleiman maintains. He says that elite circulation does not refer to the way in which elites "circulate" via different leading positions to different sectors of society (i.e., interlocking directorates), but to the way in which elites are capable of transforming themselves in a way that ultimately ensures their remaining in power (Suleiman 1978, 5). For the present purposes, however, elite circulation is understood in broader terms as comprising both the retention and loss of elite positions and the mobility of individuals between different elite groups.

In order to assess the retention of elite positions in Finland, we need first of all to consider the age of elite members. In 1991, the average age of the Finnish power elite was 51 years; in 2001 it was 54 years; and in 2011, 55 years. Before the 2005 pension reform, when retirement age was set at 63–68 years, the general retirement age was 65 years. However in the administrative elite, who are civil servants, retirement age was 63 years, whereas MPs, who account for the majority of the political elite, still have no compulsory retirement age. In the business elite, CEOs of major corporations have mostly retired at age 60, although CEO contracts signed in recent years have pushed up retirement age close to the lower end of the official age range (63 years). Many major corporations have an upper age limit for elected officials so that persons over 70, for instance, are not eligible to the boards of directors.

Table 5.15. Retention of Elite Positions in 1991–2011 by Persons

Elite Group	Has Retained Original Elite Position	Has Retained Elite Position in Any Elite Group
Political elite	12	18
Administrative elite	11	15
Business elite	7	9
Organizational elite	2	6
Mass media elite	2	3
Scientific elite	9	12
Cultural elite	5	5
Total	48	68

It is clear from the average age of elites and retirement rules that most elite members cannot retain their positions for decades. Nonetheless, 48 persons have retained their original elite position throughout the research period from 1991 to 2011 (table 5.15). This is the case if, for instance, a person who in 1991 belonged to the political elite and was in the same elite group also in 2001 and 2011. However, during their career it is possible for individuals to move from one elite group to another, or to acquire a new elite position alongside their existing one from another elite group. An example of the latter instance is when a CEO is appointed as chair of a business association. In all, 68 persons have retained their positions in some elite group throughout the research period. As the total number of elite positions in each year of study was more than one thousand, this can be considered quite a low figure for the retention of elite positions over two decades. In other words, elite turnover since the 1990s has been fairly high.

The retention of one's original or any elite position has been most common in the political and administrative elites. Retaining one's *original* elite position has been hardest and rarest in the organizational and the mass media elites. Retaining *any* elite position has been marginal and most difficult for the mass media and the cultural elites. The high retention of administrative elite positions is explained by the permanence of posts in central and local government. Even though some leading positions in central government and mayorships in major cities are now fixed term, this has not really increased the risk of losing these positions upon expiration of the term of office.

The higher retention of positions among the political elite is unexpected in that the continuity of the role of member of Parliament is dependent on re-election by voters once every four years. The average parliamentary experience and length of parliamentary career have remained quite constant since World War II: the average length of a parliamentary career has been 2.95 electoral terms. However, the figures differ widely among individual MPs: while one-quarter of all MPs have served no more than one term in parliament, one-sixth have served two or three full terms. Parliamentary experience, in turn, increases the likelihood of selection to leadership positions in the parliamentary group and parliamentary committees, and the likelihood of appointment as cabinet minister. The political elite consists predominantly of this group of MPs, so its constancy is explained by the fact that parliamentary experience increases the likelihood of re-election (Forsten 2014, 88–89; Ruostetsaari 2000).

According to Best and Higley (2014b, 176), increased elite turnover during the crisis since 2008 involved both changes and continuities. Governing elites in all EU member states except Austria, Germany, and Poland were ousted or significantly reconfigured in crisis conditions. Amid near economic meltdown in the US, control of the White House and Congress shifted from Republicans to Democrats in November and then, as the crisis ground on, back to Republican control of the House and complete control of 24 state governments two years later, with elections in 2012 not altering the pattern of divided power in Washington but tightening Republican control of state governments. However, both in the US and Europe, the turnover of the political elite consisted mainly of established parties or party coalitions changing places. There was no instance of an entire political elite, or even a large part of one, being decimated, although significant inroads occurred in Greece and Italy.

The crisis was, however, a breeding ground for relatively large turnover among individual political elite members. After the 2010 elections in the US and UK, newcomers comprised a fifth of Congress and Parliament. In the US, 65 Republican newcomers in the House of Representatives joined with 20 re-elected fiscal conservatives to form the "tea party" faction, which insisted that large cuts in government spending and a total halt to government borrowing would solve all economic and social ills. In the UK, most of the 123 newcomers, the bulk of them Conservatives, insisted that an austerity program and a pulling away from the EU would put things right. In eurozone countries, populist and usually anti-EU parties gained substantial voter support and parliamentary seats: True Finns in Finland, Syriza and Golden Dawn in Greece, the Five Star Movement in Italy, Jobbik in Hungary, the Freedom Party in the Netherlands, the UK Independence Party, the National Front in France, and Catalan separatists in Spain (Ibid.).

In Finland, too, crises have contributed to increase MP turnover. In the first parliamentary election after the great recession in 1995 and the first elections after the international financial crisis and the eurozone debt crisis in 2011, the share of newcomers was exceptionally high, even by international comparison (1995: 36.0 percent; 2011: 37.5 percent). Since World War II, higher newcomer rates have only been recorded on two occasions: in the first elections after the war in 1945 (46.0 percent), and in the 1970 "protest" elections at the height of the flight from rural areas (42.0 percent). On the other hand, MP turnover was exceptionally low (25.0 percent) in the 2003 parliamentary election, at a time of robust economic growth (Forsten 2014, 87; Ruostetsaari 2000, 71).

In many countries the financial crisis also increased turnover among the business elite. Casualties in the top echelons of banks, financial firms, and major corporations were heavy. For instance, of the 15 most senior executives in JPMorgan Chase in 2008, only three remained by April 2013, and one of them had been demoted. Citibank, Bank of America, RBS, JSBC, Deutsche Bank, and most other transnational banks had new leaders who scaled back their banks' international operations. When nationalizing, partly nationalizing, or otherwise bailing out banks and corporations, governments usually insisted on new chief executive and chief financial officers. Elite and wider personnel rosters bearing scant resemblance to pre-crisis rosters resulted from crisis-induced mergers of weakened companies with stronger ones, forced privatizations of government-owned enterprises, and selling parts of companies in order to re-capitalize. From 2008 to 2012, there were 240,000 layoffs, many of them senior, on Wall Street, and there were thousands of layoffs among banks and firms in London. All in all, between 2008–2012, a quarter of chief executive officers in 2,500 European and US business companies lost their positions (Best and Higley 2014b, 176–77). According to a survey by Booz and Company comprising 2,500 of the world's largest companies, CEO turnover has increased in the 2000s and the average career length has shortened from 8.1 to 6.3 years (*Talouselämä*, 25 Aug. 2014).

In Finland, it is harder for the business elite to retain their positions than it is for members of the political, administrative, and scientific elites. A study of 38 Finnish listed companies by Stanton Chase found that in the 1990s, on average four or five companies a year would let their CEO go and hire a new one. The CEO turnover rate has since then increased, and today six or seven companies hire a new CEO each year. In 2011, seven listed companies changed their CEO (*Helsingin Sanomat*, 13 Mar. 2014). However, the international financial crisis or the eurozone debt crisis does not account for all CEO changeovers in the 2000s, but the reasons may lie more generally in increased turbulence in the business environment and in the company owners' increased expectations of business performance.

Mobility between Elites

One area of interest in elite research has been the mobility of individuals, during their career, from one sector of society to another. In France, this phenomenon is described as *pantouflage*; in the United States, the concept of *spoils system* is used. It's also known in other countries. For example, a minister of finance may become a banker or vice versa; and a trade union leader may become a cabinet minister. This kind of mobility reflects the horizontal integration among elites: it is justified to assume that leaders moving from one sector to another share at least some values and ideologies in common, although this does not necessarily mean that the ruling class forms a closed system (Schijf 2013, 31).

The mobility of individuals between different elite groups is described in tables 5.16 and 5.17. The examination comprises all persons classified as elites (table 3.1), not only those who responded to the surveys. "Exit" refers to those individuals who for whatever reason have exited the elite. They may have lost their elite position, they may have been relegated to a lower position in some other organization, or they may have retired or died. The percentages shown in the tables are based on all elite positions, not on the number of people occupying those positions. For instance, table

Table 5.16. Circulation between Elite Groups in 1991–2001 (%)

Original Elite Group	Political	Administrative	Business	Organizational	Mass Media	Scientific	Cultural	Exit	N 1991
Political	25	3	3	6	0	0	0	63	144
Administrative	1	26	3	2	0	1	0	66	213
Business	1	3	19	7	0	4	0	66	199
Organizational	1	5	6	15	0	1	1	72	294
Mass media	1	0	1	1	26	0	1	71	120
Scientific	0	2	1	5	0	22	0	70	127
Cultural	0	0	1	1	0	0	18	80	114

Destination Elite Group

Table 5.17. Circulation between Elite Groups in 2001–2011 (%)

Original Elite Group	Destination Elite Group								
	Political	Administrative	Business	Organizational	Mass Media	Scientific	Cultural	Exit	N 2001
Political	21	3	6	7	1	1	1	62	194
Administrative	1	23	0	1	0	2	0	72	268
Business	1	1	18	3	0	4	1	72	233
Organizational	2	4	4	10	0	4	0	76	209
Mass media	0	0	0	1	19	0	1	79	135
Scientific	0	5	1	1	0	28	0	66	129
Cultural	0	0	1	0	0	0	13	86	117

5.16. shows that in 1991–2001, 25 percent of the political elite retained their position in this same elite groups, 3 percent moved into a position in the administrative elite, 3 percent into the business elite, and 6 percent into the organizational elite, while 63 percent left the elite.

A comparison of the two research periods (1991–2001 and 2001–2011) shows, firstly, that the *permanency of elite positions* has decreased. Exit from elite positions has increased significantly in all groups except the political and scientific elites, where it has decreased. As was discussed earlier, the retention of original elite positions has been easiest in the political elite. Most members of the scientific elite, then, are tenured professors, which explains the high degree of permanency in this group. In both periods the political elite has been most secure group in the sense that the numbers exiting the elite structure have been clearly lower than in other groups (63 percent in 1991–2001; 62 percent in 2001–2011). The least secure elite positions, then, have been those in the cultural elite, where 80 percent in 1991–2001 and 86 percent in 2001–2011 left the elite structure. However, the sharpest increase in the exit rate is recorded for the mass media elite.

In 1991–2001, members of the administrative and the mass media elites have remained within their own groups most often, and members of the organizational elite least often. In 2001–2011, the retention of one's position was clearly highest in the scientific elite and lowest in the organizational elite. From the former to the latter period, exiting one's group increased in all except the scientific elite, where the retention of one's position clearly increased. Retaining a position in one's original elite group decreased most in the mass media elite and least in the business elite.

Overall, mobility between elite groups has been very limited: only few people have moved from one elite group to another. In 1991–2001, mobility was highest from the business elite: 15 percent of the business elite moved to another elite group or secured an elite position in another elite group and at once retained their original elite position. In practice, 1 percent of the business elite gained an elite position in the political elite, 3 percent in the administrative elite, 4 percent in the scientific elite, and 7 percent in the organizational elite, in practice in a business and industry association. Mobility to other elites was lowest from cultural and mass media elites.

In 2001–2011, mobility to other elites was clearly highest in the political elite, with 19 percent moving to other elite groups or gaining a new elite position while retaining their original position. The political elite moved to all other elite groups, but most often to the organizational elite and the business elite. During this period, too, mobility to other elite groups was lowest from the cultural elite.

In a comparison of the two periods, *mobility into other elite groups* declined from all other groups except the political elite, from which it increased significantly (+9 percentage points). Members of the political elite have moved increasingly to the organizational and business elites.

Mobility declined most of all from the business elite (–5 percentage points). Mobility from the organizational elite to other elite groups remained unchanged.

Since the early 1990s mobility to other elites has been lowest from the cultural and mass media elites.

The increased mobility from the political elite to other elite groups can be considered a significant phenomenon, especially in view of earlier comments in the public debate that there is not enough movement of leaders from one sector of society to another—or conversely, that there is too rigorous vertical career segmentation. It has been suggested that the low level of mobility leads to a silo effect: the lack of movement across policy sectors means that knowledge and understanding of processes in other branches does not spread and that there is no effective diffusion of innovations.

One of the factors working against mobility is that the knowledge, skills, and attributes required of managers today are not necessarily the same in all policy sectors, even though business management doctrines have increasingly been applied in the public and organizational sector. Former president and CEO of a major commercial bank (Kansallis-Osake-Pankki) (1914–1934) and president of the republic (1946–1956) J. K. Paasikivi once had this comment about transferable skills: "The economist's profession is no suitable schooling for employment in government or for a politician. It dumbs down a person. My banking career was not a good school for my political career. I had to forget most of what I had learned because it would only have harmed me in my political activities" (Suomi 2013, 261). Former CEO of Nokia and chairman of the Shell board, Jorma Ollila (2013, 439) has recently made largely the same observation: "Some business managers' understanding of how society works is startlingly thin and flimsy. It seems they have no idea of the way leading politicians think, nor do they know how to talk with trade unions or their shop stewards."

It is thought that the Finnish government, too, is being hampered by the silo effect: collective collaboration among cabinet ministers is less frequent than earlier, with each minister concentrating on independently running their respective branches (e.g., Markkanen 2005). In order to break down the rigid bureaucratic separations and to increase coordination across sectoral boundaries, the government has introduced cross-sector policy programs in the 2000s. The programs have since been abandoned following the National Audit Office's (2010) assessment that they failed to achieve their original purpose of serving as strategic planning tools. Likewise, plans to rotate senior civil servants between ministries have come to nothing (Tiihonen 2009).

Career mobility between different policy sectors has long been fairly low in Finland. Careers are usually built in one and the same sector. The Finnish model of career mobility has therefore differed quite sharply from the American spoils-system, where the president, upon being appointed, handpicks people from politics, administration, business companies, organizations, and foundations to fill the highest political and administrative positions. When their appointments expire, these people often return to their original organizations (e.g., van Waarden 1992, 32–41). In the United States, cross-sectoral mobility is quite common. According to Lindsay (2014, 50), out of 51 people in his study who had two distinct positions senior enough to qualify for the US elite (i.e., a CEO of a Fortune 1000 company or its analog in government and the nonprofit world), 86 percent shifted not only companies, but between completely different sectors. "The most gifted leaders master the ability to organize and lead—talents and abilities that are moldable, even when moving from business to government or government to nonprofit life."

The Finnish mobility pattern has differed from its American counterpart in that there has been only little movement from the private sector to politics, and vice versa. The most famous movers to Parliament have included former CEO of shipbuilders Masa-Yards, Martin Saarikangas; former CEO of the retailing cooperative organization SOK, Jere Lahti; owner and managing director of newspaper publishers Suomen Lehtiyhtymä and market research company Taloustutkimus, Eero Lehti; and most recently, chair of the Centre Party, Juha Sipilä. Before his election to Parliament in 2011 and appointment as chair of the party in 2012, Sipilä owned an ICT company and was a venture investor.

Among the most famous movers from politics to business are Christoffer Taxell, chair of the Swedish People's Party (1985–1990) and long-standing member of Parliament (1975–1991) and cabinet minister (1979–1990), who took over as CEO of the industrial engineering company Partek (1990–2002); and member of Parliament for the conservative National Coalition Party (1983–1996) and Minister of Finance (1991–1996) Iiro Viinanen, who was appointed as CEO of insurance giant Pohjola (1996–2000). In addition, there has been some movement from the highest echelons of politics to the organizational elite: Matti Vanhanen, former Centre Party prime minister (2003–2010), took over as managing director of the Finnish Family Firms Associations in 2010. Jyri Häkämies, the National Coalition Party MP who served as minister of employment and the economy (2007–2012), became CEO of the Confederation of Finnish Industries EK in 2012. Furthermore, several ministerial special assistants and political permanent secretaries have moved to work for interest groups and professional lobbying firms. This has raised some concerns about risks of incompetency due to the likelihood of bias and disclosure of insider ministry information to lobbyists—which in turn has prompted calls for a quarantine period before civil servants are allowed to move from the public sector to a private firm or organization in the same branch.

Examples of the relatively low level of mobility between administration and business are provided by Ministry of Trade and Industry permanent secretary (1992–1998) Matti Vuoria, who was appointed full-time chairman of the board (1998–2003) of Fortum that was created through the merger of the state-owned energy companies Imatran Voima and Neste, and subsequently as CEO of earnings-related pension company Varma (2004–2014). Former CEO of insurers Pohjola (2001–2005) and construction company SRV (2006–2009), Eero Heliövaara, was in turn appointed director-general of the Ownership Steering Department under the Prime's Minister's Office in 2013.

6

Discussion

This study set out to explore the changes occurring at the highest levels of power in Finnish society from the early 1990s to the present day—a period that has seen the great recession of the early 1990s, Finland's accession to the European Union, and the international financial crisis and the eurozone debt crisis in the 2000s. The main focus has been on how the elite structure in Finland has changed in terms of vertical social mobility or openness, on the one hand, and horizontal mobility or coherence, on the other. With regard to vertical social mobility, the interest has focused on changes in elites' social background and other factors promoting their recruitment into elite positions. As for horizontal mobility, our key areas of interest have been elites' channels of contact with other influential groups in society, networking with various societal institutions, the attitudinal unanimity within various elites and between the elites and the citizenry, mobility between different elite groups, the accumulation of power positions, and the retention and loss of elite positions.

The following sums up the main results of the study by way of a backdrop to the discussion of how the Finnish elite structure has changed since the early 1990s. The findings are also compared with previous international studies, especially Scandinavian elite studies. Finally, we consider what the results tell us about the state of democracy in Finland.

CHANGES IN THE OPENNESS OF THE ELITE STRUCTURE

Women's share of elite positions has increased from 12 percent to 26 percent in the past two decades. There are marked group differences, however. In 2011, women accounted for 43 percent of the political elite, but for just 6 percent of the business elite. The share of women in the business elite has hardly increased at all since the early 1990s. In the power elite as a whole, the proportion of women who thought their gender had hampered their career advancement has declined significantly since 1991, but since 2001 women's experiences of the impact of their gender have taken a turn for the worse. However, an increasing proportion of both men and women felt that gender had had no effect on their career progress. Although gender may influence career advancement, there are many other factors that have a much greater impact.

Regional mobility in elite recruitment has increased since the early 1990s. The proportion of elites who lived in southern Finland (where most governmental institutions, enterprises, and NGOs are headquartered) in their youth was 65 percent in 1991, 67 percent in 2001, but just 60 percent in 2011. At the same time, there has been a slight increase in the rate of recruitment into elites from central and northern Finland. Patterns of regional mobility have changed most significantly in the political elite: until the early 2000s the political elite had a higher proportion of members recruited from northern Finland, but in the early 2010s this proportion was lower than in other elite groups.

There are marked income disparities not only between the power elite and the citizenry, but also between elite groups. Incomes are lowest in the cultural elite and highest in the business elite, whose capital gains and bonuses have pushed them into a completely different earnings bracket. In the cultural elite, incomes have become more polarized, and there are increasing numbers of both low-income and high-income earners.

High educational capital is a *de facto* prerequisite for recruitment into the elite. The proportion of elite members with a university degree increased from 82 percent in 1991 to 88 percent in 2011. Although the educational level has risen in the general population, too, the power elite is still far more educated. However, rather than widening, the gap between the power elite and the citizenry has narrowed. As both the general population and the power elite have become more highly educated, the relative benefit of education to elite recruitment has decreased since the early 1990s: ascendancy into the elite now requires not only academic qualifications, but also other resources and attributes. In fact, education is relatively less important to elite recruitment than earlier when compared with other career-advancing factors. The proportion of elite members mentioning education as a career-advancing factor has declined from 1991 to 2011, whereas tolerance of pressures and conflicts has gained increasing importance. This is possibly explained by increasing pressures and turbulence in the workplace.

There is a clear correlation between elites' and their parents' educational level: intergenerational educational inheritance is apparent at both population and elite level. However, the general trend of declining educational inheritance found in studies focusing on the general population applies to elites as well. At elite level, though, in contrast to the general population, education is more strongly inherited on the father's than the mother's side, and the inheritance effect has decreased more on the mother's than the father's side.

In more general terms, too, cultural capital has had a significant impact on elite re-cruitment. In 1991 three-fifths, but since 2001 two-thirds of elite members thought that their family background had influenced their career choice. In 2011, the elites' single most important career-advancing factor was a supportive attitude to educa-tion in their childhood home. This factor has gained increasing importance since the early 1990s. Ever fewer elite members feel—or admit—that career inheritance and having the right contacts has contributed to their career advancement.

The proportion of elite members recruited from the highest social stratum has remained highly stable since the early 1990s. However, the single largest social stra-tum in the Finnish power elite in 1991–2011 was the middle class (upper and lower functionaries), even though its share has declined since the early 1990s. Lower social strata have accounted for a growing share of the power elite: the share of offspring of blue-collar workers has increased since the early 1990s, whereas the share of de-scendants of farmers was the same in 1991 and 2011, but slightly higher in 2001. Adding together the shares of both these groups, it is apparent that the Finnish elite structure has opened up to lower social strata since the early 1990s. In other words, there has been generational mobility at elite level, meaning that the power elite has been drawn from a wider social spectrum. There has been no "glass ceiling" to elite recruitment that would have ruled out upward mobility from the lowest strata to the very highest echelons of society.

Since the early 2000s, however, the opening up of the political elite to recruitment from lower social strata has grounded to a halt, and this elite group has become de-cidedly more middle class. Recruitment from working-class backgrounds has slightly increased, while recruitment from farming backgrounds has decreased. This suggests that politics has become a less important avenue of upward social mobility, and that social mobility at elite level is increasingly independent of social background.

In the early 2010s, the elite group showing the greatest openness to recruitment from lower social strata has been the business elite. This is due to the significant increase since the early 2000s in the proportion of elite members with an agrarian background at the expense of the middle class. On the other hand, the business elite has been the least open to recruitment from a working-class background. The business elite has the second highest share (after the cultural elite) of people com-ing from the highest social stratum, although this share has slightly fallen since the early 1990s. The cultural elite has been more upper-class than other elite groups ever since the early 1990s, and the most closed elite group to recruitment from the lowest social strata.

Although a significant proportion of the power elite come from the highest social strata, the Finnish power elite is distinctly upper middle class in terms of its subjective class identification. The share of those identifying with the upper class has dropped from 13 percent to 5 percent in 2011, although this is still a much higher figure than in the whole population. In the general population hardly anyone identifies with the upper class. Identifying with the upper class does not conform to politically correct thinking among either elites or the citizenry.

The power elite come from fairly active backgrounds when looking at their parents' involvement in society. Active involvement in society is mainly inherited from the father's side, as mothers have held only few elected offices. However, the power elite's cultural capital has decreased since the early 1990s as their parents have been involved less often than before in most associations and public bodies. Based on the elective offices held by elite members' parents, it can be concluded that only a marginal proportion of parents have belonged to the elite.

Overall, the changes that have taken place in elite recruitment suggest that the Finnish elite structure has moved toward increased openness since the early 1990s. Recruitment into elites has been possible from very different family and socioeconomic backgrounds, even though cultural capital is still an important factor promoting recruitment. There is very little "inbreeding" in the reproduction of the Finnish power elite: descendants of former elite members account for a marginal proportion of new recruits. On the contrary, the Finnish recruitment pattern is best described as a *renvoyer l'ascenseur*: people rising to the ranks of the elite are expected by default to send the elevator back down again so that others from a similar background can in turn ascend to the elite.

CHANGES IN THE COHERENCE OF THE ELITE STRUCTURE

Finnish elites' lifestyles were studied here on the basis of their past and present leisure interests. A comparison of the 1991, 2001, and 2011 elites showed an increase in leisure activity during youth. The biggest relative increases were found for spending time at home and with family and friends and for involvement in associations. These changes reflect both a more privatized way of life and at once a stronger sense of community. The more active involvement of the power elite in associations and their increased interest in societal and political issues suggests they have worked from an ever younger age to build up the skills they will need later on in life. Elite groups have drifted further apart in their youth leisure pursuits, indicating a trend of increasing habitus diversification. In other words, a unified lifestyle is a less important prerequisite for recruitment into the power elite than before.

Golf, sailing, and (in earlier years) tennis are leisure pursuits that have something of an elitist aura about them. However, the Finnish power elite do not take part in these pursuits actively. The main difference between the power elite's and the general population's leisure pursuits is that the elite participate far less often in interests favored by the masses. However, elites enjoy the traditional Finnish hobby of hunting just as often as the rest of the population. Among elites, hunting has been gaining in popularity, but in the general population its popularity has waned somewhat.

As Finnish elites do not readily identify with the upper class and as they engage in rather "ordinary" leisure pursuits, it seems fair to suggest that they have internalized the conspicuous modesty ideal that is integral to Nordic political culture: it is not appropriate to give the impression that you are wealthy and successful (Daloz 2007,

181; 2010, 61). The principles of lifestyle modesty are most rigorously followed by the political elite, who depend directly on the support of ordinary citizens, that is, the electorate. However, the avoidance of ostentation is such an integral part of Finnish culture in general that other elite groups have not remained immune, either. But the winds of change are picking up. Since the early 1990s, the business elite's earnings have climbed far beyond the reach of other elites, never mind ordinary citizens, and this is now inevitably reflected in their lifestyle.

Personal contacts play a crucial part in wielding power in Finnish society. These contacts are created and maintained not only in the context of leisure pursuits, but also in various informal contact groups. While elite involvement in elective positions has decreased since the early 1990s in virtually all kinds of associations, it has increased in old boy types of networks such as Rotaries, Lions, and Freemasons. In the 2010s, personal contacts remain the most important form of influence when seeking to promote the goals of one's organization, despite the growth of electronic communications and social media.

Ever since the early 1990s, the power elite's most important channel of communication in its interaction with various institutions has been the mass media. On the other hand, the centrality of banks has decreased most in the power elite's interaction networks. Overall, the Finnish power elite's interaction network has been eroded since the early 1990s: there are fewer institutions than before with which the power elite have very close interplay. Both sending information and receiving information, key aspects of the exercise of influence, have declined in importance, while the role of more general information exchange and social interaction between elites and all societal institutions has continued to grow. The conclusion that can be drawn from these changes is that not only the density of interaction, but also the form of the elite interaction network has become increasingly fragmented and dispersed since the early 1990s. In other words, the interaction network that is made up of elite members' contacts with various institutions, which are run by elites themselves, does not tie elites to one another as closely as before.

Elites' contacts and interaction are not confined to Finland, of course. It would be reasonable to expect that foreign contacts have increased in the wake of European integration and globalization. However, the picture that emerges of the globalization of elites is somewhat contradictory. Since 1991, globalization has increased with respect to working abroad; become polarized with respect to studying abroad (both the proportions of those with no foreign studies and those studying abroad for extended periods have grown); but decreased with respect to personal contacts.

Attitudinal unanimity between elite groups and changes in the degree of unanimity were measured using responses to questions concerning various dimensions of social conflict, attitudes, and the distribution of influence in society. Different indicators yielded somewhat different, even contradictory results on how elite coherence has changed since the early 1990s. As two in three of the indicators suggest that unanimity among elites has decreased, especially since the early 2000s, it appears that the elite structure has become less coherent. Nonetheless different elite groups do share interests in common and have similar ideas of how decisions about key issues in society should be made.

Four of the seven elite groups (political, administrative, organizational, and business elites) reported having the fewest interests in common with decision-makers in the cultural sector in 2011. Identification was weakest of all between the elites of business and culture. Overall, with the exception of the cultural elite, Finnish elites are quite closely integrated with decision-makers in different sectors of society, reflecting a sense of cohesiveness, an awareness that they are an integral part of the "core of power."

The cultural elite's attitudes to the normative principles of decision-making also set them apart from other elite groups. Although the power elite have high trust in expert knowledge, they nonetheless respect the principles of democracy: four in five consider it important that decisions within their own field are made by those who are responsible to the electorate, that is, politicians. However, the cultural elite attach more importance than other elite groups to the role of experts not only in the drafting of decisions, but also in final decision-making. The support for expert power does not mean that decision-making should be evidence-based, however, as the cultural elite consider research information less important than any other elite group. The same goes for the cultural elite's views on the importance of taking into account how decisions taken impact the economy and society, and its views on the opportunities of citizens to participate in decision-making. In other words, support for stealth democracy is strongest in the cultural elite. Stealth democracy supporters believe that representative democracy works more effectively if altruistic and knowledgeable politicians make all the decisions. For instance, they are firmly in favor of using more experts and business professionals in political decision-making, at the expense of politicians (Bengtsson and Mattila 2009, 307–9; see also Hibbing and Theiss-Morse 2002).

Changes in the attitudinal distance between elites and the citizenry were analyzed, firstly, using a sum variable measuring neoliberal support for the regime; and secondly, based on views on the distribution of influence in society. Both indicators point in the same direction: the power elite's and the citizenry's attitudes have converged since the early 1990s. This raises the intriguing question as to which of the two groups has moved closer to the other, the power elite or the citizenry? It is impossible to give a clear answer based on the data available in this study. It is justified to assume, however, that under the current conditions of economic crisis, citizens have understood and taken on board the calls from elites to cut public spending and to give a stronger role to the market mechanism, while elites may have wanted to fall in line with the thinking of citizens and answer the survey items in a "politically correct" way. There are, of course, still a number of issues on which the views of elites and citizens are widely separated. These issues—European integration, membership in NATO, and nuclear energy, to mention just a few—have a symbolic function: they reflect people's hopes or fears with regard to the future development of society.

Just like the power elite, the people are not a homogeneous mass. Based on the data collected for this research, different groups of the citizenry vary in their attitudinal distance from elites. For instance, support for neoliberalism is highest—and closest to the elites' views—among the young, men, people aged under 30, supporters of the Conservatives, and those who occupy leading professional positions; and lowest in the oldest age groups (over 60), among women, the supporters of the Left Alliance, and people outside the active labor force. It is misleading, therefore, to refer to one elite and to one people. This is not true to reality. It is important that this is borne in mind in subsequent studies on the gulf that separates the elite and the people as well as in the public debate on this matter.

The accumulation of elite positions has remained quite moderate. In the past two decades, no more than 187 persons have held three elite positions or more. The accumulation of elite positions is far and away most common in the business elite, which is explained by the fact that CEOs of major corporations often occupy positions on the boards of directors of other companies and business and industry associations. The accumulation of elite positions is marginal and lowest in the mass media and cultural elites. The retention of elite positions over two decades is also fairly low. In other words, elite turnover has been fairly high since the early 1990s, and exit from elite positions has increased significantly with the exception of the political and scientific elites, where it has decreased. Elite positions in the cultural elite have been the most insecure of all.

A comparison of the two research periods (1991–2001 and 2001–2011) shows that mobility between elite groups has decreased in all groups except the political elite. Finland can be described as a vertically segmented society in the sense that the business elite has been socialized and recruited from business companies, as is the case in Germany, rather than "borrowed" from the highest echelons of state administration, as is the case in France. There has also been limited elite level mobility between politics and administration in Finland, in contrast to France and Japan. Finland has been drifting toward an American mobility pattern in that mobility from the political elite has significantly increased (Dogan 2003, 9). Increasing numbers have moved from the political elite to the organizational and business elites. Since the early 1990s, movement from one elite group to another has been lowest in the cultural and mass media elites. The growth of mobility from the Finnish political elite to other elite groups can be considered significant in view of the comments made in the public debate that there is not enough movement at the leadership level from one sector of society to another, in other words, that there is too rigorous vertical segmentation of job careers. From the point of view of elite theory, however, increased mobility is not without its problems because it may lead to the formation of an increasingly monolithic power elite, which in turn may cause it to become separated even further from the people.

Based on the results of this study it seems justified to conclude, with some caution, that the elite group showing the least resistance to changes in society, most of which have been related to the economy, has been the business elite, which has opened up significantly to lower social strata. At the same time, the position of economic institutions in interaction networks within elites and in the power structure—in elite members' own assessment—has weakened at the expense of political institutions. What, exactly, do these changes in the business elite tell us about: have political decision-makers gained the upper hand of market forces, or has the business elite, empowered by a climate of market and competition rhetoric, begun to distance itself from elite consensus? The latter seems more plausible: increasingly, voices from the Finnish business elite have been suggesting that the long-standing consensual approach to collective bargaining among the social partners and to legislation more generally stands in the way of economic growth and competitiveness.

In general, the Finnish power elite has become less coherent since the early 1990s as elite lifestyles have become more diversified, as their interaction networks with various institutions have become looser, as attitudinal unanimity among elites has decreased, and elite turnover has increased. The attitudinal distance between elites and the citizenry, on the other hand, has decreased since the early 1990s.

CHANGE IN THE TYPE OF ELITE STRUCTURE

Power is not evenly distributed in any society, but it has a tendency to concentrate to those who already have more material and intellectual resources at their disposal. Material resources include economic wealth and property, while intellectual resources consist of cultural capital such as education, energy, intelligence, and motivations, and social capital such as extensive networks. All these types of resources are more or less inheritable, but it is also possible for individuals to acquire them without the "right" home background. These various resources are most typically possessed by elites.

Since power is not evenly distributed, the existence of elites is an inevitable fact in all societies, past, present, and future. This is not, in itself, a problem for democracy, provided that elites meet certain conditions. Ultimately, democracy in a society depends, firstly, on active vertical circulation or elite openness, as stressed by classical elite theorists such as Pareto and Mosca. In other words, it has to be possible for individuals from different socioeconomic backgrounds to ascend to the elite. Secondly, it depends on low horizontal elite circulation, as stressed by Mills and democratic elitism, that is, on the separateness of elites, not so much on elite competition as such. For this reason the autonomy of elites is an important precondition for democracy.

Given the apparent connection between social mobility and equal opportunity, social mobility is generally considered a measure of the openness of society. Countries with higher social mobility are generally thought to be more open societies than countries with lower social mobility. Equality of opportunity through social mobility is considered a major objective from both a justice and democracy point of view (Härkönen 2010, 52–54, 65–66).

In the terms of the elite structure typology outlined in chapter 3 (figure 3.1), an exclusive elite structure with a low degree of openness and a high degree of coherence is least compatible with the principles of democracy. The criteria of classical democracy are most closely met by a fragmented elite structure with a high degree of openness and a low degree of coherence. A fragmented elite structure offers the best opportunities for citizens to participate and influence decision-making and, in accordance with their capabilities, to move up in the social hierarchy, all the way to the highest echelons of society. In this type of elite structure, close interaction and attitudinal unanimity between elites and citizen groups ensures that the decision-making process is responsive and that the interests of citizens are taken into account. However, very intense vertical elite circulation, which causes excessive elite turnover, does not contribute to healthy democracy because it can destabilize decision-making processes and lower the experience of leaders and the attractiveness of leadership roles (see Pakulski and Körösényi 2012, 153).

Since the early 1990s, the Finnish elite structure, viewed in the terms of the elite typology, has become more open to recruitment from below, at the same time as its coherence has decreased. Overall, the Finnish elite structure has moved away from the middle ground between an exclusive and inclusive elite type toward a more fragmented structure (see Ruostetsaari 1993; 2006). From a point of view of democracy, then, this can be seen as a positive trend.

Although people in Finland are, by international comparison, quite content with the way democracy works in their country (see Norris 2011, 111), there still remain weaknesses and areas for improvement. Cultural capital inherited from the family milieu and educational inheritance remain major preconditions for recruitment into elites. Although income disparities in Finland are still lower than in many other countries, their growth is undermining the stability and legitimacy of society. Income disparities started to increase sharply in Finland from around the mid-1990s, but this trend was brought to halt by the international financial crisis and the eurozone debt crisis. When economic growth rebounds following the long drawn-out recession, income disparities will likely start to grow again. The erosion of the welfare state and increasing inequality, driven by cutbacks in central government spending under conditions of recession, are causing increasing social inequality and a growing sense of political apathy among the underprivileged.

The basic tenet of democratic elitism is that competition among elites balances out the wielding of power and prevents any single elite group from achieving a dominant position. In contrast to the situation in Sweden (SOU 1990, 44), Finland has not had two rival political blocs. Finnish consensus has been largely based on the absence of a dominant political party or bloc, and its roots go back to the wartime period when employer and employee confederations acknowledged each other as contracting partners. No political party has managed to achieve the kind of hegemonic position that the Social Democrats have enjoyed in other Nordic parliaments, and therefore all Finnish governments since the late 1970s have been broad majority coalitions that have usually involved both right-wing and left-wing parties. This parliamentary tradition has contributed to continuation of consensus in Finnish society, at the same time as political parties have converged ideologically and turned to the growing middle classes in search for new voters.

A centralized collective bargaining system developed relatively late in Finland, at the end of the 1960s, but over the following two decades an incomes policy system and incomes policy culture became integral elements of "new consensus politics." As in the other Nordic countries, "routine corporatism," which involves the routine participation of organized interests in the preparation and formulation of public policy initiatives, has been declining in Finland (Arter 2008, 163–65). This is mainly a result of the declining use of committees in public administration for the formulation of policy proposals since the 1980s.

"Peak corporatism" refers to a regularized and culturally entrenched system of macro-economic management, which involves the government working closely with peak sectoral interest groups to achieve national incomes policy settlements that are compatible with the government's overall fiscal policy objectives. This form of corporatism flourished in high-growth Denmark, Norway, and Sweden in the 1960s. By the 1970s and 1980s, it expanded to Finland on the back of an "ideology of social partnership" and in the absence of a "winner-takes-all mentality." However, as economic growth began to slow in Denmark in the 1980s and in Finland and Sweden in the early 1990s, there was increasing pressure to move away from centralized collective bargaining toward more flexible, decentralized enterprise bargaining (Ibid., 164).

In the other Nordic countries, the role of employee and employer peak confederations has been waning, which inevitably has reduced the degree of corporatism. In Finland, however, labor market confederations play a more prominent part in political decision-making than their Swedish counterparts. Indeed, tripartism is still very much alive and well in Finland, providing an avenue through which organizations representing both employers and employees can participate in the drafting and even decision-making of major social undertakings. As recently as 2013, the government reached a centralized incomes policy agreement with peak organizations of employers and employees. An inverted illustration of the centralized nature of Finnish incomes policy is provided by the fact that employer organizations are willing to shift the focus of incomes policy-making from centralized collective wage bargaining toward decentralized bargaining at the enterprise level. Sometimes, the bargaining process is not even tripartite, but bipartite, with labor market organizations deciding amongst themselves on the content of legislation regarding tax and social policy issues (Wiberg 2014, 181). A good example is provided by the recent decision to raise the retirement age, which in most countries has been made by the government or parliament. In Finland, Katainen's Cabinet (2011–2014) delegated the *de facto* decision authority on this matter to labor market organizations, who signed an agreement in 2014.

Unlike Sweden, Finland has not had two weakly interconnected elites, with the elite representing economic power anchored to bourgeois parties and business and industry, and the elite representing political power anchored to left-wing parties and trade unions. In Sweden, there has been little direct dialogue between these rival elites (SOU 1990, 44). In Finland, even left-wing and centrist parties have had access to the exercise of economic power through the boards of directors of state-owned companies and cooperatives.

The changes seen in the Finnish elite structure over the past couple of decades are similar to those that have taken place earlier in Denmark and Norway: elites have become more open, but less cohesive (Munk Christiansen 2001; Gulbrandsen et al. 2002; Ruostetsaari 2007b; Lindvall and Rothstein 2006; Togeby et al. 2003; Østerud et al. 2004).

A Danish elite study showed that in the early 1990s, Denmark did not have one single power elite as Finland did (Ruostetsaari 1992; 1993), nor did it have two rival elites, as Sweden did. Instead, there were several more or less autonomous elite groups with relatively low levels of cohesion. Likewise, there were no indications in Denmark of the kind of elite segmentation reported in Norway in the late 1970s, that is, corporatist forums for regular meetings between business, labor market organizations, and civil servants (NOU 1982, 3). Instead, the elite structure in Denmark was relatively fragmented. In the early 1960s, Danish elites were more homogeneous and more similar to one another than they had been before and that they were later in the 1990s (Munk Christiansen et al. 2001, 244).

An elite study in Norway in the early 2000s found that the country's elite structure was not based on a one or two-elite model, nor was it cohesive. However, it was not considered adequate to refer simply to a model of several elites without additional qualifiers. The elite structure in Norway showed signs of both fragmentation and integration: in questions of social importance, elites were characterized by simultaneous coherence and incoherence. In all, it was found that the Norwegian elite structure was to a significant extent characterized by elite pluralism (Gulbrandsen et al. 2002, 277–80).

Despite the opening up of recruitment and declining coherence, there have been no dramatic changes in the Finnish elite structure since the early 1990s. Finnish elites are still interconnected enough that it is justified to speak of the existence of a single power elite, albeit in more cautious terms than in the early 1990s (Ruostetsaari 1993). Only the cultural elite differs from other elites to such an extent that it can be regarded, at best, as an "associate member" of the power elite.

HOW CAN THE MODERATE CHANGES IN THE ELITE STRUCTURE BE EXPLAINED?

How, then, to explain the absence of any major changes in the Finnish elite structure, given the many and often profound changes that have swept Finnish society since the early 1990s? Surely one would have expected these changes to have had a significant effect even on the highest echelons of society. However, the data at hand do not allow us to directly explain the absence of any major changes in the elite structure. What is evident is that the relationship between changes in society and changes in the elite structure is complex indeed (Putnam 1976, 166), and that it takes longer than two decades for the changes to filter through. This is reflected in the fact that the average age of elites in Finland is over 50 years, by which time individuals will have their own settled views and patterns of activity in society. Even though it has become more difficult to retain an elite position in Finland, even the ascendancy of new individuals to elite positions does not necessarily bring new types of elite members to the elite, because the newcomers may become socialized into elites' established practices and values. The stability of the Finnish elite structure could likely be explained by the political culture of Finnish society, which is characterized by state-centeredness, an exceptionally prominent role of associations, Finnish people's high level of trust in governmental and political institutions, but relatively low level of political involvement.

One of the key functions of associations is to serve as a source of legitimacy for the political system and as a buffer between elites and the citizenry, providing simultaneously protection for citizens against elite manipulation and protection for elites against pressures from the citizenry. Indeed, effective associations have a special meaning and significance for Finland, where collective action as well as defending and fulfilling citizens' interests still rest mainly on formally organized voluntary activity. It has been suggested that associations are more important to the Finnish political system and welfare system than anywhere else in the world. Indeed, there are large numbers of associations in Finland and citizens here belong to many associations, and it is difficult for the citizenry to find any real and effective alternative channels of influence for associations (Siisiäinen and Kankainen 2009, 129, 132).

Civil society in Finland is traditionally closely connected with the central and local governments, and NGOs are largely oriented to and dependent on the resources of these governments. Rather than confrontation, the relationship between the state and civil society can be described as a partnership, the roots of which can be traced back to the nationalist movement in the late nineteenth century. Citizens' interests in Finland have largely been processed via associations, which in exchange for their recognized status have been expected to follow the rules of the regime. In practice, this has been manifested in a respect for laws, peace and order in society, a trust in enlightenment, and profuse appreciation of formal organizations among the citizenry (Ibid., 120–22; Ylä-Anttila 2010, 31).

People in Finland have an exceptionally high number of memberships in associations: as many as nine in ten people in Finland and in the other Nordic countries belong at least to one association. In Finland, this figure has still been rising. Since the 1970s, the number of non-members has declined, and the number of those involved in several different types of associations has increased (Siisiäinen and Kankainen 2009, 132, 98). According to the 2008 European Social Survey, Finnish people were involved in NGOs during the past 12 months far more often than citizens in any other of the 24 countries taking part in the survey (Bäck and Kestilä-Kekkonen 2013, 64).

New social movements only began to develop in Finland from the late 1970s onward, later than in most other western European countries. The growth of voluntary movements has been held in check by the state-centeredness of the Finnish associations: any civic movements growing up outside the formal associations have remained small and weak and dried up quickly. Any civic movement of any significance has adopted the form of an association and been quickly integrated into the regime. However, these new social movements and associations have differed from the old tradition of Finnish civil society in that they have had less interaction with central and local governments than older associations (Siisiäinen and Kankainen 2009, 94–97; Ylä-Anttila 2010, 32).

Finnish people also show exceptionally high levels of trust in the regime and its institutions. Their trust in democracy, parliament, the government, political parties, the civil service, trade unions, and the press has in fact grown since the early 1990s (Norris 2011, 71–88; Karvonen 2014, 139). In a 2012 comparison of citizen trust in the government among OECD countries, Finland ranked sixth after Switzerland, Luxembourg, Norway, Sweden, and New Zealand (OECD 2014). Likewise, trust in governmental institutions such as the legal system, the police, and defense forces is very high in Finland, and has continued to strengthen since the early 2000s. In a comparison of 24 European states in 2004, Finland ranked first in terms of citizen trust in the police and second in citizen trust in the legal system (Borg 2013, 59–63; Listhaug and Ringdal 2007).

Robert Putnam (1993, 167) defines social capital as connections among people—the social networks and the norms of mutual cooperation that arise from them. According to the European Social Survey 2002–2003, Finland ranked third (after Denmark and Norway) in mutual trust among people, with Greece coming last (Grönlund and Setälä 2006, 164). Indeed it is apparent that the high level of trust in Finland both in political institutions and in governmental institutions is largely explained by Finnish people's high levels of social capital. This interpretation differs from that suggested by Norris (2002, 161), according to which social capital does not increase trust in governmental institutions such as parliament, the government, or public administration. What does apply in the Finnish case is Norris's finding that trust among people is associated with the impartiality and incorruptibility of public administration (see Grönlund and Setälä 2006, 160–61). International comparisons have shown that there is very little corruption in Finland. A survey conducted by the European Commission in 2007 found that only Denmark (75) had a higher proportion of respondents than Finland (73 percent) who disagreed with the statement that "corruption is a major problem in our country" (European Commission 2008).

Putnam (2000) suggests that the decline of political participation in western democracies—declining party memberships and voter turnout at elections—is explained by the decline of social capital. Finland's voter turnout rates are among the lowest one-third in western democracies, and they have been falling more sharply than in many other countries, especially the Nordic countries (Norris 2011). As

Finland is characterized by high levels of social capital, its low levels of political participation cannot be explained in the way proposed by Putnam.

Political participation presupposes more than just social capital: it also requires objectives that are pursued by political action and a conviction that such action will contribute to achieving those objectives (Grönlund and Setälä 2006, 158–59). Indeed, Finnish people's subjective civil competence—the sense that one can understand political processes and participate in them meaningfully—is at a much lower level than in Europe on average. In 2008, Finnish citizens' subjective civil competence was the third lowest among 23 European countries (Kestilä-Kekkonen 2014, 49–51).

In terms of difficulties in understanding politics, Finns display patterns that are clearly different not just from their Nordic neighbors, but from western Europe more generally. When the 2008 European Social Survey asked "How often does politics seem so complicated that you can't really understand what is going on?", Finns, along with respondents from eastern, southern and southeastern Europe, were among those who said this was often the case. Citizens of other Nordic countries, as well as throughout western Europe, found it easier to comprehend politics. The low level of civic competence cannot, however, be explained by Finns' political ignorance. On the contrary, the level of political knowledge in Finland is closely similar to that in Scandinavia. Nordic citizens appear politically quite knowledgeable compared with other countries. Furthermore, Finland's highly acclaimed school system and high level of education would also seem to contradict the idea of large-scale political ignorance in the country (Karvonen 2014, 141–43).

A more credible explanation for the level of low civic competence in Finland is that politics here is in fact more difficult to understand than in many other countries. The consensual style of campaigning and policy-making makes it difficult for citizens to judge the political alternatives that are on offer in elections. For instance, political parties rarely rule out a partnership in the government with any other party before the elections. Similarly, cabinet coalition parties are collectively responsible for the government's output, and they are bound by strong formal commitments to explicit rules of parliamentary behavior. In short, it is very difficult for citizens to tell where the political parties stand on crucial issues, what the main lines of political conflict are, and who is really responsible for the way the country is governed (Ibid., 143).

One of the factors that may have contributed to upholding the legitimacy of the regime is the prevailing political culture in Finland, which weaves together a high level of trust in the regime, low levels of political participation, a civil society that integrates citizens with public authorities, and low belief in one's chances to have a say in political decisions. These distinctive features of the political culture have served as a buffer between changes in society and elites, relieving the pressures of change on elites. However, elites cannot let themselves be lulled into the false sense that the Finnish regime will retain its stability and legitimacy even in the near future. The glue of the Finnish regime that has held civil society and the state as well as elites and the citizenry together is at risk of being eroded.

NEW CHALLENGES FOR ELITES

Associations' role as a mediator and protective buffer between elites and the citizenry is weakening. This is due, firstly, to the shift in the focus of organized activity from the political arena to cultural, sports, and other leisure pursuits (Siisiäinen and Kankainen 2009, 98). Associations also have a less prominent role than before in political recruitment: ascent to parliament requires less training than before in local and regional political party organizations and civic associations but instead more educational and professional qualifications as well as more frequent and intensive public exposure (Ruostetsaari 2000). Another indication of the changing role of associations is the reduced involvement of Finnish elites in their activities since the early 1990s, even though leisure associations have retained their role as a means of attachment to civil society.

Although voter turnout in Finland is fairly low by international comparison, Finnish people are by no means politically indifferent. On the contrary, interest in politics is higher than in Europe on average: in 2010 just 7 countries out of 23 ranked ahead of Finland (Kestilä-Kekkonen 2014, 48). Public interest in politics has fact increased in all population groups since the early 1990s (Paloheimo and Borg 2009, 359–62; Karvonen 2014, 140; Haavisto 2014). Young people's attitudes to politics, though, are ambivalent: at the same time as they are increasingly interested in politics and have increasing trust in political institutions, they are less inclined to directly participate in politics (Myllyniemi 2014, 20). The populist True Finns's landslide victory in the 2011 parliamentary elections served as a warning signal to elites that citizens may be mobilized in new ways and that the balance of party support may shift even rapidly and substantially.

Rosanvallon (2008) argues that political systems based on liberal representative democracy have recently developed in a way that underscores the tensions between representative democracy and citizens' direct opportunities to exercise influence. Citizens and political parties have drifted further apart in Finland than in any other Nordic country (Wass and Wilhelmsson 2009, 71). In Finland as many as three in four feel that parties have been losing touch with ordinary people's everyday problems (Haavisto 2014).

In the absence of clearly formulated interests and related identities that representatives could work to promote, elected representatives have become more and more detached from their voters. Voting has come to resemble the Schumpeterian picture of democratic elitism where the main concern is to elect people into positions of power, leaving actual issues of substance and policy directions largely indeterminable. This is a particular concern in Finland where citizens can never know at the ballot box exactly how their votes will be used: which political parties will form the government coalition, and what objectives will they adopt in the government program. One would expect this to incentivize citizens to make clear their views on different issues and to influence them between elections as well (Paloheimo and Borg 2009, 363). However, traditional direct forms of participation such as signing appeals, contacting the authorities, and attending demonstrations have not increased to any noticeable degree in Finland since the early 1990s (Borg 2013), although the arrival of the Internet has changed forms of participation.

Expectations with regard to representation have changed in Finland as well. Rather than working to push interests through and demonstrating ideological camaraderie, representatives are first and foremost expected to show empathy and presence. Several studies have shown that citizens remain sensitive, or are even more sensitive than before to the behavior, empathy, or the lack of empathy shown by rulers than they are to the actual content of their decisions (Rosanvallon 2013, 26, 279; Hibbing and Theiss-Morse 2002). For instance, the electoral funding scandal surrounding the political elite since 2008 severely eroded the legitimacy of most parties in Finland and impacted the outcome of the 2011 parliamentary election (Borg 2012). Apart from less favorable policy outputs, other factors contributing to the victory of the populist True Finns were the recession that was triggered by the international financial crisis in 2008 and the Finnish government's involvement in the financial bailout of Greece and Portugal.

People in power are expected first and foremost to show that they are able to share and that they are sensitive to everyday concerns. Neighborliness consists of a voluntary gesture of coming closer, an active presence, a demonstration of solidarity. The politics of presence consists of these kinds of characters of "an exemplary neighbor" (Rosanvallon 2013, 279–80). International comparisons have shown that the political elite in Finland and other Nordic countries are expected to demonstrate "conspicuous modesty" and a common touch with the people. MPs in Finland, for instance, must be careful to avoid giving the impression of wealth and success, as the electorate expect them to have dedicated their lives to serving their country (Daloz 2007). Nothing works better to alleviate the hatred of the gentry than a politician demonstrating his or her abilities before moving into politics, especially if these abilities are in a field respected by ordinary people, such as house building or woodwork (Huoviala 2013).

Finland's candidate-centered electoral system leans itself ideally to a politics of presence. Even though the Nordic countries are often considered the archetypes of party-dominated electoral systems that leave limited room for individual candidates, the Finnish proportional electoral system is unique not only in the Nordic countries, but even more widely. In the Finnish open party list system, the ranking of candidates running for each party is determined solely by the amount of votes received by each candidate (Bengtsson et al. 2014, 84; Karvonen 2004). Given this electoral system, political parties in Finland—in contrast to the other Nordic countries—cannot in practice decide which MPs get elected, because they cannot prioritize their candidates. Each candidate, including leading politicians, have to run not only against candidates representing rival parties, but also other candidates from their own political party. It follows that all MPs have an incentive to maintain contact with their voters.

Presence defines representation in a whole new way. No longer is the aim to create a bond of obligation between the rulers and the ruled, but to demonstrate that the rulers understand what the ruled are having to endure in their lives. Empathy is seen as palpable proof that the rulers are not insulated in their own small world. The distance between representatives and represented is reduced not by giving the latter direct power over the former, or by establishing some form of resemblance between them. These two traditional techniques of social appropriation must be complemented by physical proximity and display of concern. While campaign promises are increasingly seen as tenuous and inconsequential, presence is palpable, direct, and effective. Empathy always keeps its promises, even if they are modest. For the politician, though, even the choice of who to empathize with is ultimately a political choice (Rosanvallon 2013, 295–97).

The media has become a key instrument for the new politics of presence. Its role is not limited to telling people what those in power are doing or saying, but its primary role is to show them. Empathetic power thus responds to the crisis of representation by striving to make modern politics—which has lost its meaning—more understandable and more visible. Presence through the media can be seen as a response to the disintegration and growing complexity of the decision-making processes. The irregularity of legislative work may give the impression that nothing is happening as representatives do much of their work beyond the public gaze in parliamentary committees, and even the work of administration is abstract and hard to grasp. In this situation it is easy for empathetic power to gain exposure for its commonsensical truth (Ibid., 282–83).

There are some signs that people in Finland are beginning to lose their trust in political institutions. In the aftermath of the international financial crisis in 2007–2012, public trust in the government fell much more sharply than in the OECD countries on average. The only countries that saw an even deeper loss of trust were the country's most severely affected by the debt crisis: Ireland, Portugal, Greece, and Slovenia (OECD 2014, 139). The loss of trust is problematic because it is in the nature of democracy that it needs to wield only a minimum of coercive power when citizens feel that the system is legitimate and when they adapt voluntarily. The loss of trust and support for political institutions may adversely affect this relationship and the operation of democratic institutions. Elites lose the economies of efficiency that are produced by the trust of citizens: they have to spend more time persuading and informing citizens that their interests will be represented. For citizens, too, declining trust in political institutions gives rise to new costs as suspicious citizens have to spend more time monitoring political institutions. The transaction costs of the democratic system thus increase along with citizens' declining trust in political institutions (Dalton 2011, 12).

It is equally important not to overemphasize the significance of citizens' trust to the political system: trust may involve a trap. For democracy to work, it is necessary for people to believe in democracy, and the better it works, the more people believe in it. But the more people believe in democracy, the less likely it is that they are aware that something is wrong (Runciman 2013, 324). Critique of political institutions and suspicions about politics are part and parcel of democratic politics—a scarcity of critique and suspicion is not necessarily a sign of healthy democracy (Dalton 2011, 201).

A good example is provided by the international financial crisis that started from the United States and that can be regarded as a failure of democracy: leading democratic states failed to realize what was going wrong before it was too late. The excesses associated with the economic boom ahead of the crisis found different expressions in different countries. In the United States, Ireland, and Spain, the principal symptom was a real estate bubble; in the UK, it was an oversized banking sector; in Italy and Greece, an oversized and ineffective public sector; in Germany, excessive confidence in export markets created by the euro; and in Finland, an ICT sector blinded by the rapid growth and success of Nokia and the failure of the paper industry, long the backbone of the country's economy, to adapt to the changing markets. Nowhere did the system self-repair in time. The first attempts to redress the situation only got under way when it was already too late. The damage had already been done (Runciman 2013, 275–76).

According to Runciman, this was in fact a dual failure. The democratic system that had emerged victorious at the start of the twenty-first century, was supposed to have two security valves. On the one hand, democratic public opinion was supposed to rectify any excesses by politicians and civil servants: if the political leaders went too far, they could be halted by the voters. On the other hand, civil servants, including bankers within the independent central banking systems, were to guard against any excesses by voters: if the voters went too far, the technocrats could stop them. The safety valves, however, didn't work. Rather than guarding each other, it seems that the two sides of democratic life—public opinion and expert opinion—have lulled each other. Both were confident that the other side would sound the alarm when things got out of hand (Runciman 2013, 276.)

Citizens' waning interest in electoral democracy and the growing wave of criticism against political parties has been tackled by introducing various forms of direct participation and influence at both the central and local government level in Finland and within the EU context. For instance, since 2012 a minimum of one million citizens from at least seven EU countries have been able to launch a citizens' initiative that calls upon the European Commission to present a legislative proposal. Since 2012, citizens in Finland have had access to the same tool: Parliament is required to consider any initiative that attracts more than 50,000 signatures. The government's recent report on democracy policy also underscores the importance of increasing direct citizen participation and influence. (VNS 3/2014).

Citizens' increased expectations of direct involvement may create a paradox, however: any reforms concerning them may lead to increased fragmentation of political interests, which may undermine citizens' support for the regime. The fact that more and more interest groups are pushing for specific goals through referenda, appeals, and public hearings may even exacerbate the tensions related to complex governance. In other words, present-day democracies are hampered not only by the articulation of overlapping and conflicting interests, but also by the absence of such institutions and processes that might aggregate and balance different interests into coherent policy programs that are acceptable to all the participants. Most studies concerning direct democracy suggest that this imbalance is further accentuated by the increasing number of such reforms (Dalton 2011, 205). In other words, the key to strengthening democracy is that feedbacks from direct participation are integrated with representative democracy and administrative processes so that citizens feel their views are heard and that they really count.

The international financial crisis and the eurozone debt crisis with its bailout packages has led to the "adjustment" of public finances in many countries, that is, to a vicious circle of cutbacks in welfare services and tax hikes, at the same time as corporate and dividends taxes have been considerably eased and business directors continue to enjoy high salaries and bonuses. There is a sense among citizens that they are being encouraged by the stick, while the elites are encouraged by the carrot. As far as the legitimacy of the regime is concerned, the key is the sense of trust experienced by citizens, as well as their prospects of getting ahead in life. Social mobility has an important role in this. If young people even from challenging backgrounds believe they have a real chance to get an education and to earn a decent living regardless of whether their parents can afford to pay for their studies, then trust can be an important bridge to the future. If they are denied this opportunity, then Finland—as well as many other countries—may well find itself struggling in the international competition and at the same time see an increase in inequality (Blom, Kankainen and Melin 2012, 29).

Bibliography

Abbink, Jon, and Tijo Salverda, eds. *The Anthropology of Elites. Power, Culture, and the Complexities of Distinction.* Basingstoke: Palgrave Macmillan, 2013.

Agger, Roger, Daniel Goldrich, and Bert Swanson. *The Rulers and the Ruled.* New York: Wiley, 1964.

Aguiar, Luis L. M., and Christopher J. Schneider, eds. *Researching Amongst Elites. Challenges and Opportunities in Studying Up.* Farnham: Ashgate, 2012.

Ahola, Sakari. *Eliitin yliopistosta massojen korkeakoulutukseen. Korkeakoulutuksen muuttuva asema yhteiskunnallisen valikoinnin järjestelmänä.* Koulutussosiologian tutkimuskeskus. Raportti 30. Turku: Turun yliopisto, 1995.

Ahola, Sakari, and Jani Tolonen. "Katsaus koulutusalan periytymiseen suomalaisilla yliopisto-opiskelijoilla." *Tiedepolitiikka* 38 (2013): 47–56.

Alapuro, Risto. "Valta ja valtio—miksi vallasta tuli ongelma 1900-luvun vaihteessa?" In *Talous, valta ja valtio,* ed. Pertti Haapala, 237–54. Tampere: Vastapaino, 1990.

Aldrich, Howard E. *Organizations and Environments.* Englewood Cliffs, N.J: Prentice-Hall, 1979.

Alestalo, Matti, and Hannu Uusitalo. "Eliittien sosiaalinen tausta ja yhteiskunnan muutokset Suomessa." *Sosiologia* 5 (1972):193–207.

Allardt, Erik. "Elämäntapa, harkinta ja muoti ihmisten valintojen perustana." In *Kymmenen esseetä elämäntavasta,* ed. Kalle Heikkinen, 3–34. Helsinki: Yleisradio, 1986.

———. *Sosiologia I.* Helsinki: WSOY, 1983.

Arter, David. *Scandinavian Politics Today.* Manchester: Manchester University Press, 2008.

Asp, Kenneth. *Mäktiga massmedier. Studier i politisk opinionsbildning.* Stockholm: Academilitteratur, 1986.

Aula, Maria Kaisa. *Poliitikkojen ja toimittajien suhteet murroksessa?* Tutkimus-ja kehitysosasto, Tutkimusraportti 5. Helsinki: Yleisradio, 1991.

Bachrach, Peter. *The Theory of Democratic Elitism. A Critique.* Boston: Little, Brown, 1967.

Bäck, Maria, and Elina Kestilä-Kekkonen. "Sosiaalinen pääoma ja poliittinen osallistuminen Suomessa." *Politiikka* 55 (2013): 59–72.

Bang, Paul Henrik, and Torben Bech Dyrberg. "Demo-elitism and Ordinary Politics." Paper presented at the conference "Connecting people through governance—a new mode of governmentality and involvement," Nordic Governance Summit at COS, Copenhagen October 11–12, 2001.

Barnes, John A. "Network Analysis: Orienting Notion, Rigorous Technique or Substantive Field of Study?" In *Perspectives on Social Network Research*, eds. Paul W. Holland and Samuel Leinhardt, 403–23. New York: Academic Press: New York, 1979.

Bengtsson, Åsa, and Mikko Mattila. "Suoran demokratian ja häivedemokratian kannatus Suomessa." In *Vaalit* yleisödemokratiassa, eds. Sami Borg and Heikki Paloheimo, 303–24. Tampere: Tampere University Press, 2009.

Bengtsson, Åsa, Kasper M. Hansen, Ólafur Þ. Harðarson, Hanne Marthe Narud, and Henrik Oscarsson. *The Nordic Voter. Myths of Exceptionalism.* Colchester: ECPR Press, 2014

Berg, Annukka. "The Discursive Dimensions of a Decent Deal: How Nuclear Energy Evolved from Environmental Enemy to Climate Remedy in the Parliament of Finland." In *The Renewal of Nuclear Power in Finland*, eds. Matti Kojo and Tapio Litmanen, 91–125. Basingstoke: Palgrave Macmillan, 2009, 91–125.

Best, Heinrich, and Maurizio Cotta, eds. *Parliamentary Representatives in Europe 1848–2000. Legislative Recruitment and Careers in Eleven European Countries.* Oxford: Oxford University Press, 2000.

Best, Heinrich, and John Higley. "Introduction." In *Political Elites in the Transatlantic Crisis*, eds. Heinrich Best and Maurizio Cotta, 1–23. Basingstoke: Palgrave Macmillan, 2014a.

Best, Heinrich, and John Higley. "Conclusions." In *Political Elites in the Transatlantic Crisis*, eds. Heinrich Best and Maurizio Cotta, 170–80. Basingstoke: Palgrave Macmillan, 2014b.

Best, Heinrich, György Lengyel, and Luca Verzichelli. *The Europe of Elites. A Study into the Europeanness of Europe's Political and Economic Elites.* Oxford: Oxford University Press, 2012.

Birch, Anthony. *Concepts & Theories of Modern Democracy.* 2nd edition. London: Routledge, 2001.

Björklund, Anders and Markus Jäntti. "Intergenerational Income Mobility and the Role of Family Background." In *Oxford Handbook of Economic Inequality*, eds. Wiemer Salverda, Brian Nolan, and Timothy M. Smeeding, 491–520. Oxford: Oxford University Press, 2009.

Blom, Raimo, Tomi Kankainen, and Harri Melin. *Jakaantunut Suomi. Raportti ISSP 2009 Suomen aineistosta.* Julkaisuja 10. Tampere: Yhteiskuntatieteellinen tietoarkisto, 2012.

Boas, Taylor C. and Jordan Gans-Morse. "Neoliberalism: From New Liberal Philosophy to Anti-Liberal Slogan." *St Comp Int Dev* 44 (2009): 137–61.

Bonacich, Philiph. "Technique for Analysing Overlapping Membership." In *Sociological Methodology* 1972, ed. Herbert Costner, 176–85. San Francisco: Jossey-Bass, 1972.

Borg, Sami. "Indikaattorikatsaukset." In *Demokratiaindikaattorit 2013,"* ed. Sami Borg, 17–94. Selvityksiä ja ohjeita 52. Helsinki: Oikeusministeriö, 2013.

——— (ed.). *Muutosvaalit 2011.* Selvityksiä ja ohjeita 16. Helsinki: Oikeusministeriö, 2012.

———. *Puolueet ja edustuksellinen kunnallisdemokratia. Tutkimus poliittisesta edustautumisesta ja legitimiteetistä.* Kunnallistieteiden julkaisusarja nr 1. Tampere: Tampereen yliopisto,1998.

Borg, Sami, and Ilkka Ruostetsaari. "Suuret ikäluokat ja valta." *Hyvinvointikatsaus* 1 (2002), 51–58.

Bourdieu, Pierre. *Distinction. A Social Critique of the Judgement of Taste.* London: Routledge, 1989.

———. "Sport and Social Class." *Social Science Information* 17: 1978, 819–40.

———. *The State Nobility. Elite Schools in the Field of Power.* Cambridge: Polity Press, 1996.

Brannen, Peter. "Working on Directors: Some Methodological Issues." In *Research Methods for Elite Studies*, eds. George Moyser and Margaret Wagstaffe, 166–80. London: Allen and Unwin, 1987.

Breen, Richard, ed. *Social Mobility in Europe.* Oxford: Oxford University Press, 2004.

Breen, Richard, and Jan O. Jonsson. "Inequality of Opportunity in Comparative Perspective: Recent Research on Educational Attainment and Social Mobility." *Annual Review of Sociology* 31 (2005): 223–43.

Burdeau, Georges. "Die Politische Klasse." In *Demokratische Elitenherrschaft*, ed. Wilfred Rörlich, 251–68. Darmstadt: Wissenschaftliche Buchgesellschaft, 1975.

Burnham, James. *The Managerial Revolution.* 2nd edition. Westport: Greenwood Press, 1975.

Burt, Ronald S. *Toward a Structural Theory of Action. Network Models of Social Structure, Perception, and Action.* New York: Academic Press, 1982.

Burton, Michael, and John Higley. "Invitation to Elite Theory. The Basic Contentions Reconsidered." In *Power Elites and Organisations*, eds. G. William Domhoff and Thomas R. Dye, 219–38. Beverly Hills: Sage, 1987.

———. "Political Crises and Elite Settlement." In *Elites, Crises and the Origins of Regimes*, eds. Mattei Dogan and John Higley, 47–70. Oxford: Rowman and Littlefield, 1998.

———. "The Study of Political Elite Transformations." *International Review of Sociology* 11 (2001): 181–99.

Canovan, Margaret. *Populism.* London: Junction Books, 1981.

———. "Trust the People! Populism and the Two Faces of Democracy." *Political Studies* 47 (1999): 2–16.

Castells, Manuel. *The Rise of the Network Society. Vol. 1 of the Information Age, Economy, Society and Culture.* Oxford: Blackwell, 1996.

Cawson, Alan, ed. *Organized Interests and the State. Studies in Meso-Corporatism.* London: Sage, 1985.

Central Chamber of Commerce. *Miehet johtavat pörssiyhtiöiden liiketoimintoja—naiset päätyvät tukitoimintoihin.* Helsinki: Keskuskauppakamari, 2011.

———. *Nais-ja miesjohtajien välinen palkkaero kaventuu: Naisjohtajan euro 95 senttiä.* http://kauppakamari.fi/2015/01/22/nais-ja-miesjohtajan-valinen-palkkaero-kaventuu-naisjohtajan-euro-95-senttia, accessed January 22, 2015.

Christmas-Best, Verona, and Ulrik Kjær. "Why so Few and Why so Slow? Women as Parliamentary Representatives in Europe from a Longitudinal Perspective." In *Democratic Representation in Europe. Diversity, Change, and Convergence*, eds. Maurizio Cotta and Heinrich Best, 77–101. Oxford: Oxford University Press, 2007.

Clegg, Stewart R. *Frameworks of Power.* London: Sage, 1989.

Compston, Hugh. *Policy Networks and Policy Change. Putting Policy Networks Theory to the Test.* Basingstoke: Palgrave Macmillan, 2009.

Conti, Nicoló, Maurizio Cotta, and Pedro Tavares de Almeida, eds. *Perspectives of National Elites on European Citizenship. A South European View.* London: Routledge, 2012.

Cotta, Maurizio. "Facing the Crisis: The European Elite System's Changing Geometry." In *Political Elites in the Transatlantic Crisis*, eds. Heinrich Best and Maurizio Cotta, 59–80. Basingstoke: Palgrave Macmillan, 2014.

Cotta, Maurizio, and Heinrich Best, eds. *Democratic Representation in Europe: Diversity, Change and Convergence.* Oxford: Oxford University Press, 2007.

Crenson, Matthew A. *The Un-Politics of Air-Pollutions: A Study of Non-Decision Making in the Cities*. Baltimore: John Hopkins University, 1971.

Dahl, Robert A. "A Critique of the Ruling Elite Model." *American Political Science Review*, 52 (1958): 463–69.

———. *Modern Political Analysis*. 3rd edition. Englewood Cliffs, N.J.: Prentice-Hall, 1976.

Daloz, Jean-Pascal. "Political Elites and Conspicuous Modesty: Norway, Sweden, Finland in Comparative Perspective." In *Comparative Studies of Social and Political Elites*, eds. Fredrik Engelstad and Trygve Gulbrandsen, 171–10. Amsterdam: Elsevier, 2007.

———. *Rethinking Social Distinction*. London: Palgrave Macmillan, 2013.

———. *The Sociology of Elite Distinction. From Theoretical to Comparative Perspectives*. London: Palgrave Macmillan, 2010.

Dalton, Russel J. *Democratic Challenges, Democratic Choices. The Erosion of Political Support in Advanced Industrial Democracies*. Oxford: Oxford University Press, 2011.

Dexter, Lewis Anthony. *Elite and Specialized Interviewing*. Colchester: ECPR Press, 2006.

Diani, Mario. "Introduction: Social Movements, Contentious Actions and Social Networks: 'From Metaphor to Substance'?" In *Social Movements and Networks. Relational Approaches to Collective Action*, eds. Mario Diani and Dough McAdam, 1–18. Oxford: Oxford University Press, 2009.

DiMaggio, Paul, and Togir Mukhtar. "Arts participation as cultural capital in the United States, 1982–2002: Signs of decline?" *Poetics* 32 (2004): 169–94.

Dogan, Mattei. "Introduction: Diversity of Elite Configurations and Clusters of Power." In *Elite Configurations at the Apex of Power*, ed. Mattei Dogan, 1–15. Leiden/Boston: Brill, 2003.

Dogan, Mattei, and John Higley. *Elites, Crises and the Origins of Regimes*. Oxford: Rowman and Littlefield, 1998a.

———. "Elites, Crises, and Regimes in Comparative Analysis." In *Elites, Crises and the Origins of Regimes*, eds. Mattei Dogan & John Higley, 3–27. Oxford: Rowman and Littlefield, 1998b.

Domhoff, G. William. *The Power Elite and the State. How Policy is Made in America*. New York: Aldine de Gruyter, 1990.

——— (ed.). *Power Structure Research*. Beverly Hills, CA: Sage, 1980.

Ekholm, Peter. *Ymmärrystä yli rajojen: Valtakunnallisten maanpuolustuskurssien vaikuttavuus*. Strategian laitos, Julkaisusarja 2, Tutkimusselosteita No 32. Helsinki: Maanpuolustus-korkeakoulu, 2006.

Engelstad, Fredrik. "Democratic Elitism—Conflict and Consensus." In *Democratic Elitism: New Theoretical and Comparative Perspectives*, eds. Heinrich Best and John Higley, 61–77. Leiden and Boston: Brill, 2010.

———. "Elite Compromise, Crisis and Democracy: The United States, Norway and Italy Compared." In *Political Elites in the Transatlantic Crisis*, eds. Heinrich Best and Maurizio Cotta, 138–54. Basingstoke: Palgrave Macmillan, 2014.

Engelstad, Fredrik, and Trygve Gulbrandsen, eds. *Comparative Studies of Social and Political Elites*. Amsterdam: Elsevier, 2007.

Erikson, Robert, and John H. Goldthorpe. *The Constant Flux. A Study of Class Mobility in Industrial Societies*. Oxford: Clarendon Press, 1992.

Erikson, Robert, and Seppo Pöntinen. "Social Mobility in Finland and Sweden: A Comparison of Men and Women." In *Small States in Comparative Perspective. Essays for Erik Allardt*, eds. Risto Alapuro, Matti Alestalo, Elina Haavio-Mannila, and Raimo Väyrynen, 138–62. Oslo: Norwegian University Press, 1985.

Erola, Jani. "Luokkarakenne ja luokkiin samastuminen Suomessa." In *Luokaton Suomi? Yhteiskuntaluokat 2000-luvun Suomessa*, ed. Jani Erola, 27–44. Helsinki: Gaudeamus, 2010.

Etzioni-Halevy, Eva. *Classes and Elites in Democracy and Democratization*. New York and London: Garland, 1997.

———. *The Elite Connection. Problems and Potential of Western Democracy*. Cambridge: Polity Press, 1993.

———. "Élites, Inequality and the Quality of Democracy in Ultramodern Society." *International Review of Sociology* 9 (1999): 239–50.

Eulau, Heinz. "Elite Analysis and Democratic Theory: The Contribution of Harold D. Lasswell." In *Elite Recruitment in Democratic Polities. Comparative Studies Across Nations*, eds. Heinz Eulau and Moshe M. Czudnowski, 7–28. New York: Sage, 1976.

European Commission. The Attitudes of Europeans towards Corruption. Special Eurobarometer 291. http://ec.europa.eu/public_opinion/archives/ebs/ebs_291_en.pdf, 2007, accessed December 12, 2014.

EVA. *Erilaisuuksien Suomi. Raportti suomalaisten asenteista 2001*. Helsinki: Finnish Business and Policy Forum, 2001.

———. *Maailman paras maa*. Helsinki: Finnish Business and Policy Forum, 2011.

———. *Suomi etsii itseään. Raportti suomalaisten asenteista 1991*. Helsinki: Finnish Business and Policy Forum, 1991.

Finnish Constitution (1999/731). http://www.finlex.fi/fi/laki/kaannokset/1999/en19990731.pdf, accessed December 18, 2014.

Forsberg, Tuomas, and Tapio Raunio. "Johdanto. Muuttuva maailma, muuttuva politiikka." In *Politiikan muutos*, eds. Tuomas Forsberg and Tapio Raunio, 9–40. Tampere: Vastapaino, 2014.

Forsten, Timo. "Keitä kansanedustajat ovat?" In *Eduskunta. Kansanvaltaa puolueiden ja hallituksen ehdoilla*, eds. Tapio Raunio and Matti Wiberg, 77–90. Helsinki: Gaudeamus, 2014.

Foucault, Michel. *The History of Sexuality. 2. The Use of Pleasure*. London: Penguin, 1992.

———. "The Subject and Power." In *Power. Essential Works of Foucault 1954–1984*, ed. James D. Faubion, 326–48 . Vol. 3. New York: The New Press, 2000.

Foundation for Municipal Development. *Kansalaismielipide ja kunnat. Ilmapuntari 2011–2012*. Helsinki: Kunnallisalan kehittämissäätiö, 2012.

Galaskiewicz, Joseph. "Interorganizational Networks Mobilizing Action at the Metropolitan Level." In *Networks of Power. Organizational Actors at the National, Corporate, and Community Levels*, eds. Robert Perrucci and Harry R. Potter, 81–96. New York: Aldine de Gruyter, 1989.

Gallager, Michael, Michael Laver, and Peter Mair. *Representative Government in Modern Europe*. Second edition. London: McGraw-Hill, 1995.

García de León, María Antonia, María José Alonso Sánchez, and Helena Rodrigues Navarro. "The Élites' Cultural Capital." In *Gendering Elites. Economic and Political Leadership in 27 Industrialized Societies*, eds. Mino Vianello and Gwen Moore, 35–49. London: Macmillan, 2000.

Giddens, Anthony. *Central Problems in Social Theory. Action, Structure and Contradictions in Social Analysis*. London and Basingstoke: Macmillan, 1979.

Grönlund, Kimmo, and Maija Setälä. "Sosiaalinen pääoma." In *Suomen demokratiaindikaattorit*, ed. Sami Borg, 154–72. Oikeusministeriön julkaisu 1. Helsinki: Oikeusministeriö, 2006.

Gulbrandsen, Trygve, Fredrik Engelstad, Trond Beldo Klausen, Hege Skjeie, Mari Teigen, and Øyvind Østerud. *Norske makteliter.* Oslo: Gyldendahl Norsk Forlag, 2002.

Haavisto, Ilkka. *Neljäs Suomi. EVA:n arvo-ja asennetutkimus 2014.* Helsinki: Taloustieto, 2014.

Habermas, Jürgen. *The Philosophical Discourse of Modernity.* Cambridge: Polity Press, 1990.

Hague, Rod, and Martin Harrop. *Comparative Government and Politics. An Introduction.* 5th edition. Basingstoke: Palgrave, 2001.

Härkönen, Juho. "Sosiaalinen periytyvyys ja sosiaalinen liikkuvuus." In *Luokaton Suomi? Yhteiskuntaluokat 2000-luvun Suomessa,* ed. Jani Erola, 51–66. Helsinki: Gaudeamus, 2010.

Haveri, Arto, and Ari-Veikko Anttiroiko. "Kuntajohtaminen: haasteena paikallisten kilpailuja yhteistyösuhteiden hallinta." In *Governance. Uuden hallintavan jäsentyminen,* eds. Ilari Karppi and Lotta-Maria Sinervo, 191–11. Hallintotieteiden keskus. Tampere: Tampereen yliopisto, 2009.

Heikkinen, Sakari. "Suomen talous polkee pitkään paikallaan." *Helsingin Sanomat,* June 28, 2014.

Heiskala, Risto. "Kansainvälisen toiminnan muutos ja Suomen yhteiskunnallinen murros." In *Uusi jako. Miten Suomesta tuli kilpailukyky-yhteiskunta?,* eds. Risto Heiskala and Eeva Luhtakallio, 14–42. Helsinki: Gaudeamus, 2006a.

———. "Sosiaaliset innovaatiot ja hegemonisen mallin muutokset: kuinka tulkita Suomen 1990-luvun murrosta?" In *Uusi jako. Miten Suomesta tuli kilpailukyky-yhteiskunta?,* eds. Risto Heiskala and Eeva Luhtakallio, 202–17. Helsinki: Gaudeamus, 2006b.

Heiskala, Risto, and Anu Kantola. "Vallan uudet ideat: Hyvinvointivaltion huomasta valmentajavaltion valvontaan." In *Valta Suomessa,* ed. Petteri Pietikäinen, 124–48. Helsinki: Gaudeamus, 2010,

Heiskala, Risto, and Eeva Luhtakallio eds. *Uusi jako: miten Suomesta tuli kilpailukyky-yhteiskunta?* Helsinki: Gaudeamus, 2006.

Heiskanen, Ilkka. *Muuttuivatko laitokset, ja miksi ja miten? Taide-ja kulttuurilaitosten institutionaalinen muutos 1990-luvulla.* Tilastotietoa taiteesta nro 28. Helsinki: Taiteen keskustoimikunta, 2001.

Helén, Ilpo. "Michel Foucaultin valta-analytiikka." In *Sosiologian teorian nykysuuntauksia,* ed. Risto Heiskala, 270–315. Helsinki: Gaudeamus, 1994.

Helsingin Sanomat 22.11.2001, 13.1.2002, 14.9.2010, 4.12.2010, 31.12.2011, 4.3.2012, 10.8.2013, 20.7.2013, 17.12.1013, 24.1.2014, 4.2.2014, 11.2.2014, 13.3.1014, 3.10.2014, 25.10.2014, 28.12.2014, 30.1.2015.

Henriksson, Marketta, and Ilkka Kajaste. "Budjettien stressitestaus luo jännitteitä euroalueelle." *Helsingin Sanomat,* November 12, 2014.

Herkman, Juha. *Politiikka ja mediajulkisuus.* Tampere: Vastapaino, 2011.

Hertz, Rosanna, and Jonathan B. Imber eds. *Studying Elites Using Qualitative Methods.* London: Sage, 1995.

Heuru, Kauko. *Itsehallinnon aika.* Helsinki: Kunnallisalan kehittämissäätiö, 2001.

Hewitt, Christopher J. "Elites and the Distribution of Power in British Society." In *Elites and Power in British Society,* eds. Philiph Stanworth and Anthony Giddens, 45–64. Cambridge: Cambridge University Press, 1974.

Hibbing, John, and Elisabeth Theiss-Morse. *Stealth Democracy. Americans' Beliefs about How Government Should Work.* Cambridge: Cambridge University Press, 2002.

Higley, John. "Democracy and Elites." In *Comparative Studies of Social and Political Elites,* eds. Fredrik Engelstad and Trygve Gulbrandsen, 249–63. Amsterdam: Elsevier, 2007.

Higley, John, Ursula Hoffman-Lange, Charles Kadushin, and Gwen Moore. "Elite Integration in Stable Democracies." *European Sociological Review* 7 (1991): 35–53.

Higley, John, and György Lengyel. "Introduction: Elite Configurations after State Socialism." In *Elites after State Socialism. Theories and Analysis*, eds. John Higley and György Lengyel, 1–21. Oxford: Rowman and Littlefield, 2000.

Higley, John, and Gwen Moore. "Elite Integration in the United States and Australia." *American Political Science Review* 75 (1981): 581–97.

———. "Political Elite Studies at the Year 2000: Introduction." *International Review of Sociology* 11 (2001): 175–180.

Higley, John, and Jan Pakulski. "Epilogue: Elite Theory versus Marxism: The Twentieth Century's Verdict." In *Elites after State Socialism. Theories and Analysis*, eds. John Higley and György Lengyel, 229–41. Oxford: Rowman and Littlefield, 2000.

Hirvikorpi, Helena. *Jos on valta, on myös vastuu. Asmo Kalpalan elämä.* Helsinki: WSOY, 2012.

Hix, Simon, and Bjørn Høyland. *The Political System of the European Union.*—3rd edition. Basingstoke: Palgrave Macmillan, 2011.

Hoffman-Lange, Ursula. "Elite Research in Germany." *International Review of Sociology* 11 (2001): 201–16.

———. "Surveying National Elites in the Federal Republic of Germany." In *Research Methods for Elite Studies*, eds. George Moyser and Margaret Wagstaffe, 27–47. London: Allen and Unwin, 1987.

Hout, Michael, and Thomas A. DiPrete. "What We Have Learned: RC28's Contributions to Knowledge about Social Stratification." *Research in Social Stratification and Mobility* 24 (2006): 1–20.

Hulkko, Kustaa, and Jorma Pöysä. *Vakaa markka. Teot ja tarinat.* Jyväskylä: Atena, 1998.

Hunter, Floyd. *Community Power Structure.* New York: Anchor Books, 1963.

Huoviala, Kari. "Kätevyys on valtti politiikassa." *Aamulehti*, August 17, 2013.

Husa, Jaakko. *Non liquet? Vallanjako, perusoikeudet ja systematisointi—oikeuden ja politiikan välisiä rajankäyntejä.* Julkaisuja A-sarja N:o 254. Helsinki: Suomalainen lakimiesyhdistys, 2004.

Ilmonen, Kaj. "Luottamus Suomessa 1990-luvulla." In *Lama ja luottamus*, eds. Kaj Ilmonen, Anne Kovalainen and Martti Siisiäinen, 20–41. Forskningsrapporter 55. Helsinki: Svenska handelshögskolan, 2002.

Jääsaari, Johanna. "Sukupolvet, elämäntapa ja politiikka." *Politikka* 28 (1986): 258–81.

Jokinen, Kimmo, and Kimmo Saaristo. *Suomalainen yhteiskunta.* Helsinki: WSOY, 2002.

Julkunen, Raija. *Suunnanmuutos. 1990-luvun sosiaalipoliittinen reformi Suomessa.* Tampere: Vastapaino, 2001.

Kantola, Anu. *Markkinakuri ja managerivalta. Poliittinen hallinta Suomen 1990-luvun talouskriisissä.* Helsinki: Loki-kirjat, 2002.

———. "Modernin julkisuuden teoria ja käytännöt." In *Hetken hallitsijat*, ed. Anu Kantola, 17–41. Helsinki: Gaudeamus, 2011b.

———. "Tyhjää vai täyttä julkista elämää?" In *Hetken hallitsijat*, ed. Anu Kantola, 164–79. Helsinki: Gaudeamus, 2011a.

Kantola, Anu, and Juho Vesa. "Skandaalit ja julkinen elämä Suomessa." In *Hetken hallitsijat*, ed. Anu Kantola, 42–64. Helsinki: Gaudeamus, 2011.

Kantola Anu, Juho Vesa, and Salli Hakala. "Notkean myrskyn silmässä: vaalirahaskandaali." In *Hetken hallitsijat*, ed. Anu Kantola, 65–88. Helsinki: Gaudeamus, 2011.

Karila, Alpo. *Kuntien talouden ohjaus ja sen muutos.* Helsinki: Suomen Kuntaliitto, 1998.

Kartovaara, Leena. *Suomalainen eliitti "Kuka on kukin" -teoksen valossa vuosina 1909, 1934 ja 1970.* Sosiologian pro gradu-tutkielma. Helsinki: Helsingin yliopisto, 1972.

Karttunen, Marko. *Evidence of Partisan Emphasis on EMU during 1994–1999: Comparing Finnish Parties.* Acta Politica 38. Department of Political Science. Helsinki: University of Helsinki, 2009.

Karvonen, Lauri. *Parties, Governments and Voters in Finland. Politics under Fundamental Societal Transformation.* Colchester: ECPR Press, 2014.

———. "Preferential Voting: Incidence and Effects." *International Political Science Review* 25 (2004): 203–26.

Kauppi, Niilo, and Mikael Rask Madsen, eds. *Transnational Power Elites. The New Professionals of Governance, Law and Security.* London: Routledge, 2013.

Kenis, Patrick, and Volker Schneider. "Policy Networks and Policy Analysis. Scrutinizing a New Analytical Toolbox." In *Policy Networks: Empirical Evidence and Theoretical Considerations,* eds. Bern Marin and Renate Maynts, 25–59. Frankfurt am Main: Campus Verlag, 1991.

Kestilä-Kekkonen, Elina. "Puoluedemokratian haasteet Euroopassa: Syrjäyttävätkö uudet poliittisen osallistumisen muodot edustuksellisen demokratian?" In *Politiikan muutos,* eds. Tuomas Forsberg and Tapio Raunio, 41–76. Tampere: Vastapaino, 2014.

Kiander, Jaakko. *Laman opetukset. Suomen 1990-luvun kriisin syyt ja seuraukset.* Julkaisuja 27:5. Helsinki: Valtion taloudellinen tutkimuskeskus, 2001.

Kiander, Jaakko, and Pentti Vartia. *Suuri lama. Suomen 1990-luvun kriisi ja talouspoliittinen keskustelu.* Helsinki: Taloustieto, 1998.

Kivinen, Markku. "Luokkateoria ja yhteiskunnalliset jaot." In *Yhteiskunnalliset jaot. 1990-luvun perintö?,* eds. Timo Piirainen and Juho Saari, 140–59. Helsinki: Gaudeamus, 2002.

Knight, Alan. "Historical and Theoretical Considerations." In *Elites, Crises and the Origins of Regimes,* eds. Mattei Dogan and John Higley, 29–45. Oxford: Rowman and Littlefield, 1998.

Knoke, David. *Political Networks. The Structural Perspective.* New York: Cambridge University Press, 1990.

———. "Organization Sponsorship and Influence Reputation of Social Influence Associations." *Social Forces* 61 (1983): 1065—87.

Kohn, Melvin L. "Social Class and Parent-Child Relationship: An Interpretation." *The American Journal of Sociology* 68 (1963): 471–80.

Korkman, Sixten. "Eurooppäättäjiä syytä arvostella." *Suomen Kuvalehti* 25–26 (2013): 14–15.

———. "Onko eurovaltio itsenäinen?" *Helsingin Sanomat,* November 11, 2014.

Kuisma, Markku, and Teemu Keskisarja. *Erehtymättömät. Tarina suuresta pankkisodasta ja liikepankeista Suomen kohtaloissa.* Helsinki: WSOY, 2012.

Kulha, Keijo. *Kuilun partaalla. Suomen pankkikriisi 1991–1995.* Helsinki: Otava, 2000.

Kunelius, Risto, Elina Noppari, and Esa Reunanen. *Media vallan verkoissa.* Tiedotusopin laitos, julkaisuja, sarja A 112. Tampere: Tampereen yliopisto, 2009.

Kuusela, Hanna, and Matti Ylönen. *Konsulttidemokratia. Miten valtiosta tehdään tyhmä ja tehoton.* Helsinki: Gaudeamus, 2013.

Lahire, Bernard. "From the habitus to an individual heritage of dispositions. Towards a sociology at the level of the individual." *Poetics* 31 (2003): 329–55.

Laumann, Edward O., and David Knoke. "Policy Network of the Organizational State: Collective Action in the National Energy and Health Domains." In *Networks of Power. Orga-*

nizational Actors at the National, Corporate and Community Level, eds. Robert Perrucci and Harry R. Potter, 17–53. New York: Aldine de Gruyter, 1989.

Laitinen, Ahti. "Yhteiskunnan oikeudellistuminen ja kontrolli globalisoituvassa maailmassa." In *Oikeus—Kulttuuria ja teoriaa. Juhlakirja Hannu Tolonen*, eds. Jyrki Tala and Kauko Wikström, 71–86. Oikeustieteellinen tiedekunta. Turku: Turun yliopisto, 2005.

Lasswell, Harold, and Abraham Kaplan. *Power and Society*. New Haven: Yale University Press, 1950.

Lavapuro, Juha. *Uusi perustuslakikontrolli*. Helsinki: Suomalainen lakimiesyhdistys, 2010.

Lehväsvirta, Leena. *Kuntien hallinto muuttuvassa toimintaympäristössä*. Helsinki: Suomen Kuntaliitto, 1999.

Lindsay, D. Michael, with M. G. Hagar. *View from the Top. An Inside Look of How People in Power See and Shape the World*. Hoboken, New Jersey: Wiley, 2014.

Lindvall, Johannes, and Bo Rothstein. "Sweden: The Fall of the Strong State." *Scandinavian Political Studies* 29 (2006): 47–63.

Listhaug, Ola, and Kristen Ringdal. "Trust in Political Institutions: The Nordic Countries Compared with Europe." Paper presented at the Norwegian Political Science Meeting, NTNU, Trondheim, Norway, 3–5 January 2007.

Mäkelä, Klaus. "Kulttuurisen muuntelun yhteisöllinen rakenne Suomessa." *Sosiologia* 22: 1985, 247–60.

Mann, Michael. *Sources of Social Power. Vol. 1. A History of Power from the Beginning to A.D. 1760*. Cambridge: Cambridge University Press, 1986.

Markkanen, Tapani. *Mauri Pekkarinen. Politiikan pikkujättiläinen*. Jyväskylä: Atena, 2005.

Marsh, David, ed. *Comparing Policy Networks*. Buckingham: Open University Press, 1998.

Martikainen, Tuomo. *Puuttuva punainen viiva*. Helsinki: Tilastokeskus, 1988.

Martikainen, Tuomo, and Hanna Wass. *Vaienneet äänet. äänestäminen vuosien 1987 ja 1999 eduskuntavaaleissa*. Vaalit 2001: 2. Helsinki: Tilastokeskus, 2001.

Mattila, Mikko. *Policy Making in Finnish Social and Health Care. A Network Approach*. Acta Politica no. 12. Helsinki: Helsinki University Press, 2000.

Meisel, James. *The Myth of the Ruling Class. Gaetano Mosca and the "Elite."* Ann Arbor: University of Michigan Press, 1958.

Merikallio, Katri, and Tapani Ruokanen. *Matkalla. Martti Ahtisaaren tarina*. Helsinki: Otava, 2011.

Michels, Robert. *Puoluelaitos nykyajan demokratiassa*, (orig. *Zur Soziologie des Partaiwesens in der modernen Demokratie*, 1911, translated by Timo Kyntäjä) Helsinki: WSOY, 1986.

Mills, C. Wright. *The Power Elite*. New York: Oxford University Press, 1956.

Money value converter. http://www.rahamuseo.fi/arvo_laskuri/laskuri_web.html, accessed February 8, 2014.

Moore, Gwen. "The Structure of a National Elite Network." *American Sociological Review* 44 (1979): 673–92.

Moring, Tom, and Juri Mykkänen. "Vaalikampanja." In *Vaalit yleisödemokratiassa. Eduskuntavaalitutkimus 2007*, eds. Sami Borg and Heikki Paloheimo, 28–59. Tampere: Tampere University Press, 2009.

Mosca, Gaetano. *The Ruling Class*. New York and London: McGraw-Hill, 1939.

Möttönen, Sakari. *Tulosjohtaminen ja valta poliittisten päätöksentekijöiden ja viranhaltijoiden välisessä suhteessa*. Helsinki: Suomen Kuntaliitto, 1997.

Moyser, George, and Margaret Wagstaffe, eds. *Research Methods for Elite Studies*. London: Allen and Unwin, 1987a.

Moyser, George, and Margaret Wagstaffe. "Studying Elites: Theoretical and Methodological Issues." In *Research Methods for Elite Studies*, eds. George Moyser and Margaret Wagstaffe, 1–24. London: Allen and Unwin, 1987b.

Munk Christiansen, Peter, Birgit Møller, and Lise Togeby. *Den danske elite*. København: Hans Reitzels Forlag, 2001.

Murto, Eero, Pekka Väänänen, and Raimo Ikonen. *Sisäpiirit EU-Suomessa, Unioni ja muut eliitit*. Helsinki: Edita, 1996.

Myllymäki, Arvo. *Suomen pääministeri—presidentin varjosta hallitusvallan käyttäjäksi*. Helsinki: Talentum, 2010.

Myllyniemi, Sami. *Vaikuttava osa. Nuorisobarometri 2013*. Helsinki: opetus- ja kulttuuriministeriö, nuorisoasiainneuvottelukunta, nuoritutkimusverkosto, 2014.

National Audit Office. *Politiikkaohjelmat ohjauskeinona*. Valtiontalouden tuloksellisuustarkastuskertomukset 212. Helsinki: Valtiontalouden tarkastusvirasto, 2010.

Naumanen, Päivi, and Heikki Silvennoinen. "Koulutus, yhteiskuntaluokat ja eriarvoisuus." In *Luokaton Suomi? Yhteiskuntaluokat 2000-luvun Suomessa*, ed. Jani Erola, 67–88. Helsinki: Gaudeamus, 2010.

Nieminen, Liisa. *Eurooppalaistuva valtiosääntöoikeus—valtiosääntöistyvä Eurooppa*. Julkaisuja A-sarja No: 259. Helsinki: Suomalainen lakimiesyhdistys, 2004.

Noponen, Martti. "Kansanedustajien sosiaalinen tausta." In *Suomen kansanedustusjärjestelmä*, ed. Martti Noponen, 115–47. Helsinki: WSOY, 1989.

Norris, Pippa. *Democratic Phoenix. Reinventing Political Activism*. Cambridge: Cambridge University Press, 2002.

———. *Democratic Deficit. Critical Citizens Revisited*. New York: Cambridge University Press, 2011.

NOU 1982:3. *Maktutredningen. Norges offentlige utredninger*. Oslo/Bergen/Tromsö: Universitetsforlaget, 1982.

OECD. *Society at a Glance. The Crisis and its Aftermath. OECD Social Indicators*. http://www.keepeek.com/Digital-Asset-Management/oecd/social-issues-migration-health/society-at-a-glance-2014_soc_glance-2014-en#page1, accessed December 12, 2014.

Official Statistics of Finland (OSF). *Statistical Yearbook of Finland*. Helsinki: Statistics Finland, 2001.

———. *Statistical Yearbook of Finland*. Helsinki: Statistics Finland, 2011.

———. *Statistical Yearbook of Finland*. Helsinki: Statistics Finland, 2012.

———. *Statistical Yearbook of Finland*. Helsinki: Statistics Finland, 2013.

Ojanen, Tuomas. "Tuomioistuimet. Oikeusturvan takaajat ja lainsäätäjän vartijat." In *EU ja Suomi. Unionijäsenyyden vaikutukset suomalaiseen yhteiskuntaan*, eds. Tapio Raunio and Matti Wiberg, 165–83. Helsinki: Edita, 2000.

Ollila, Jorma, and Harri Saukkomaa. *Mahdoton menestys. Kasvun paikkana Nokia*. Helsinki: Otava, 2013.

Østerud, Øyvind, Fredrik Engelstad, and Per Selle. *Makten og demokratiet*. Trondheim: Gyldendal Akademisk, 2004.

Paastela, Jukka. *Valhe ja politiikka. Tutkimus hyveestä ja paheesta yhteiskunnallisessa kanssakäymisessä*. Helsinki: Gaudeamus, 1995.

Pakulski, Jan, and András Körösényi. *Toward Leader Democracy*. London: Anthem Press, 2012.

Paloheimo, Heikki. "Divided Government in Finland: From a Semi-presidential to a Parliamentary Democracy." In *Divided Government in Comparative Perspective*, ed. Robert Elgie, 86–105. Oxford: Oxford University Press, 2001.

Paloheimo, Heikki, and Sami Borg. "Eduskuntavaalit yleisödemokratian aikakaudella." In *Vaalit yleisödemokratiassa. Eduskuntavaalitutkimus 2007*, eds. Sami Borg and Heikki Paloheimo, 357–76. Tampere: Tampere University Press, 2009.

Pareto, Vilfredo. *The Mind and Society. A Treatise on General Sociology.* New York: Dover, 1963.

Parry, Geraint. *Political Elites.* London: Allen and Unwin, 1969.

Parsons, Talcott. "Power and the Social System." In *Power*, ed. Steven Lukes, 94–143. Oxford: Blackwell, 1986.

Passy, Florence. "Social Networks Matter. But How?" In *Social Movements and Networks. Relational Approaches to Collective Action*, eds. Mario Diani and Dough McAdam, 21–48. Oxford: Oxford University Press, 2009.

Pekkarinen, Jukka, and Visa Heinonen. "Talouspolitiikka ja kansantaloustieteellinen asiantuntemus Suomessa." In *Asiantuntemuksen politiikka -professiot ja julkisvalta Suomessa*, eds. Juri Mykkänen and Ilpo Koskinen, 84–99. Helsinki: Yliopistopaino, 1998.

Peltonen, Lasse."Sotkuinen demokratia' ja Tampere-foorumi—talkootoimintaa julkisen tilan puolesta." *Kunnallistieteellinen aikakauskirja* 2 (2002): 168–83.

Pentikäinen, Mikael. *Luottamus.* Helsinki: Otava, 2014.

Peterson, Richard A. "Understanding audience segmentation: From elite and mass to omnivore and univore." *Poetics* 21 (1992): 243–58.

Petersson, Olof. "Introduktion." In *Maktbegreppet*, ed. Olof Petersson, 7–26. Helsingborg: Carlssons, 1987.

———. *Maktens nätverk. En undersökning av regeringskansliets kontakter.* Helsingborg: Carlssons, 1989.

Pfeffer, Jeffrey, and Gerald R. Salancik. *The External Control of Organizations. A Resource Dependence Perspective.* New York: Harper and Row, 1978.

Pietilä, A-P. *Pankkikriisin peitellyt paperit.* Helsinki: Art House, 2008.

Pietiläinen, Tuomo, and Tutkiva työryhmä. *Wahlroo$. Epävirallinen elämäkerta.* Helsinki: Into, 2013.

Pohjola, Matti. "Taantuma ei ollut ennätyksellisen syvä." *Helsingin Sanomat,* December 1, 2010.

Pokka, Hannele. *Porvarihallitus.* Helsinki: WSOY, 1995.

Pöntinen, Seppo. *Social Mobility and Social Structure. A Comparison of Scandinavian Countries.* Commentationes Scientiarum Socialium no. 20. Helsinki: Helsingin yliopisto, 1983.

Presthus, Robert. *Men at the Top.* Oxford: Oxford University Press, 1964.

Purhonen, Semi, Jukka Gronow, Riie Heikkilä, Nina Kahma, Keijo Rahkonen, and Arho Toikka. *Suomalainen maku. Kulttuuripääoma, kulutus ja elämäntyylien sosiaalinen eriytyminen.* Helsinki: Gaudeamus, 2014.

Putnam, Robert D. *Bowling Alone: The Collapse and Revival of American Community.* New York: Simon and Schuster, 2000.

———. *The Comparative Study of Elites.* Englewood Cliffs: Prentice Hall, 1976.

———. *Making Democracy Work. Civic Traditions in Italy.* Princeton: Princeton University Press, 1993.

Ranki, Risto. *Haltia vai haltija? Harri Holkerin hallituksen talouspoliittinen ministerivaliokunta.* Helsinki: Edita, 2000.

Raunio, Tapio. "Euroopan unioni poliittisen järjestelmänä." In *Integraation teoria*, eds. Teija Tiilikainen and Teemu Palosaari, 115–42. Helsinki: Gaudeamus, 2007.

———. "Poliittinen järjestelmä: konsensusta kansallisen edun hengessä." In *Eurooppalaistuminen. Suomen sopeutuminen Euroopan integraatioon*, eds. Tapio Raunio and Juho Saari, 41–71. Helsinki: Gaudeamus, 2006.

————. "Politiikkaa yhdentyvässä Euroopassa: eduskunta, EU ja ulkopolitiikka." In *Eduskunta. Kansanvaltaa puolueiden ja hallituksen ehdoilla*, eds. Tapio Raunio and Matti Wiberg, 226–42. Helsinki: Gaudeamus, 2013.

Raunio, Tapio, and Matti Wiberg. "The Eduskunta and the Parliamentarisation of Finnish Politics: Formally Stronger, Politically Still Weak?" *West European Politics* 31 (2008): 581–99.

————. "How to Measure the Europeanisation of a National Legislature?" *Scandinavian Political Studies* 33 (2010): 74–92.

————. "Johdanto: Eduskunta Suomen poliittisessa järjestelmässä." In *Eduskunta. Kansanvaltaa puolueiden ja hallituksen ehdoilla*, eds. Tapio Raunio and Matti Wiberg, 7–38. Helsinki: Gaudeamus, 2014.

Roos, J. P. *Liikunta ja elämäntapa. Nautintoa vai itsekuria?* Nykykulttuurin tutkimusyksikön julkaisuja 14. Jyväskylä: Jyväskylän yliopisto, 1989.

————. *Suomalainen elämä. Tutkimus tavallisten suomalaisten elämäkerroista*. Hämeenlinna: SKS, 1987.

Rosanvallon, Pierre. *Demokraattinen oikeutus. Puolueettomuus, refleksisyys, läheisyys*. Original publication *La légitimité démocratuque impartialité, réflexivite, proximité*. Tampere: Vastapaino, 2013.

————. *Vastademokratia. Politiikka epäluulon aikakaudella*. Original publication *La contre-démocratie. La politique á l'âge de la défiance*. Tampere: Vastapaino, 2008.

Runciman, David. *The Confidence Trap. A History of Democracy in Crisis from World War I to the Present*. Princeton: Princeton University Press, 2013.

Ruostetsaari, Ilkka. "The Anatomy of the Finnish Power Elite." *Scandinavian Political Studies* 16 (1993): 305–27.

————. "Eduskunnan valta ja asema eliittien ja kansalaisten silmin." In *Eduskunta. Kansanvaltaa puolueiden ja hallituksen ehdoilla*, eds. Tapio Raunio and Matti Wiberg, 91–108. Helsinki: Gaudeamus, 2014b.

————. "Eliitti ja kansa—kaksi eri maailmaa? Päättäjien ja kansalaisten asenne-erot vuosina 1991–2011." *Yhteiskuntapolitiikka* 78 (2013b): 272–85.

————. "Elites and Democracy: Are They Compatible?" In *Comparative Studies of Social and Political Elites*, eds. Fredrik Engelstad and Trygve Gulbrandsen, 265–74. Amsterdam: Elsevier, 2007a.

————. *Energiapolitiikan määräytyminen. Julkisten, kollektiivisten ja markkinaperusteisten toimijoiden asema Suomen energiasektorin politiikkaverkostossa*. English Summary: Determination of Energy Policy. The Position of Public, Collective and Market-based Actors in the Policy Network of Finland's Energy Sector. Acta Universitatis Tamperensis, Ser. A, Vol. 278. Tampere: Tampereen yliopisto, 1989.

————. *Energiavalta. Eliitti ja kansalaiset muuttuvilla energiamarkkinoilla*. Tampere: Tampere University Press, 2010.

————. "Euroeliitissä vai politiikan sivuraiteilla? Europarlamentaarikoiden asema suomalaisessa valtarakenteessa." *Politiikka* 3 (2003b): 194–211.

————. "Finland: From Political Amateurs to Political Class." In *The Political Class in Advanced Democracies*, eds. Jens Borchert and Jürgen Zeiss, 107–23. Oxford: Oxford University Press, 2003c.

————. "From Political Amateur to Professional Politician and Expert Representative: Parliamentary Recruitment in Finland since 1863." In *Parliamentary Representatives in Europe 1848–2000. Legislative Recruitment and Careers in Eleven European Countries*, eds. Heinrich Best and Maurizio Cotta, 50–87. Oxford: Oxford University Press, 2000.

———. "Nordic Elites in Comparative Perspective." *Comparative Sociology* 6 (2007b): 158–89.

———. "Opening the Inner Circle of Power: Circulation in the Finnish Elites in the Context of Major Societal Changes 1991–2011." *Comparative Sociology* 12 (2013a): 255–88.

———. *Politiikan professionalisoituminen ja poliittisen luokan muotoutuminen Suomessa.* Politiikan tutkimuksen laitoksen julkaisuja 3. Tampere: Tampereen yliopisto, 1998.

———. "Populistiset piirteet vennamolais-soinilaisen puolueen ohjelmissa." In *Populismi. Kriittinen arvio,* ed. Matti Wiberg, 94–146. Helsinki: Edita, 2011.

———. "Social Upheaval and Transformation of Elite Structures: The Case of Finland." *Political Studies* 54 (2006): 23–42.

———. "Suomen poliittinen järjestelmä: Valtasuhteiden muutokset 1990-luvun alun jälkeen." In *Politiikan muutos,* eds. Tuomas Forsberg and Tapio Raunio, 77–122. Tampere: Vastapaino, 2014a.

———. "Suomi murroksessa 1991–2011: Muuttuiko eliittirakenne?" *Politiikka* 54 (2012): 269–84.

———. *Toimenkuva katoamassa vai valoa ikkunassa? Paikallisen poliittisen järjestötoiminnan tila Suomessa.* Oikeusministeriön julkaisu 10. Helsinki: Oikeusministeriö, 2005.

———. *Vallan ytimessä. Tutkimus suomalaisesta valtaeliitistä.* Helsinki: Gaudeamus, 1992.

———. *Valta muutoksessa.* Helsinki: WSOY, 2003a.

Ruostetsaari, Ilkka, and Sami Borg. "Sukupolvien valta-asemien muutos eliiteissä ja eduskunnassa." *Yhteiskuntapolitiikka* 69 (2004): 147–58.

Ruostetsaari, Ilkka, and Jari Holttinen. *Luottamushenkilö ja valta. Edustuksellisen kunnallisdemokratian mahdollisuudet.* Helsinki: Kunnallisalan kehittämissäätiö, 2001.

———. "Kunnallisten luottamushenkilöiden rooli ja professionalisoituminen." *Kunnallistieteellinen aikakauskirja* 4 (2004): 277–91.

Ruuskanen, Olli-Pekka, Alex Snellman, and Mika Widgren. "Yhteiskunnan huipulla: Eliittirakenne muutoksessa 1809–2009." In *Valta Suomessa,* ed. Petteri Pietikäinen, 34–55. Helsinki: Gaudeamus, 2010.

Saari, Heikki. *Jacke. Jacob Södermanin elämä.* Helsinki: Siltala, 2014.

Sailas, Raimo. "Perustuslakimme taipuu eurokriisin kenttäoikeudessa." *Kanava* 41 (2013): 30–31.

Salminen, Janne. "Suomen perustuslaki ja eurooppalainen yhdentymiskehitys." In *Perustuslakihaasteet,* ed. Matti Wiberg, 61–76. Helsinki: Edita, 2010.

Salverda, Tijo, and Jon Abbink. "Introduction: An Anthropological Perspective on Elite Power and the Cultural Politics of Elites." In *The Anthropology of Elites. Power, Culture, and the Complexities of Distinction,* eds. Jon Abbink and Tijo Salverda, 1–28. Basingstoke: Palgrave Macmillan, 2013.

Sänkiaho, Risto. "Puolueiden kannattajakunnan rakenne." In *SVT. Kansanedustajain vaalit 1991,* 37–46. Helsinki: Tilastokeskus, 1991.

Sartori, Giovanni. *Democratic Theory.* Detroit: Wayne State University Press, 1962.

Saumalaiset osallistujina. Oikeusministeriön julkaisuja 5. Helsinki: Oikeusministeriö.

Savolainen, Raimo. *Keskusvirastolinnakkeista virastoarmeijaksi. Senaatin ja valtioneuvoston alainen keskushallinto Suomessa 1809–1995.* Helsinki: Edita, 1996.

Saukkonen, Pasi. "Suomalaisen yhteiskunnan poliittinen kulttuuri." In *Suomalaisen politiikan murroksia ja muutoksia,* ed. Kari Paakkunainen, 27–51. Politiikan ja talouden tutkimuksen laitoksen julkaisuja 1. Helsinki: Helsingin yliopisto, 2012.

Schijf, Huibert. "Researching Elites: Old and New Perspectives." In *The Anthropology of Elites. Power, Culture, and the Complexities of Distinction*, eds. Jon Abbink and Tijo Salverda, 29–44. Basingstoke: Palgrave Macmillan, 2013.

Schumpeter, Joseph A. *Capitalism, Socialism and Democracy*. Eighth impression. London: Allen and Unwin, 1959.

Schwarzmantel, J. J. *Structures of Power. An Introduction to Politics*. Brighton: Wheatsheaf Books, 1987.

Scott, John. *Who Rules Britain?* Cambridge: Polity Press, 1991.

Scott, John, and Catherine Griff. *Directors of Industry: The British Comparative Network 1904–1976*. Glasgow: Polity Press, 1984.

Shore, Cris, and Stephen Nugent, eds. *Elite Cultures. Anthropological Perspectives*. London: Routledge, 2002.

Siisiäinen, Martti, and Tomi Kankainen. "Järjestötoiminnan kehitys ja tulevaisuuden näkymät Suomessa." In *Suomalaiset osallistujina*, 90–137. Oikeusministeriön julkaisu 5. Helsinki: Oikeusministeriö, 2009.

Sipponen, Kauko. *Kansalainen—isäntä vai renki*. Helsinki: WSOY Lakitieto, 2000.

Sirniö, Outi. *Sosiaalinen liikkuvuus Suomessa 1985–2005*. Sosiologian pro gradu–tutkielma. Helsinki: Helsingin yliopisto, 2010.

Soini, Timo. *Peruspomo*. Helsinki: WSOY, 2014.

SOU 1990:44. *Demokrati och makt i Sverige*. Stockholm: Statens offentliga utredningar, 1990.

Statistics Finland. (2011), Income and Consumption. http://www.stat.fi/tup/suoluk/suoluk _tulot_en.html, accessed February 2, 2014.

———. "Long-term economic disparities in Finland." http://tilastokeskus.fi/til/tjt/2011/05/ tjt_2011_05_2013-05-22_tie_001_fi .html, accessed April 1, 2014.

Stenvall, Jari. *Herrasmiestaidosta asiantuntijatietoon. Virkamiehistön asiantuntemuksen kehitys valtion keskushallinnossa*. Helsinki: Hallintohistoriakomitea, 1995.

Strömbäck, Jesper. "Four Phases of Mediatization: An Analysis of the Mediatization of Politics." *Press/Politics* 13 (2008): 228–46.

Suleiman, Ezra N. *Elites in French Society. The Politics of Survival*. Princeton: Princeton University Press, 1978.

Sund, Ralf. *Uhrataan puoluesihteeri*. Helsinki: WSOY, 2002.

Sundberg, Jan. "Puolueiden organisaatiot ja niiden suhteet etujärjestöihin." In *Suomen puolueet ja puoluejärjestelmä*, eds. Heikki Paloheimo and Tapio Raunio, 61–84. Helsinki: WSOY Oppimateriaalit, 2008.

Suomen Kuvalehti 18.9.1998.

Suomi, Juhani. *Toisinajattelevan tasavaltaa*. Helsinki: Tammi, 2013.

Suvanto, Antti, and Jyrki Vesikansa, eds. *Modernismi taloustieteessä ja talouspolitiikassa. O-ryhmän kirjoituksia ja kirjoituksia O-ryhmästä*. Helsinki: Kansantaloudellinen Yhdistys and Gaudeamus, 2002.

Talouselämä 18.10.2013, 4.4.2014, 25.8.2014.

Taloussanomat 30.7.2011.

Tarkiainen, Lasse, Pekka Martikainen, Mikko Laaksonen, and Tapani Valkonen. "Disparity in Life Expectancy between Income Quintiles, 1988–2007." *Suomen Lääkärilehti* 48 (2011): 3651–57.

Tarkka, Jukka. *Uhan alta unioniin. Asennemurros ja sen unilukkari EVA*. Helsinki: Otava, 2002.

Therborn, Göran. *European Modernity and Beyond: the Trajectory of European Societies 1945–2000*. London: Sage, 1995.

Tiihonen, Seppo. *Ministeriön johtaminen. Poliittisen ja ammatillisen osaamisen liitto*. Tampere: Tampere University Press, 2006.

———. "Poliittisen hallinnan ja hallintopolitiikan muutoksia 1980- ja 1990-luvulla." In *Uusi jako. Miten Suomesta tuli kilpailukyky-yhteiskunta?*eds. Risto Heiskala and Eeva Luhtakallio, 82–104. Helsinki: Gaudeamus, 2009.

Tirronen, Pekka. *Juristien ylivalta: ministeriöiden ylimpien virkamiesten koulutustaustasta*. Yleisen valtio-opin hallinto-opin suuntautumisvaihtoehdon pro gradu-tutkielma. Helsinki: Helsingin yliopisto, 1990.

Togeby, Lise, Jørgen Gould Andersen, Peter Munk Christiansen, Torben Beck Jørgensen, and Signild Allgårda. *Power and Democracy in Denmark. Conclusions*. Aarhus: University of Aarhus, 2003.

Tuori, Kaarlo. "Kansallinen ja ylikansallinen demokratia." In *Uusi ja vanha demokratia*, 6–15. Eduskunnan tulevaisuusvaliokunnan julkaisu 7. Helsinki: Eduskunta, 2013.

———. *Oikeuden ratio ja voluntas*. Helsinki: WSOYpro, 2007.

Uimonen, Risto. *Iiro Viinanen. Henkilökuva*. Jyväskylä: Minerva, 2010.

———. *Median mahti*. Helsinki: WSOY, 2009.

———. *Nuori pääministeri*. Helsinki: WSOY, 1995.

Useem, Michael. *The Inner Circle. Large Corporations and the Rise of Business Political Activity in the US and U.K.* New York: Oxford University Press, 1984.

Uusitalo, Hannu. *Valtion korkeimpien hallintovirkamiesten ja talouselämän johtajiston sosiaalinen tausta 1970-luvulla*. Julkaisuja, Sarja A-8. Turku: Turun kauppakorkeakoulu, 1980.

Väisänen, Kari. *Vaihtoehdoton valtakunta*. Helsinki: Taloudellinen tiedotustoimisto, 2013.

Väyrynen, Raimo. *Suomi avoimessa maailmassa. Globalisaatio ja sen vaikutukset*. Helsinki: Sitra/Taloustieto, 2000.

Viinanen, Iiro, and Kalle Heiskanen. *Vaaran vuodet. Muistelmia ja päiväkirjamerkintöjä 1991–1995*. Helsinki: Paasilinna, 2014.

Virkkunen, Janne. *Päivälehden mies*. Helsinki: WSOY, 2013.

Virtanen, Matti. *Fennomanian perilliset. Poliittiset traditiot ja sukupolvien dynamiikka*. Helsinki: SKS, 2001.

VNS 3. "Avoin ja yhdenvertainen osallistuminen." Valtioneuvoston demokratiapoliittinen selonteko. Helsinki: Valtioneuvosto, 2014.

Vogt, Henri. "Euroopan integraatio ja demokratia." In *Integraation teoria*, eds. Teija Tiilikainen and Teemu Palosaari, 81–114. Helsinki: Gaudeamus, 2007.

Vuolle, Pauli, and Risto Telama. "Liikunta elämän sisältönä." In *Näin suomalaiset liikkuvat*, eds. Pauli Vuolle, Risto Telama, and Lauri Laakso, 269–78. Liikunnan ja kansanterveyden julkaisuja 50. Jyväskylä: Liikunnan ja kansanterveyden edistämissäätiön tutkimuslaitos, 1986.

Waarden, Franz van. "Dimensions and Types of Policy Networks." *European Journal of Political Research* 21 (1992): 29–52.

Waris, Heikki. *Suomalaisen yhteiskunnan rakenne*. Helsinki: WSOY, 1948.

Wass, Hanna, and Pilvi Torsti. "Limittyvät sukupolvet ja jaetut näkemykset: suomalaisten yhteiskunnalliset sukupolvet ja sukupolvittaiset erot poliittisessa käyttäytymisessä." *Politiikka* 53 (2011): 167–84.

Wass, Hanna, and Niklas Wilhelmsson. "Äänestysaktiivisuus Suomessa—raportti vaaliosallistumisen tutkimisesta, äänestysaktiivisuuden trendeistä ja osallistumistutkimuksen kehitystarpeista." In *Suomalaiset osallistujina,* 20–90. Oikeusministeriön julkaisu 5. Helsinki: Oikeusministeriö, 2009.

Westlake, Martin. *Britain's Emerging Euro-Elite? The British in the Directly-Elected European Parliament 1979–1992.* Aldershot: Dartmouth, 1994.

Wiberg, Matti. *Hallitseeko hallitus?* Helsinki: Kunnallisalan kehittämissäätiö, 2009.

———. "Innostunut eliitti ja epäilevät kansalaiset—yleinen mielipide Euroopan integraatiosta." In *Päätöksenteko Euroopan unionissa. Selkeä johdatus monimutkaiseen vallankäyttöön,* eds. Tapio Raunio and Matti Wiberg, 282–303. Helsinki: Gaudeamus, 1998.

———. "Lainsäädäntömme EU-vaikutteisuus luultua olennaisesti pienempää." *Oikeus 33* (2004): 200–6.

———. *Politiikka Suomessa.* Helsinki: WSOY, 2006.

———, ed. *Populismi. Kriittinen arvio.* Helsinki: Edita, 2011.

———. "Puolueryhmät eduskunnassa." In *Eduskunta. Kansanvaltaa puolueiden ja hallituksen ehdoilla,* eds. Tapio Raunio and Matti Wiberg, 163–83. Helsinki: Gaudeamus, 2014.

Winkler, John T. "The Fly on the Wall of the Inner Sanctum: Observing Company Directors at Work." In *Research Methods for Elite Studies,* eds. George Moyser and Margaret, 129–46. Contemporary Social Research 14. London: Allen and Unwin, 1987.

World Bank. "Gini index." http://data.worldbank.org/indicator/SI.POV.GINI, accessed November 5, 2014.

Wrong, Dennis H. *Power. Its Forms, Bases and Uses.* Oxford: Basil Blackwell, 1979.

Ylä-Anttila, Tuomas. *Politiikan paluu. Globalisaatioliike ja julkisuus.* Tampere: Vastapaino, 2010.

Zannoni, Paolo. "The Concept of Elite." *European Journal of Political Research* 1 (1978): 1–30.

Index

accumulation of elite positions, 181–84, 199
age of elite members, 57
attitudinal unanimity: between elites, 148–56, 187–98; between elites and citizenry, 157–61, 198–99, 201
Americanization, 172
austerity, 14, 186

Bachrach, Peter, 22, 30
bailout packages, 11, 14, 163, 208, 211
banking crisis, 8-9, 11,173–74
bankrupt, 8-9, 104, 173–74
blue-collar workers, 53, 84, 195
Bourdieu, Pierre, 55, 71, 74–75, 110–11, 188, 121-122, 135
budgetary control, 163
Burnham, James, 17, 31n1, 43

capital: cultural, 71, 73–74, 79, 92, 105–6, 110–11, 123, 195–196, 200-201; economic, 74–75, 110–11, 135; educational, 75, 79, 194; social, 110–13, 135, 137, 200, 205–6; symbolic, 118
career advancement, 92, 94–96, 137, 195; career choices, 93–94; elective offices, 102–5; key life stages, 99–102; promoting factors, 96–99, 194–95
career mobility, 30, 52, 90, 191

centrality, 135, 197
civic competence, 206
civil society, 166, 204–7
class identification, 89–91, 195
competitiveness state, 174
composition of the elite structure, 40–43; administrative elite, 41–42; business elite, 41–42; cultural elite, 41, 43; mass media elite, 41, 43; organizational elite, 41–43; political elite, 40–42; scientific elite, 41, 43
concentration of power, 18–19, 21, 161, 169, 174–75, 181
consensus, 105, 130, 136–37, 153, 200–202, 206
conspicuous modesty, 123–24, 196, 208
constitutional changes 15, 130, 162, 164–66, 170
contacts: informal, 124–28; personal, 124–28
corporatism, 19, 105, 175–77, 202–3
corruption, 15, 205
culture: high 111, 117, 121–22; popular, 111. See also political culture

data, 46–47
decision making, 18, 35, 37–38
decisional approach, 33–35, 39

democracy, 15, 21–22, 26–28, 30, 198,
    200–201, 209–211; direct, 207,
    210–11; representative, 18, 198, 207;
    stealth, 155–56, 198. *See also* political
    participation
democratic elitism, 21–28, 30–31, 200–
    201, 207
demo-elite perspective, 22–26,
Denmark, 162, 202–3, 205
deregulation of financial markets, 8–9, 11,
    158, 168, 172–73
distinctions: cultural, 110–11; social, 121
distribution of power, 18–19, 35

education, 19, 29, 33, 55, 96, 194, 206;
    inheritance of, 71–74, 79–81, 194, 201;
    background, 34; inequality, 71; level,
    74–79
elective offices: inheritance of, 105–7, 196;
    of elite members, 102–5
electoral funding scandal, 12, 14–15, 47, 208
elite: circulation, 181–92, 200; coherence
    of, 19, 25–31, 51, 82, 104, 109, 136,
    160, 180, 196–200, 203; cohesiveness
    of, 19–20, 29–30, 33, 35, 51, 136, 198;
    concept of, 3, 22–25, 40; confrontations,
    27; consensus, 27, 30–31; cooperation,
    26–28; dartboard model of, 25, 181;
    degeneration, 28; inner core, 140,
    153, 181, 198; positions, 27, 40–43;
    self-consciousness of, 19, 25, 29, 136;
    solidarity, 27; unanimity, 29–30. *See also*
    elite consensus; power elite; separations
    of elites
elite structure, 23, 29, 31,40–43; coherence,
    109, 196–200, 203; exclusiveness, 29,
    201; fragmentation, 29, 197, 201, 203;
    inclusiveness, 29, 201; openness, 51, 94,
    193–96, 200–201, 203; segmentation, 29
elite theory, 2, 17–18, 29, 44, 199; classical
    19, 20, 25–26, 28–29, 33, 200. *See also*
    democratic elitism
elite typology, 29, 196–200
elite circulation, 29–31; vertical, 29, 31;
    horizontal, 29, 31
elites: accountability of, 21–22; autonomy
    of, 26–27, 30–31, 33, 200; career of,
    28; circulation between, 28; competition

among, 21–22, 27, 30; cooperation
    between, 28; exclusivity, 29; influence
    of, 43–46; interaction between, 28–29,
    30, 33, 201; mobility between, 30–31;
    openness of, 28–29, 31, 82, 84, 195–96;
    responsiveness of, 26–27, 31; separation
    of, 26; social background of, 28–31,
    33–35, 40, 50, 82, 193–96; sub-elites,
    22–23, 26; typology of, 29, 200–201;
    unity of, 29–30
electoral system, 208
energy policy, 155, 157–58
equality of opportunity, 52, 200
Etzioni-Halevy, Eva, 3, 20, 22–23, 25–27,
    30–31
Euro zone debt crisis, 10–14, 55, 68, 163–
    64, 173, 186–87, 201, 211
European Central Bank, 163–64
European Commission, 163–64, 167, 210
European Council, 162, 165, 168
European Economic Area, 10, 165
European Fiscal Compact, 163
European integration, 2, 161–64, 171, 197
European Parliament, 164
European Union, 11, 145, 147–48, 161–68,
    170–71, 177, 186
Economic and Monetary Union, 148,
    162–63
experts, 39, 44, 151–56, 167–68, 198
Europeanization, 64, 161, 167, 170

farmers, 84, 195
Foucault, Michel, 36–37
France, 50, 111–12, 121–23, 165, 187, 199

glass ceiling, 62, 195
gender, 97, 59–62, 193–94
generation: concept of, 55; of elites, 57–59
Germany, 86, 163, 186–87, 199, 210
Giddens, Anthony, 37–38
globalization, 7, 64, 112, 145, 172, 197
governmentalization of politics, 169
Great Britain, 79, 86, 111, 123, 186–87,
    210
Greece, 186, 205, 208–10
gulf: between elites and citizenry, 12, 30,
    157, 181; concerning leisure pursuits,
    122–23. *See also* attitudinal unanimity

habitus, 56, 75, 92, 112, 121, 196
Hobbes, 20
Hunter, Floyd, 31n1, 33, 34

income, 68-71; disparities, 10, 54, 68–71,
    111, 194, 201; distribution, 157; level
    of, 68–71
incomes policy, 176–77, 202
influence: concept of, 38; distribution of,
    159–61, 198; indirect, 38–40; of elite
    groups, 43–46; of experts, 150–56,
    167–68. *See also* experts
institutional positions, 35
interaction: among elites, 27, 124–28,
    137–48, 197; content, 135; density, 138,
    197; form, 135, 197; intensity, 137. *See
    also* interaction networks
interaction networks, 97, 100, 200; density,
    137–41; direction, 141–45; forms of
    influence, 128–31; international contacts
    145–48; utilization of mass media,
    131–32
interest groups, 18–19, 23, 202
international contacts, 97, 99; foreign
    institutions, 147–48; personal contacts,
    146–47, 197; studying abroad, 145,
    197; working abroad, 145–46, 197. *See
    also* interaction networks
international financial crisis, 10–13, 55, 68,
    173, 186–87, 201, 208–11
Italy, 186, 210

judicialization of politics, 170

labor market organizations, 23, 131, 202
legitimacy, 14, 18, 21, 35, 204, 206, 208,
    211
leisure pursuits, 115–24, 196–97. *See also*
    lifestyles
liberalization of financial markets, 8, 173,
    175
lifestyles, 29, 110–13, 121, 196–97. *See also*
    leisure pursuits

marital status, 60–62
market forces, 159–61, 200
Marx, Karl, 17–18, 90
Marxism, 2, 3, 17–18, 33, 44, 73

masses, 20–22, 25–26, 43, 111, 122, 181,
    196
mediatization of politics, 132, 178–80
Meisel, James, 19, 29
meritocracy, 1, 51
Michels, Robert, 6, 31n1, 43
middle class, 54, 84, 90, 112, 195, 202
Mills, C. Wright, 3, 17, 20, 22, 29, 31,
    31n1, 33, 44, 49, 82, 125, 136, 200
mobility: between elites, 187–92, 199;
    downward, 73, 79; regional, 65–67, 194;
    upward, 72, 74, 86, 121, 195. *See also*
    social mobility
Mosca, Gaetano, 6, 17, 19–21, 28, 31,
    31n1, 43, 157, 184, 200

native tongue, 63
neo-liberalism, 8, 54, 158–59
network analysis, 132–36
new institutionalism, 36
New Public Management, 168–69
Nokia Corporation, 10, 114, 125–26, 182,
    210
Nordic countries, 2, 31, 53–54, 60, 63,
    72, 123, 131, 147–48, 157, 176, 196,
    201–2, 204–8
normative principles, 153–56, 198
Norway, 11, 68, 124, 202–5

occupational status, 53; of parents', 82–83
old boy networks, 13–15, 197
omnivorousness, 122
overlapping membership 18, 34

pantouflage, 187
Pareto, Vilfredo, 6, 17, 20–21, 23, 28,
    30–31, 31n1, 43, 184, 200
parlamentarization, 15, 165–66
permanency of elite positions, 190, 199
personal contacts, 99, 116–17, 128–29,
    137, 197
personification of politics, 163, 178–79
plebiscitary democracy, 21
prestige, 136
pluralism, 1, 17–18, 20–22, 33, 34, 38, 44
political class, 19, 25
political culture, 112, 196–97, 204, 206
political decision-makers, 12, 21–22;
    decision-making process, 38–39

political knowledge, 206
political participation, 59, 95, 205–6,
    207, 210–11; direct, 22, 38–40, 155;
    indirect, 38–40. *See also* democracy
political scandals, 12–13, 15, 27, 179
politicization of justice, 170
populist political parties, 14, 157, 186,
    207–8
positional approach, 33–35, 39–40
power: actual, 134; concept of, 35–38;
    formal, 38–40; informal, 38–40;
    potential, 131–32; symbolic, 75
power elite, 22, 28–30, 40, 50; coherence
    of, 104, 200; inner circle of, 20, 25–26;
    outer fringes, 20
power resources, 18, 23–24, 26, 34–36, 38,
    134–35, 200
power relations: governmental and
    political institutions, 161–67; judiciary;
    courts of law, 170–72; labor markets
    organizations, 175–77; market forces,
    172–75; mass media, 177–81; public
    administration; civil servants, 167–70
power structure, 18, 23, 37–38
presidential powers, 164–66
privatization, 8, 158, 168, 187
public, 22–23, 26–27
public opinion, 26, 210
Putnam, Robert D., 2, 3, 49, 51, 204–6

recruitment into elites, 28–29, 33–35, 40,
    49, 193–96
recession: great, 8, 11, 100, 104, 112, 121,
    173, 175, 186; new, 11, 175
reconciling career and family, 62
regulation, 173, 175
reputational method, 33–35, 38–40
research methods, 33–35
residential area, 67
retention of elite positions, 184–87, 199
rules of the political game, 27–28, 30
ruling class, 17, 28
Russia, 63, 68, 124

Sartori, Giovanni, 21–22
Schumpeter, Joseph, 21–22, 30, 155, 207

semi-presidentialism, 165–66
separation of powers, 44
social background, 20, 29, 33, 49–51, 72,
    92, 94, 200. *See also* social background
    of elites
social inheritance, 67
social media, 129–32, 180–81, 197, 208
social mobility, See mobility 1, 50–55, 82,
    86, 92, 195, 200
social movements, 23–24, 205
social networks, 92, 96, 121, 205
social status, 100–11
social stratum, 29, 50, 52, 82–89, 195; of
    fathers', 85
social class, 33, 50–51
societal conflicts, 149–50
societal upheavals, 5, 7
socioeconomic inequality, 26–27, 111
Soviet Union, 8–9, 55, 120, 173,
spoils system, 187, 191
state-centeredness, 204–5
stealth democracy, 155–56, 198
Sweden, 11, 63, 68, 86, 124, 130–31, 201,
    202–5

taste, 111, 118,121–23
trust: among elites, 14, 135; in expert
    knowledge, 198; in institutions, 173,
    204–9; in politicians, 155, 207; in
    regime, 158, 205–6
turnover of elite members, 184–87

underprivileged, 23, 26–27, 201
unemployment, 8,11,54
upper class, 51–52, 84, 89–90, 112, 121,
    195; functionaries, 53
United States, 40, 60, 62, 66, 68, 70, 76–
    77, 79, 84, 90, 114, 122–23, 165, 179,
    186–87, 191–92, 199, 210

Weber, Max, 21, 30, 35, 90
welfare state, 10, 57, 89, 111, 158, 174,
    201, 204, 211
women's representation, 59–62, 193–94
working class, 90, 112, 195

voter turnout, 59, 205–7

About the Author

Ilkka Ruostetsaari is professor of political science at the University of Tampere, Finland. Previously he has been Senior Research Fellow at Academy of Finland and professor of political science at the University of Turku. He has specialized in elite study and power structures since the early 1990s.